HITTING PAUSE

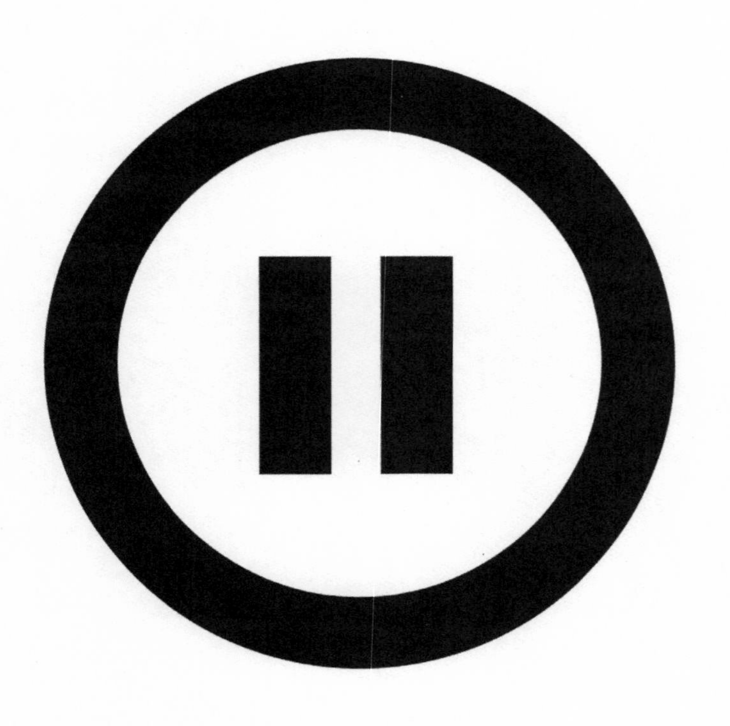

HITTING PAUSE

65 Lecture Breaks to Refresh and Reinforce Learning

Gail Taylor Rice

Foreword by Kevin Barry

Stylus
STERLING, VIRGINIA

Published by Stylus Publishing, LLC.22883 Quicksilver Drive
Sterling, Virginia 20166-2102

Library of Congress Cataloging-in-Publication Data
Names: Rice, Gail Taylor, 1945- author.
Title: Hitting pause : 65 lecture breaks to refresh and reinforce learning/ Gail Taylor Rice ; foreword by Kevin Barry.
Description: First edition. | Sterling, Virginia : Stylus Publishing, LLC, [2018] | Includes bibliographical references and index.
Identifiers: LCCN 2017030390 (print) |
LCCN 2017054044 (ebook) |
ISBN 9781620366547 (Library networkable e-edition) |
ISBN 9781620366554 (Consumer e-edition) |
ISBN 9781620366530 (pbk. : alk. paper) |
ISBN 9781620366523 (cloth : alk. paper)
Subjects: LCSH: Lecture method in teaching. | Active learning.
Classification: LCC LB2393 (ebook) |
LCC LB2393 .R53 2018 (print) |
DDC 371.39/6--dc23
LC record available at https://lccn.loc.gov/2017030390

13-digit ISBN: 978-1-62036-652-3 (cloth)
13-digit ISBN: 978-1-62036-653-0 (paperback)
13-digit ISBN: 978-1-62036-654-7 (library networkable e-edition)
13-digit ISBN: 978-1-62036-655-4 (consumer e-edition)

Printed in the United States of America

All first editions printed on acid-free paper
that meets the American National Standards Institute
Z39-48 Standard.

First Edition, 2018

10 9 8 7 6 5 4 3

To Rick, my best friend and favorite teacher

EPIGRAPH

Our students live in cacophony. Clamour, chatter and din fill their ears, and may even injure them. . . . We can educate ourselves to be models of intellectuals who trust and value silence, who practice what we have always known; when no one is speaking, someone is learning. We can create oases of silence where cool springs of insight trickle and flow.

—R. Marken, 2008, p. 115

CONTENTS

FOREWORD

It has been known for millennia that active/engaged learning strategies could have a positive impact on student outcomes. In western thought, the idea goes back as far as the *Socratic method*, defined by LEARN NC as "a student-centered approach that challenges learners to develop their critical thinking skills and engage in analytic discussion" (www.learnnc.org/lp/pages/4994).

Jumping forward to the early twentieth century, Dewey and Dewey (1915) called for engaging students in experiential learning and metacognitive reflection about their experiences. The call for engaged practice continued with Chickering and Gamson's (1987) summary of research on higher education teaching and learning in their book *Applying Seven Principles for Good Practice in Undergraduate Education*. In *How Learning Works: Seven Research-Based Principles for Smart Teaching*, Ambrose, Bridges, DiPietro, Lovett, and Norman (2010) presented a series of cases that illustrate learning principles including, among others, the importance of attending to motivation, goal-directed practice, and self-regulation in creating learning experiences. Even more recent is the confirmation from neuroscience that engaged practices make a difference in student learning. Books like *Make It Stick: The Science of Successful Learning* (Brown, Roediger, & McDaniel, 2014) and *Small Teaching: Everyday Lessons From the Science of Learning* (Lang, 2016c) bring neuroscience research to the practitioner with confirmation that things like interleaving practice and providing students opportunities to make predictions prior to hearing explanations impact learning outcomes.

Research on practice in higher education indicates that instructors have taken notice of the importance of making their classrooms active, learner-centered spaces. The pure dissemination style classroom is becoming less common, and use of active learning strategies is increasing. The 2013–2014 Higher Education Research Institute (HERI) faculty survey results indicated increases in percentage of faculty using learner-centered approaches such as discussion (69.6% to 80.0%), project-based learning (18.0% to 45.5%), incorporating student-selected topics (8.5% to 26.3%), cooperative learning (25% to 60.7%), and peer evaluation (10% to 28%), while "heavy reliance on lecture" has dropped "more than 5 percentage points" (to 50.6%) since the survey was first administered in 1989–1990 (Eagan et al., 2014). These numbers are encouraging but, given the information in Maryellen Weimer's

(2012) recent article, there is still room for incorporation of engaged learning methods. When asked, 57% of students endorsed the use of "in-class activities/demonstrations," but only 21% indicated that these were used by the "typical professor." Clearly, there is still an opportunity to change practice to bring more active/engaged learning into higher education classrooms.

After more than 20 years collaborating with instructors to help them incorporate learner-centered/engaged activities in their classes, I have found that the effort is most successful when three conditions have been met. First, the instructor must commit to reserving time for the activity so that it is not rushed or omitted due to time constraints. It is clear that good intentions are not enough; this change must be carefully planned, and hard choices about what can be moved out of class time must be made. Second, the activity must have a clear structure and detailed instructions that ensure all students will engage meaningfully in the activity. Too many times I have seen (and been the purveyor of) activities that didn't include a clearly communicated purpose or detailed instructions. In these cases, time is wasted, and the goals of the activity are often undermined by the lack of clarity. Third, the structure of the activity must include time to identify the progress that has been made as part of the activity. To paraphrase Dewey (1933), we don't learn by experience but by reflecting on experience. This final step provides the opportunity to reflect on learning experience and create an awareness of what learning has occurred. The pauses described in this book provide a wide variety of activities that can be used for purposes including focusing attention, enhancing retention of information, and emphasizing key learning outcomes.

Kevin Barry
Director, Kaneb Center for Teaching and Learning
University of Notre Dame

ACKNOWLEDGMENTS

Writing acknowledgments is a humbling experience; it helps me remember that every good idea I have about teaching and learning has been a gift. It is a privilege to take the gifts I have received over the years and put them together in new ways. I know that I have forgotten to attribute credit to appropriate individuals who have shared their ideas with me through print or in person. I hope you will get in touch with us so we can fix this in the next printing.

Thank you to my students who have been my teachers and colleagues in my journey to develop this work.

Thank you to Richard Hart, president of Loma Linda University, and Provost Ronald Carter, also of Loma Linda University, who model servant leadership and value good teaching and faculty development. Thank you to Craig Jackson, my dean, who has believed in me and encouraged me every step of the way. No request was so big that he couldn't find a way to support it. He provided opportunities for me to study with incredible teachers and learn in wonderful settings.

Thank you to Elizabeth Armstrong, director of the Harvard Macy Institute, for accepting me as a scholar and then inviting me to join the teaching faculty in the program. The first time I heard her speak about the cycle of learning, I began to see how my ideas for this book might be actualized.

Thank you to my Loma Linda University colleagues Laura and Alan Alipoon, Edd Ashley, Lee Berk, Rafael Canizales, Sondra Caposio, Tim Cordett, Willie Davis, Marie DeLange, Marilyn Eggers, Bertha Escobar-Poni, Peter Gleason, Carla Gober Park, Elaine Hart, Nancy Heine, Patti Herring, Mike Iorio, Eric Johnson, Everett Lohman, Iris Mamier, Arthur Marshak, Ernest Medina, Todd Nelson, Ehren Ngo, Doyle Nick, Kerby Oberg, Hans Schaepper, Tim Seavey, Brian Sharp, Tammi Thomas, Karla Lavin Williams, Beverly Wood, Nelia Wurangian Caan, Zane Yi, and my faculty development committee.

Thank you to my USC colleagues Dixie Fisher, who constantly was thinking exactly the same as I was; Julie Nyquist; Win May; and Bev Wood.

Thank you to my Adventist University of Health Science colleagues Deanna Flores, Edwin Hernandez, Dan Lim, Charlotte Henningsen, Deena Slockett, and the Faculty Development Committee.

Thank you to my Harvard Macy Institute colleagues Tom Aretz, Constance Bowe, Debra Boyer, Victoria Brazil, Ted Carrick, Ambrose Cheng, Eugene Corbett, Alan Dow, Leslie Ellis, Susan Farrell, Todd Fowler, Elizabeth Gaufberg, Stuart Goldman, Holly Gooding, Paul Haidet, Mark Hanson, Gordon Harper, Jeffery Hunt, Lisa Jacobson, Nicolas Thibodeau Jarry, Bob Kegan, Jean Klig, James Kwan, Alan Leightner, Lauren Maggio, Karen Mann, Neil Mehta, Jacek Mostwin, Deb and Andre Navedo, Dan Pratt, Subha Ramani, Joseph Rencic, Elizabeth Rider, Carla Romney, John Venson, Curtis Whitehair, Terry and Dan Wolpow, and many others.

Thank you to the following, whose ideas have shaped my work: Elizabeth Barkley, James Lang, Barbara Millis, Maryellen Weimer, Itiel Dror, Todd Zakrajsek, Terry Doyle, Laurie Richlin, Kevin Barry, Larry Michaelsen, and countless others.

Thank you to the following educators who work with trainers who have shaped my thinking about the importance of bringing fun to higher education: Michele Deck, Bob Pike, Dave Arch, Vicki Halsey, and Sharon Bowman.

Thank you to my Loma Linda University technical assistants Intithar Elias, Arthur Kroetz, Geoffrey Chien, Pravin Aaron, Kitty Sachdeva, Hsiaoyun Hu, Cheng-yung Wu, Shaili Kapadia, Priti Shinde, Khusboo Kapuria, and countless others who have served as graduate assistants.

Thank you to my family, which values good teaching and loves good learning. Our daughter, Alison Rice, professor at the University of Notre Dame, spent hours moving commas and periods around, and Rosa, our granddaughter, illustrated a concept for the book.

Thank you to John von Knorring, president of Stylus Publishing. John has been a continual source of encouragement and inspiration. Thank you to Stylus for making it possible to share my ideas and to develop an expanded community of learning as a result.

Finally, thank you to my husband, Rick, who helped me edit this book. He has taken time from his busy schedule to help me dispense with unnecessary words. At one point, recalling the slogan, "Teach less better," he wrote in the margin, "Write less better." He is a master teacher and mentor with a wonderful sense of humor.

INTRODUCTION

Carl teaches in the department of humanities at his college. He has been teaching for 30 years. He has always enjoyed teaching, but lately he has noticed a change. He doesn't look forward to his classes like he used to. It appears that his students have also lost their enthusiasm for his classes. Last semester students made the following comments on their course evaluations: "The instructor just read his PowerPoint slides to us" and "This class was really boring" and "I was really disappointed in this class—I do not feel like I learned anything." Carl wonders why the course that used to be popular with students is barely filling up now. The lectures that used to be fine are not working so well anymore. This close to the end of his career, Carl isn't sure he is ready to make drastic changes. Carl is not alone; he has a lot of colleagues who would like to know what it will take to keep their own high excitement about teaching their subject as well as how they can improve learning in their classrooms without totally reinventing themselves as professors.

If we are seasoned professors, we may think our students today are so different from what students used to be that we don't know how to relate to them anymore. We wonder if it is possible to teach well if we don't know about the latest Internet teaching tools. We ask ourselves, How do we make our classes interactive without totally redesigning them? Is it possible to take those lesson plans that have stood the test of time and update them with some simple tweaks? Will anything help us increase student motivation to listen and learn? Is there a way to improve our teaching without a total revamp of our course and lecture outlines? Can we keep our PowerPoint slides and find ways to build student interest into what we have already developed?

After completing her doctoral degree, Emma joins the faculty at a local college. Like many who are in the early stages of a higher education teaching career, Emma wonders how to start, asking, How do we design a course? How do we plan our classes? Should we develop illustrated lectures and handouts like the ones we had in college and graduate school? Do we need a degree in education? Most of us haven't taken a single class on how to teach and have very little time to attend conferences or offerings from our campus's teaching and learning center. We may hear about some new developments in teaching but figure that right now all we can manage is to stay one class session ahead of our students. Our lecture plans are just that—plans to lecture. We have little time to even think about what we might do as an alternative to standing in front of our class and talking.

Whether we are new or seasoned professors, most of us can relate to these difficult questions. This book addresses these questions and attempts to provide answers and possible solutions to these dilemmas. It is based on two fundamental principles: Shorter segments of instruction are better than longer ones, and students who pause periodically to actively participate in instruction will learn better than those who don't (Wilson & Korn, 2007). This book is for faculty members in higher education, those of us who are responsible for learning. We now know it is not what we teach that counts, it's what our learners learn. It's not enough to merely spout information. If our students don't learn, we haven't taught, no matter how much information we provide.

Many of us were taught by teachers who thought that a teacher's job is to talk. They saw learners as listeners. "If we don't say it," they thought, "our students won't learn." These teachers believed the following:

- I have too much content to cover; I'll never be able to get it all in.
- It is my responsibility to explain every single important idea in class.
- If only I can get my students to listen to me, they will learn.

But today's teachers are more and more aware of the fallacies of this kind of thinking. Cognitive scientists, educational psychologists, college professors, and adult learning specialists tell us we should try to keep in mind the following principles when planning our teaching:

- Whoever is doing the work is doing the learning (Doyle, 2011).
- Whoever is doing the talking is doing the learning (Bowman, 2009; Halsey, 2011).
- Learners learn by discussing, engaging, applying, analyzing, and problem-solving with others (Jensen, 2008).

As a result, we realize we can't fill the entire class period with our talk. We need to break up our lectures into reasonably spaced chunks, we should allow students opportunities for collaborative work, and we might try to increase active learning in our classrooms. The problem is that the challenge of providing these engaging learning experiences takes significant time and energy, and until recently we haven't had the resources to help us with this daunting task.

We are increasingly aware of the fact that despite our best intentions, very little learning occurs in many of our classrooms. The cartoon in Figure I.1 says it all: We are doing the talking, no one is doing the learning.

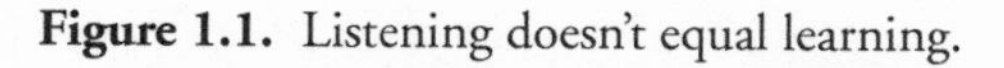

Figure 1.1. Listening doesn't equal learning.

"They don't give us time to learn anything in school; we have to listen to the teacher all day."

Note. From HERMAN © 1977 LaughingStock International inc. Reprinted by permission of ANDREWS MCMEEL SYNDICATION for UFS.

If we slip into a colleague's classroom, we see a lot of what Jensen (2008) calls "nonstop learning" (p. 220), which is when teachers talk and there are no pauses for students to interact with what they are hearing. This is what we observe: The teacher is in the front of the room at the podium, PowerPoint slides are up on the screen, and the only break occurs when the instructor momentarily stops explaining and asks a question. If anyone responds, usually a student near the front of the room answers before anyone else has a chance to think of an answer. If instructors who think that their students are actively engaged because one person has come up with an answer to a question could observe their classrooms from the back of the room, they might notice that many of their students are looking at e-mail, texting on their mobile phones, and not paying attention. We rarely observe colleagues putting students into groups to solve a problem or a dilemma or to work on an application activity. When we see what a difference such simple activities make in the learning experience of our students, we realize it is worth what it takes to seek resources to help us develop these purposeful pauses to energize our classrooms.

Whatever approach we take to teaching, it is essential to present concepts in small segments and give students occasional breaks so they can retrieve information and engage with the concepts being introduced (Agarwal, 2017). One literature professor has a useful metaphor to help her manage learning periods in need of pausing: She conceives the classroom as a play with various scenes. As her class proceeds, she moves her students from one scene to the next with opening and closing acts for each of the scenes. Another teacher uses a narrative metaphor and considers starting and closing pauses as bookends for the class period. He pauses at the start to set the stage for the story to follow and then pauses at the end to bring it back full circle.

Hit Pause

We can put away our electronic devices when we need a break from a steady flow of input. When we need to stop the music, the video, or the voice that is talking too fast, all we need to do is hit the pause button. Hitting the pause button provides that needed rest to catch our breath, look back over what has come before, reflect, meditate, refresh, and prepare ourselves before we resume.

Students might wish that there was a pause button connected to their college professors. How helpful it would be if their instructors recognized the need to stop talking occasionally so that learners could rewind, take a moment to check for understanding, and prepare to continue.

When instructors stop talking and allow learners to reflect on what they have learned, they turn a routine lecture into a powerful learning experience. Jensen (2008) suggests that "not learning breaks" are "necessary for the brain to process and transfer learning from short- to long-term memory" (p. 220).

College students would probably be surprised if their instructor did hit the pause button during class because they are not used to expecting learning to happen during class. Ask typical college students when they learn or how they prepare for their exams, and they will usually say they pull out their class notes or the teachers' handouts right before the exam and begin studying in earnest only then. I've observed countless college and graduate students enter the classroom, pick up the instructor's printed handout, and find a seat near the back of the room. Confident that the handout contains everything that is important to know, they feel quite comfortable closing their eyes and taking a nap during class, especially when the teacher is showing PowerPoint slides in a darkened room. These students assume that learning is reserved for the wee hours of the morning, when memorizing key concepts from the handouts in preparation for the exam the next day.

Students who plan to relax during class may resist the professor's efforts to pause midway through for students to think about a particular concept and solve a problem. But these learning pauses are just what students need for efficient learning and retention. These students studying during the midnight hours to prepare for the final exam will actually recognize concepts they grappled with during those classroom learning pauses. They will probably remember very little else from the lecture or the handout from a few weeks before, but they will not forget the idea they debated with the person sitting next to them.

Pauses inject stimulating experiences at critical moments in learning, and these powerful moments can be liberating. Professors can rely on these pauses to provide active learning opportunities and require minimal changes to their lesson plan. They won't have to flip their classrooms or switch to team-based learning. If they hit pause in the right way at the right times, they can rehabilitate their lectures and improve learning in their classes.

Benefits of Pausing

Well-timed pauses can provide students with the benefits of active learning—increased interest, motivation, and retention. Learning pauses help students focus so that their attention is not lost. Pauses allow students to personalize learning and improve retention. Pauses allow students to check their understanding and practice retrieval and increase interest, arouse curiosity or anticipation, or help activate prior knowledge. A pause may also give learners opportunities to predict outcomes, which increases their interest in learning more about a topic. Closing pauses ask students to commit to action and increase the likelihood of transferring their knowledge into practice.

Pausing benefits instructors as well as students. When instructors pause, we can get feedback from our students about what they have learned and how they respond to our instruction. Pausing also gives us a chance to catch our breath as we look ahead and plan how the rest of the class period will proceed.

Although using pauses is critical to effective lecturing, it is essential to any profitable learning session. A starting pause will get learners ready for instruction and not be distracted by other thoughts. How important is it to avoid streaming nonstop information before finding out where learners are, what they already know, and what their expectations are? This is true for any kind of learning, not just a lecture, such as a laboratory or skills practicum, clinic orientation, team-based learning class, discussion class, a short one-on-one conference with a student or patient, and online instruction. It is important to pause at the start of instruction, but it may be even more important for learners in all settings to have the opportunity to look back at the close of instruction—whether it is a five-minute tutorial, an online module, a conference address, or a class session—and wrap it up by identifying what they valued and what actions they plan for following up. This final pause is just as necessary after an interactive learning experience, such as a simulation or objective structured clinical examination, as it is after listening to a lecture, observing a panel discussion, or viewing a film or video presentation. Brian Sztabnik (2015) says it well in the following:

> That is the crux of lesson planning right there—endings and beginnings. If we fail to engage students at the start, we may never get them back. If we don't know the end result, we risk moving haphazardly from one activity to the next. Every moment in a lesson plan should tell.

Recall the following questions:

- Is it possible to teach well using lectures?
- If so, can we plan good lectures?
- Can we make our lectures interactive without totally redesigning them?
- Is it possible to take those lectures that have stood the test of time and update them with some simple tweaks that will allow us to increase student motivation to listen and learn?
- Can we do this without a total revamp of our lesson plans? Can we teach effectively without changing our lectures into discussions and active learning events?
- Is it possible to keep most of those PowerPoint slides and find ways to build student interest into what we have already developed?

The answer to the questions about saving lectures is a resounding yes. We can do this by building introductory pauses, concluding pauses, and intermediate pauses into our lectures, which does not require changing the lesson plan, although it does require deciding what can be removed from our lecture to make space for the pauses. Focusing on how we start and end learning and adding pauses to our teaching will encourage student engagement and interest, increase active participation and transfer of learning, and cause students to leave our classrooms and laboratories inspired with the value of what they have learned. As we apply the latest findings from cognitive science to our teaching plans, we will discover the joy of pausing with our students to allow learning to sink in, to take on its own life, and to embed itself into each learner's experience.

How to Approach This Book

This book presents suggestions for planned pauses in learning design. There are critical moments when these pauses are most likely to have the desired effect, so we focus on pausing at the beginning and at the close of instruction. We also provide ideas for midpauses for longer learning periods.

Part one provides additional information about the benefits of pausing instruction. Part two summarizes brain science support for the pause. Part three presents classroom stories of how pausing helped achieve objectives. The book concludes with three appendixes with descriptions of 65 techniques teachers can use with just about any topic and a variety of audiences.

We describe these techniques briefly and then give step-by-step instructions for carrying them out. We suggest ways to vary the techniques to fit particular disciplines or settings, including online teaching. Each pause technique begins with Starting Pause (SP), Midpause (MP), or Closing Pause (CP) and the number of the pause, which is consecutive from 1 to 65. For example, if we want to refer the reader to the Dump Bucket Starting Pause, we use (SP 16), which is described in detail in Appendix A.

Those of us who are already convinced that pauses will help improve our next online module, classroom presentation, lab orientation, or one-on-one instruction may want to go directly to the appendixes and start looking in for an idea to use. Those of us who are a bit skeptical about this whole idea of pauses may want to read part two, which provides references to studies from cognitive science that support the importance of curiosity, prediction, a positive environment, awareness of thinking (metacognition), and activating prior knowledge, all characteristics of learning pauses that promote learning. Those of us who have too much content to cover and worry that pauses will waste our time may want to read about the studies in Chapter 4 suggesting that less is more. If it appears that our students or our subjects are too sophisticated for these kinds of approaches, the experience of the statistics teacher described on page 92 may be helpful.

Many of the ideas in this book are well established. The minute paper, an excellent pause to close out learning, was popularized by Angelo and Cross (1993) and has been widely used. Many faculty members have developed good ways to pause teaching and have been doing so throughout their teaching careers. We owe a tremendous debt to Elizabeth Barkley, along with Claire Major, who have done so much to help us understand the importance of pausing with our learners. Their extensive research, clear writing style, and detailed examples are exemplary (Barkley, 2010; Barkley & Major, 2015). Regarding those essential first five and last five minutes of class, some authors provide specific suggestions about how to harness the power of the start and close of the class session when students are more attentive (Finley, 2015; Harrington, 2014; Honeycutt, 2016; Lang, 2016a, 2016b, 2016c; Sipe, n.d.).

In an era when there is so much competition for the attention of our students, any strategies that will assist in minimizing distraction and keeping students focused on learning will be of great benefit indeed.

PART ONE

BENEFITS OF PAUSING

I

WHY WE NEED TO PAUSE

As a new college instructor, I was excited to attend my first national conference on teaching and learning. It was organized by a group that described itself as being opposed to lectures. There would be no plenary addresses and no large group session, only small-group breakouts at this conference. Presenters were told to plan for interactive learning sessions with no lecturing. I thought I would be experiencing all kinds of new ways to teach when attending these engaging learning opportunities, but I was in for a surprise. Every single session started out the same way. Presenters stood behind a lectern and talked. Most did eventually get around to some kind of large-group discussion or small-group activities, but virtually all of them started by lecturing.

I did learn from the conference, and I have been hooked on teaching and learning conferences ever since, but I have to admit that I was baffled that even a conference that advertised itself as committed to alternatives to lecturing consisted of an awful lot of lecturing.

The Predominance of the Lecture

If nearly every session at a conference where lecturing is discouraged starts with a presentation that looks a lot like a lecture, it shouldn't surprise us that the lecture is pretty dominant in most of academia. Register for a national meeting of any academic society and attend a large-group session or a breakout workshop. You can probably expect to sit quietly, listen to someone talk, and take notes. In fact, it isn't that unusual to go to an academic meeting and discover that the time is devoted to the reading of a paper. Find a college or university, slip into any undergraduate or graduate class, and you are likely to hear a fairly traditional lecture.

Considered the standard model of academic teaching, the large college lecture continues to dominate college classrooms, particularly the humanities, comprising well over 80% of all courses (Dennick & Exley, 2004; Kimball & Milanowski, 2009; Neuman, 2001).

An example of the fact that professors love to lecture and will continue to use it as an appropriate way to teach appeared in an article by Molly Worthen (2015), a university professor, who stated the following in support of the traditional lecture:

> In the humanities there are sound reasons for sticking with the traditional model of the large lecture course. . . . Lectures are essential for teaching the humanities' most basic skills: comprehension and reasoning, skills whose value extends beyond the classroom to the essential demands of working life and citizenship.

History of the Lecture

The lecture has a long tradition. The word *lecture* means "to read." Lecturing started centuries ago when people read texts and listeners copied what they heard word for word. Religion scholars would travel hundreds of miles to hear monks read from ancient scrolls. Early academics had only oral instruction as a method to learn as they listened and copied down what they heard (Garside, 1996; Thelin, 2011). Before the printing press, before the Internet, this was how new information was shared, so it made sense to think of it as a good way to learn—probably because it was the *only* way to learn.

Lecture Continues Despite Criticisms

To Stanford physics professor Carl Wieman, the college lecture is the educational equivalent of bloodletting, a common way to treat illnesses from ancient Greek times until the late nineteenth century (Westervelt, 2016). Although medical practices have changed significantly over time, educational approaches have not. Wieman suggests that the typical college lecture today does as much good as bloodletting did a hundred years ago. Whatever learning occurs takes place despite the lecture, rather than because of it (Westervelt, 2016).

Wieman's concern about undergraduate education and our overreliance on lecturing is not new. Traditional lectures have been under scrutiny for some time. Earlier criticisms focused on limitations of the lecture. Bligh (2000) suggested that lectures are really only good for transmitting information, and that other ways of teaching are better suited to all the additional objectives teachers have for their students, such as changing attitudes, developing behavioral skills, or promoting deep thought.

The biggest concerns with the lecture approach focus on our tendencies to monopolize the classroom conversation with "teacher talk." We do not allow anyone else to speak when we are behind the lectern providing a constant stream of information. When active learning proponents emerged (Bonwell & Eison, 1991), a number of professors began to criticize traditional lectures as old-fashioned and inappropriate ways to teach students, particularly students who were becoming more and more visual and less aural in their learning style as well as increasingly used to fast-moving media and highly stimulating technology.

Finkel (2000) tells us, "Educational research over the past twenty-five years has established beyond a doubt a simple fact: What is transmitted to students through lecturing is simply not retained for any significant length of time" (p. 3). Our students actually learn only when we cut away from the traditional lecture where we are the only ones talking. Evaluations of alternative approaches to lecturing reveal that students achieve deeper understanding, have lower failure rates, and improve test performance by as much as 50%. Wieman (2014) argues,

> In fact, the data on the power of these techniques are so persuasive, it's almost unethical to teach undergraduates any other way. I know you can double how much a student learns depending on what method the instructor is using. (cited in Westervelt [2016])

Despite the fact that there is overwhelming evidence that the lecture method is "substantially less effective" (Wieman, 2014, p. 8319) than active learning methods of teaching, we professors continue to spend a good bit of our time doing exactly what Bligh describes as lecturing, that is, "more or less continuous expositions by a speaker who wants the audience to learn something" (Bligh, 2000, p. 4). When we speak to very large audiences, when we do our TED talks, when we have opportunities to give plenary addresses, when we have a specific objective of providing information in a short amount of time, for example, we find the lecture to be a compelling way to teach.

Improving the Lecture

Because lecturing continues despite various criticisms, it is helpful to consider what Phillip Boffey suggested about lecturing at Harvard University back in 1962, when he asserted that it wasn't necessary to get rid of the lecture but instead to improve it. And that is our focus now as well. Rather than try to reinvent what we have been doing in our classrooms and clinics, suppose we look for ways to effectively rehabilitate our lectures. Our solution for rehabilitating lectures taps into what we know about engagement and cooperative learning. Nelson (2010) reminds us that "effort spent improving lectures is wasted unless the pedagogy already has been transformed to use effective cooperative learning" (p. 123). We might discover that "some comparatively simple changes could make a big difference" (Brown, Roediger, & McDaniel, 2014, p. 9).

Pauses Could Save Lectures

This brings us to the central premise of this book: By adding pauses to our lectures, we can create engaging cooperative learning experiences and improve learning outcomes. Learning pauses help us chunk information, which is critical to good learning. Students will learn more when we talk less and insert strategic pauses into the lecture. Harrington and Zakrajsek (2017) tell us that "incorporating lecture pauses where active learning strategies are used helps to maintain student attention" (p. 55). A *lecture pause* occurs when instructor talk stops, and students are asked to think about their learning and what they will do with it. These learning pauses represent the powerful small changes that can maximize learning. Ideally, learning pauses occur at the start and the close of all learning experiences; midpauses may be necessary as well, depending on the length and complexity of the session. Many of our colleagues think these pauses are only needed for long, tedious sessions where attention is bound to wander. But even a five-minute, one-on-one instruction will benefit from pausing to find out where the student is, what his or her perceived needs and prior experiences are and pausing to close with the student's summary of what she or he is taking away from this instruction.

James Lang (2016a) encourages faculty members to take a few minutes at the beginning of class to pause for students to ponder the topic of the day. His complementary article contains ideas for closing pauses, such as asking students to consider how the class helped answer the questions raised at the beginning (Lang, 2016b). In these two articles and his book, Lang (2016a, 2016b, 2016c) provides a number of ways teachers can achieve quite different results by making small adjustments in their classroom teaching.

A number of authors offer specific intentional educational activities to help faculty members add active learning experiences to their classroom lectures. Honeycutt (2016) suggests that focusing activities minimize distractions, maintain momentum, and create more time for learning. Major, Harris, and Zakrajsek (2016) is another valuable resource that gives readers strategies for pausing teacher talk for student learning. The authors wrote, "We assert that presenting mini-lectures and *pausing* [emphasis added] between segments can improve the pacing of a given lecture. It provides students with an opportunity to collect their thoughts and reflect upon their learning" (p. 12). The practice of the pause has great promise for increasing the impact of our lectures. When we pause and allow students to make meaning of the lecture, they move beyond just acquiring new information, they can progress beyond recall and understanding. They start to analyze, apply, or evaluate.

In contrast, when only the teacher talks, students are unlikely to focus. Wieman (2014) describes teaching physics at Stanford this way, saying that most of the time

> only 10% [of the students] would actually remember the answer. A lot of them are asleep, or lost, and I don't know whether they're getting anything out of it. If I'm standing up there talking at them, I have no clue what they're absorbing and not absorbing. . . . If I'm just lecturing the whole time, what a terrible waste that would be. Half the material would be over their head, and half the material would be completely trivial to them.

But when the teacher takes a break and invites students into the conversation, the lecture takes on new energy, and higher cognitive learning occurs. It is only when we pause that we give students opportunities to connect to prior experiences, to personalize, generalize, analyze, evaluate, create, and value.

Dan Schwartz, dean of Stanford's Graduate School of Education, reflected on Wieman's use of these learning pauses and his abandonment of the pure lecture method in the following: "The large lecture, and racing through material, doesn't allow you to slow down to see the beauty of what you're learning" (as cited in Westervelt, 2016).

This book shows that new instructors can develop powerful lectures, and seasoned professors can resurrect lectures by simply slowing down and helping students see the beauty of what they are learning. We do this by making what Lang (2016a, 2016b, 2016c) refers to as small changes, providing learning pauses that allow students to enter the conversation and transforming the lecture from a monologue to a dialogue.

Problems When Planning Lectures

When I observed a fellow faculty member teach at my campus, I could see how she had earned the reputation for being a good lecturer. I watched her deliver a well-crafted 50-minute presentation. All 150 of the students were in their places ready for class to start. They paid close attention to the instructor as she carefully proceeded through her PowerPoint slides and ended exactly on time. The professor provided detailed information on the topic of the day.

At the end of the session, the students applauded, gathered their laptops and notes, and left the room. During the hour no student spoke. The instructor asked no questions. No cases were discussed and no probing dilemmas presented.

A couple of days later I sat down with the teacher to share my notes and discuss my observations. I showed her how she reduced tension when she told the class that a particularly difficult concept would not be on the test. I complimented her on how nicely organized her outline was, and how well her slides matched the outline she had posted on the website. I described the close attention the students paid to her monologue and the notes I observed them writing on the printed outlines. She seemed a little surprised when I mentioned before I left that I would be happy to look at her lesson plan for her next session if she would like and perhaps offer a suggestion or two. She asked me what I might have suggested if I had looked ahead of time at this lesson.

I responded that she might have paused for a moment at the beginning of class to ask her learners to think about their previous experiences with the topic. I also suggested that she might have paused midway during her fast-paced monologue to ask the students a question or two, to allow for a brief testing or review of pathogens discussed in an earlier lesson. Maybe she could have given her students a matching activity about the oral pathogens they were studying. Any of these pauses would not have taken more than a couple of minutes, but my colleague looked at me with a shocked expression and responded, "Oh, no. I wouldn't think of doing something like that. I have my class timed down to the second. I know exactly how much I can cover, and I have no time to waste with stuff like that."

When I mentioned how much talking is correlated with learning, she responded, "I know—it is so gratifying for me to rehearse these lectures, as it helps me to really nail down the information in my own head." She didn't get it. This wasn't about her, it was about her students.

My colleague thinks what so many of us have thought for so long. Our job is to lecture; we have the knowledge needed to fill the empty containers of our students.

Pauses Could Have Helped

Many of my colleagues would give this lecture high ratings, but how would a learning specialist rate it? What would Nobel laureate and Stanford physics professor Wieman have said about it? Would a cognitive scientist suggest that she could turn this lecture from a performance into a learning experience with a few simple pauses? Our new, devoted research professor doesn't have to give up her lecture to be effective. She can keep her PowerPoint slides and her well-constructed outline. All she has to do is make some small changes, such as adding a starting pause to allow the students to think about the cold sore they had when they were kids, a little Beat the Clock (MP 35) pause midway, and a paired Exam Question Challenge (CP 58) pause at the end. It could have been an exciting ending if the instructor promised a couple of bonus points for any pair whose question got used on the final exam. At a cost of five to seven minutes of lecture time, she could have transformed her performance into a significant learning experience.

The following illustrates how pausing can make a big difference. Neil Mehta, a colleague of mine, was wondering how to educate residents and faculty about giving formative feedback. He had observed that the institutional culture was about providing mostly summative feedback at the end of the rotation. He wanted to give this audience a sense of how students feel when they start a clinical rotation, how intimidated they might be, and how faculty and residents can help them navigate this new setting and learn.

So he chose an scenario involving an airplane and made each person go through this exercise online (Mehta, n.d.). Feedback from his audience indicated that the exercise helped them realize the importance of formative, nonjudgmental, timely, and specific feedback. He has since made his exercise available to other educators who have used it for their training sessions on feedback.

Mehta shared the following airplane exercise with me, and I decided to use it as a starting pause the next time I was asked to lecture on the topic of feedback for health professional faculty

> You are a student learning to fly a small airplane. You are about to go up in the plane for the first time with your instructor. You see the cockpit in front of you, full of complicated instruments. You are hoping for lots of help from your instructor as you fly this plane for the first time. During this simulated flight, the instructor says hardly anything about how you are doing, what specifically you are doing well, or what needs improvement. When you are finally back on the ground, you are feeling lucky to be alive, but extremely frustrated. (N. Mehta, personal communication, July 17, 2017)

After students started the session with the pause to fly a plane, wondering whether they would live or die through the experience, they talked about their feelings about feedback, their personal experiences with feedback in the past, and what they would like to get from the workshop. This frustrating experience with flying seemed to be a perfect preparation for the learning session about the importance of providing appropriate feedback to their students. Afterward, they were ready to hear the lecture about feedback; they listened more carefully and asked better questions as they now desired to be more effective in providing feedback to their students.

At the end of the seminar, I handed out three-inch-by-five-inch cards and asked participants to answer the following questions: How will what they have discussed today affect their working with medical students in the weeks to follow? What, specifically, will they do to improve the feedback they provide to their students? These questions resulted in comments like the following:

> Now that I have experienced inadequate feedback (flying the airplane), I will be more aware of what kind of feedback I am giving to my students.
>
> I will be sure to make time for providing feedback, as it is certainly essential to a good learning experience,
>
> I will try to be sure that my feedback is timely, frequent, and specific.
>
> I will be sure to listen to my students before I launch into telling them what I think.

Teaching Without Beginning and Closing Pauses

Contrast the preceding example with what happened the first few times I attempted to teach this seminar. I provided the same information and used the same lecture outline. Without the pauses, however, there were no questions, no discussion, and no statements of commitment or plans for action. The faculty members left the room as quickly as possible, anxious to get back to their work. With no beginning pause or concluding pause, my early teaching efforts on this important topic were a waste of everyone's time and resulted in little, if any, change in attitude or behavior.

When I introduced the lecture with the pilot activity previously described, the entire learning experience changed. I didn't rework the lecture, I didn't develop a new case or alter the content, and I didn't try to flip the session. I simply began by giving learners a chance to feel the frustration of not getting feedback when they needed it. This simple experience helped them to be more sensitive to the fact that we all need feedback sometimes. When I again paused the lecture at the end, I provided them with an opportunity to think about personal applications and specific action plans. To generate major improvements in our students' learning, we don't have to overhaul the valuable lecture notes that we have developed over time. A good way to start is to add pauses at appropriate times throughout the lecture period.

Good teaching requires not only transferring information but also motivating the learner to think about the learning experience and see the beauty of the learning. Motivating teachers help their students desire new information at the start and help them look back at the value gained from the learning experience at the close.

When we pause during a teaching session, we have less time to cover the content, but we can be sure that what we teach will be well learned. We hear often that less is more; instead of trying to cover too much material at one time, we would have better results if we taught less information more thoroughly (Dror, 2011; Jensen, 2005; Medina, 2011).

In the Epigraph (p. vi , this volume), Marken's (2008) reference to pauses as *silences* reminds us of our responsibility to "create oases of silence where cool springs of insight trickle and flow" (p. 115). Learners who have experienced the gift of a teacher's silence at the start of the session are curious about the topic, anticipate it, and respond positively to the lecture as the discussion ensues. Most important, when their teachers have become silent and listened to them at the closing of the session, students will know how to use what they have learned and why it is valuable. Perhaps our silence might inspire insight in a way our talk was never able to achieve.

PART TWO

BRAIN SCIENCE SUPPORT FOR THE PAUSE

2

PAUSING SUPPORTS IDEAL LEARNING

When we add pauses to our teaching plan, we are essentially changing the class session from a traditional lecture to what we might consider an interactive lecture classroom. This interactive approach inserts purposeful learning pauses into a series of short lectures and brings the power of collaborative learning and engagement into what would otherwise be a presentation dominated by teacher talk.

Benefits of Pausing

Inserting pauses into our teaching will affect learning in important ways. We can expect to improve the classroom environment through the development of collaborative relationships among students, and we will give and receive important feedback on student learning. Data abound that learning and retention show amazing improvement when the flow of teacher talk takes an occasional break for students to respond to challenges presented in understanding and applying important concepts.

Pauses Tap Into the Power of Collaborative Learning

Higher education classrooms have become quite solitary affairs. Our students enter their classroom, find a seat, consult their text messages or e-mail, and expect to sit quietly for the entire class period without saying a word to anyone. Many of our students are used to spending little if any time at all on campus beyond attending class; they pride themselves on making it as far as they have in higher education on their own, and they probably have quite full lives outside the academic realm. These students are not making connections with their classmates and tend to resist cooperative learning approaches. Without our help, they rarely ask for and discover the resources available to them in their colleagues—their peers—who can help them accomplish challenging tasks that might not be possible for them to achieve alone.

When we ask students to spend a minute or two during a short lecture break to talk with a classmate across the room about their learning, we change the learning environment. New relationships form during these pauses, and these relationships may be just as important to the quality of the learning as the content of the task. Bowman (2011) describes it as the following:

> Relationships create a feeling of psychological safety. When learners feel safe with each other and the instructor, they are more willing to ask questions, make mistakes, be open to new ideas, try new skills and take some risks. In effect, they learn better. (p. 125)

Pauses provide more for students than just focus and energy. Pausing the lecture helps students with the normal human desire for connection and social support. These pauses provide students with a number of positive outcomes, such as increased self-esteem, social awareness, sensitivity, and improved listening and communication skills needed for success in the workplace.

Nearly all the pauses in this book involve sharing ideas among two or more students and thus will tap into the powerful benefits of collaborative learning, connecting students to resources they might otherwise remain quite oblivious to.

Pauses Provide Feedback

When learners talk to a classmate, they give and receive feedback from their peers. If they need help understanding a concept, they can request it. If they notice something that needs clarification, their peers can provide it. They can correct each other's misconceptions and suggest alternative ways to look at a subject. They can fill in details for each other or expand an idea with additional perspectives. This feedback helps learners take charge of their own learning. Now they know what they need to study in more depth, they have a better idea of how to approach academic tasks, and they know where they can go for additional assistance and feedback—to not only the instructor but also their colleagues.

When we as faculty members begin working pauses into our lecture plans, we encounter a number of unexpected benefits beyond enhancing our students' learning. We may even become a bit addicted to those pauses that give us the gift of feedback, which tells us that our students have understood the concept we just tried so hard to explain or, perhaps, tells us that we need to try another way to get the idea across.

The little break from having to concentrate on what we will say next gives us a moment to reset and refocus. That pause to allow our students to find their applications and make connections between the theoretical concept and a real-world issue frees us to interact with students, ask and answer questions, and note how certain students are thinking, while giving us opportunities to provide that needed feedback.

Pauses Increase Retention

Because pauses allow learners to switch from listening to talking, they have powerful effects. Talking enhances learning; we talk to understand, remember, and learn. Perhaps Bowman (2011), writer of many practical books that apply brain science to learning for the training world, has said it best, "The person doing the most talking about the topic is doing the most learning about the topic" (p. 126).

Why is talking so important to learning? One cannot be passive if one is speaking. To respond to a question, learners must first comprehend the question, then they need to consider what they think about the issue and put it into their own words. The process of formulating a verbal response requires the learner to revisit the ideas several times. Repetition alone will increase retention.

Wolfe (2001) and many others suggest that the best way to learn is to teach. When we ask students to share their notes with each other or to quiz each other on an important concept or to explain their thinking, we give them opportunities to teach and, therefore, are reinforcing learning in the most powerful ways. Richard Rice, teaching medical students a course on suffering and God's relation to the world, had a question from a student about a particular concept of God that had been discussed in a previous course the quarter before. Rice glanced around the room and noticed that a number of the students present had taken the course that had addressed this question at some length. He asked those who had been in the previous course to pair up with someone who hadn't taken the course and explain the concept to their partner in five minutes. After the students returned to their seats, Rice asked the teacher students if they understood it better now that they had explained it, and the answer was a very strong yes (R. Rice, personal communication, October 22, 2014).

One of the early studies that showed better learning and test outcomes when teacher talk was substituted with student talk assessed outcomes from a large number of college physics classes (Hake, 1998). This landmark study showed tremendous differences in outcomes between courses taught in the traditional lecture method and those with more collaborative approaches. Students who learned more cooperatively showed gains two to three times greater than their classmates in the traditional classrooms. Essentially, the worst class that paused for some student talk outperformed the best class where teacher talk prevailed. Similar results have been reported by educational researchers many times (Millis, 2010).

Characteristics of Good Learning Pauses

When we consider giving students a voice, we are referring to very specific directed activities, not just a turn-and-talk opportunity without directions and expectations. For ideal learning to result from a lecture break, it is essential for the teacher-planned pause to meet certain criteria. We explore what cognitive science suggests to make all learning pauses particularly successful in this chapter. Chapters 3, 4, and 5 contain particular considerations for pauses at different stages of learning.

Cognitive science researchers provide insights on how to shape these learning pauses for maximum benefits. It may be helpful to review some concepts that will make our learning pauses even more effective.

Good Pauses Create a Positive and Safe Environment

Emotions play a powerful role in learning by triggering the release of the neurotransmitters adrenaline, norepinephrine, and vasopressin, which signal the brain to pay attention. Medina (2011) tells us that "emotionally charged events persist much longer in our memories and are recalled with greater accuracy than neutral memories" (p. 80).

Well-known author David McCullough caught my attention on a morning news show recently, saying that when you're happy, you think better (McCullough, 2017). This comment may seem obvious, but it is worth considering in the context of teaching and learning. Cavanagh (2016) explored the role of emotions in learning, stating, "Happier, more optimistic teachers could lead to more academic gains in students" (p. 99). Jensen (2008) draws our attention to the importance of creating a positive learning environment from the beginning of class. "The bottom line," he states, "is that unless students are in a good emotional state for learning, you have no more important job" (p. 145). He further suggests that students frame learning to make it "relevant, important, and compelling" as well before the lecture begins. Framing further creates a positive mood and an emotional invitation to learn by hooking students into wanting to know what is to follow.

A pleasant environment influences learning in important ways. When students enter a learning space where they feel safe to open themselves to new possibilities, new ways of thinking and learning can occur that might not have otherwise been possible. Before opening themselves to explore attitudes and beliefs, learners must feel that their ideas will be treated with respect. We can create this kind of learning environment through consciously planning to begin learning in a positive and accepting way. Learning pauses throughout the class period can continue to assure students that their professor values their input and welcomes their ideas.

As engineers of learning spaces and experiences, we may become so engrossed in organizing our content that we forget to think about including an uplifting, upbeat, happy element in our teaching plan. When we focus on fostering a positive environment in the class, however, improved learning will result. David Rock (2008), cofounder of the NeuroLeadership Institute, said, "There is a large and growing body of research which indicates that people experiencing positive emotions perceive more options when trying to solve problems, solve more non-linear problems that require insight, collaborate better and generally perform better overall" (p. 46).

Shaun Achor (2011a), Harvard psychology professor, tells us that when we are in a positive mood dopamine is released in the brain, which literally "turns on all of the learning centers in the brain." He reports that students taking math tests do significantly better when they are in a positive state of mind. Doctors in a positive mood show

> almost three times more intelligence and creativity than doctors in a neutral state, and they make accurate diagnoses 19 percent faster. . . . Our brains are literally hardwired to perform at their best, not when they are negative or even neutral, but when they are positive. (Achor, 2011b, p. 15)

Those of us who would like to increase the positive tone of our classrooms might invite a colleague to observe us for the express purpose of looking for ways we might improve. As painful as it is to look at a recording of ourselves in the classroom, this is also worth doing so we can look for body language. Are we leaning forward? Are we moving around the room or standing absolutely still and wooden? Are we welcoming student comments and making positive responses to them? Are we smiling? Do we look relaxed and comfortable? Have we planned for something interesting during the period? Do our students ever say that class was fun? Do they ever say that the time flew? Students tell us that when they are doing the talking, they are having fun. When they are doing the talking, they are doing the learning. When they are pausing to do something other than listen to teacher talk, they are learning.

In selecting examples of pauses for this book, I have tried to provide a range of possibilities from quite cerebral and dignified to rather playful. You may not feel particularly comfortable with some of the more lighthearted approaches to pausing in your setting, but you may be surprised at how well your students may react to even the less dignified pauses suggested in the appendixes. It is important to note that it seems that when the questions we ask students to consider are significant, it is okay to do this in a playful way. Read the statistics class example in the introduction to the Pauses. An adult learning specialist wasn't too far off track when he said, "Adults are just babies in big bodies" and "Learning is directly proportional to the amount of fun one is having" (Pike, 2003, p. 3). Creating a positive environment cannot help but contribute to learning.

Good Pauses Are Purposeful and Metacognitive

Students in higher education, increasingly focused on short-term goals of passing courses, checking off requirements, completing degrees or certificates, and possibly passing board exams, often appear uninterested in learning for learning itself. One of the beauties of the lecture pause is that it requires students to begin thinking about their learning. When we regularly ask our students to look back at what they have learned and place it into a particular context or apply it to a question students raised earlier in class, we give them an opportunity to pause from the race to take in volumes of information and see how important learning is and how it will contribute to their success.

Weimer (2012) writes about metacognition when she says,

> It is terribly important that in explicit and concerted ways we make students aware of themselves as learners. We must regularly ask, not only "What are you learning?" but "How are you learning?" We must confront them with the effectiveness (more often ineffectiveness) of their approaches. We must offer alternatives and then challenge students to test the efficacy of those approaches.

When we offer our students a chance to talk about the benefits of becoming more aware of how their brain works, when we ask them to explain how they came to a particular conclusion, when we ask for their summary or a ranking or an evaluation, we give them metacognition training and an orientation toward lifelong learning. We help them to not only think about their thinking but also evaluate their thinking and develop new ways of thinking. Cross (2007) suggests that "setting people up to learn how to learn ignites a process of perpetual self-improvement. Enlightened self-interest kicks in" (p. 78).

Learning how to learn may be the most valuable skill we help students develop. They often have no idea how little they actually grasp course concepts and are sometimes shocked when they get an exam back with a low grade. These same students rarely think about what they could learn from a poor exam performance, shrugging it off as an unlucky coincidence or, more likely, the result of a poorly written test that really didn't cover the material the teacher presented in the course. Students frequently have illusions of fluency (Brown et al., 2014); that is, thinking they know much more than they do. When asked to predict how well they will do on an exam, it is common for them to have an unrealistic assessment of their readiness. Known as an exam wrapper, this metacognitive approach is helpful to assist students to think about how they prepared for an exam, what worked, and what they might do differently the next time.

Similar to using an exam wrapper to help students assess their study habits and how they might have done better on their exam, the idea of a Lecture Wrapper (CP 63) helps students to metacognitively evaluate how they approach learning in class. Lovett (2008) suggests we consider using the Lecture Wrapper pause technique to train students to learn to listen for key elements and be able to duplicate the instructor's outlines. In Lovett's study, students were asked to list the three most important concepts from the day's lecture on several successive occasions. Students turned in their cards with their ideas of the important points, and then the teacher told students what the three most important concepts were intended to be. The students' ability to match their responses with the teachers' responses improved from 45% the first time and 68% the second time to 75% the third time they were asked to finish class with this pause technique. Instructors discovered that this activity taught students how to listen better and appreciate the beauty of a well-delivered lecture (Lovett, 2008).

The concept of wrapping is an excellent metacognitive technique we might incorporate into our closing pauses to help students learn better from the lecture, bring closure to concepts, and make action plans for future learning. Nilson (2013) suggests that "incorporating the right wrappers could redeem the well-delivered lecture as a highly respectable teaching method" (p. 45).

The following are some ways to include metacognition in our lecture pauses:

- Be explicit in explaining metacognition and its potential impact. For example, tell the class, "Metacognition is becoming more aware of our thinking and our learning and how we can improve by analyzing ourselves as thinkers and learners. We will be doing metacognitive thinking when we pause to anticipate or look back over our learning together."

- Include starting pauses to help learners examine their prior experiences and current thinking. Ask, "What do you already know about this topic, and how does your earlier experience affect your learning?"
- Allow learners to frequently look over their notes and identify areas that need clarification. Ask them what they don't understand or how you can assist them to identify gaps and areas they would like help with.
- Frequently give students details about why you are asking them to pause or how a particular pause benefits them at this point in learning by saying, for example, "Research supports the benefits of breaking learning up into smaller sections, so we are going to stop a minute to see if you can answer this question" or "The benefits of physical movement include increasing oxygen to the brain and thus help you to think better, so we are going to walk around the room for a minute before we find a partner to share our ideas with."
- Ask learners to think about how you approached a particular challenge and how it might apply to other fields of study. For example, you could ask "We have used inductive reasoning to try to understand the philosophical concept of God's actions in the world. How would this way of thinking help you with other concepts in other courses you are studying?"
- During the closing pause, ask students to talk about how their thinking has changed during this particular class. This can be especially valuable as a closing activity at the end of the course and not just at the end of a particular class session.
- Ask for reflection on the learning process. Journal or online discussion assignments are often a good place to address such considerations as how their personal life benefits from how they have learned in this course.
- Model metacognitive thinking when describing how we approach problems in our discipline. When we can laugh with our students at mistakes we have made and describe how we learned from them and moved forward, we are teaching that learning and improving are more likely when we analyze our errors and find ways to turn them into positive outcomes.

According to Kolb (2014), there are four phases in ideal learning (set, content, application, and closure), and there are four questions to be answered in ideal learning (why, what, how, and if). Metacognitive questions for learners to address while pausing during the four phases might include the following:

Phase 1: Starting Pauses

- Why am I attending this class?
- Why will this be useful to me?
- Why should I care about this topic?

Phase 2: Midpauses

- What should I learn and how can I be effective in learning it?
- What resources do I need to help me learn well?
- What will be important to me from this topic?
- What am I learning and what do I need to review?
- What do I need clarification or assistance with?

Phase 3: Midpauses

- How can I use this information in a practical way?
- How are my strategies working?
- How can I improve the way I apply these concepts?
- How will I evaluate my ability to apply?

Phase 4: Closing Pauses

- If I am going to remember this important information, what do I need to do?
- If this is truly important, what are my next steps?
- If I am to improve, what do I need to focus on?
- If I were to teach this class, how would I change it?

The beauty of the metacognitive learning pause is that it helps our students increase their awareness of how they learn and how they can learn better. Perhaps as they learn more about their learning, they will have the ultimate survival tool in the end (Bjork, 1994).

Good Pauses Personalize Learning

We can add value to the pauses we take with our students when we ask them to think about their personal experiences with a particular concept. When information takes on a personal meaning, entire neural fields are activated, and information becomes personally relevant and authentic (Jensen, 2008). Medina (2011) states, "The more personal an example, the more richly it becomes encoded and the more readily it is remembered" (p. 115). Harrington and Zakrajsek (2017) suggest that connecting material to ourselves "is a natural and efficient learning system, powerful because our memory for the familiar is much stronger than our memory for the unfamiliar, and what could be more familiar than our own lives?" (p. 86).

Medical educators, such as Elizabeth Armstrong, director of the Harvard Macy Institute for Health Professional Education, recognize the importance of personalized learning. To prepare learners for new content, she suggests that

> personal meaning and motivation should be set for what is to follow. . . . Any effective educational encounter begins with the learner. In our professional development courses, the participants bring questions, goals, issues, and real-world projects that set the stage for learning to be anchored in tasks and goals the learner has defined. . . . These group and individual exercises both provide a clear starting point for the learning process and also help the learners clarify what they hope to accomplish and why they should actively engage in the course work. This creates an environment that places the learner at the center. The teacher gets to know and care about the participants as individuals. Through activating, articulating, and reflecting what they already know and value, the participants ready themselves to listen to and evaluate the new information the course provides. (Armstrong & Parsa-Parsi, 2005, p. 680)

Armstrong (2016) makes the point again in a powerful way in talking about a large-group case discussion when she says,

> I use the discussion method without summaries from me at the end because I believe that learners have to reflect on the experience of the case discussion to construct their own knowledge. They need to create their own summary—I cannot and should not give it to them. I believe that this is the way that they learn. (p. 681)

I realized the importance of bringing personal meaning into the learning experience at an activity Todd Zakrajsek, educator and author, shared at a Lilly Conference on higher education. Zakrajsek handed each of us a sheet of paper with instructions and blanks to fill in at the beginning of the activity. The front half of the room had pink handouts. Those of us in the back got green handouts. Zakrajsek flashed a series of about 50 words up on the screen. The instructions on the green handout were to write down the number of syllables each of the words contained. The words were all common household items, such as mayonnaise, barbecue, or flashlight. After recording the number of syllables for each word on the list in blanks provided on the handout, we were asked to write down as many of the words as we could remember. I tried as hard as I could to remember what the words were, but I could only come up with five of them. I was feeling dumb, as I noticed others in the room were writing down many more words than I had been able to write down.

Zakrajsek explained the activity to us and asked us to report how many words we remembered. He was quick to point out that the better students were sitting at the front of the room, where everyone had received a pink handout. The pink handouts distributed to those in the front of the room contained a different set of instructions from the green ones. The instructions on the pink handout asked those in the front to write in the blanks how many times they had interacted with each item in the past week. No wonder the front half of the room remembered an average of 16 to 18 words, whereas the back half of the room could only come up with 5 or 6 of the words. Those who remembered more had been attaching personal meaning to each of the words. Those of us who only counted syllables hadn't considered what the words meant at all, certainly not what they meant to us individually. When I saw the word "mayonnaise," I only counted 3 syllables, wrote down 3, and proceeded to the next word without a thought. If I had been asked to write down how many times I had interacted with mayonnaise during the past week, I might have thought about the fact that I had been trying to eat a low carbohydrate diet and had avoided sandwiches completely, which means I would have written down 0 for mayonnaise. I would have remembered more because I would have thought about what each of those words meant to me personally during the learning activity.

When we pause our lectures to allow our students to respond to a learning task, we find that a personal element is frequently present. Many of the closing pauses ask learners to think about how what they have just learned will contribute to their personal or professional success. Other pauses for the close of the learning session request students to share what they personally value from the class, and why they chose a particular concept. Starting pauses may include answering a question, such as, What has been your experience with this topic? or Have you known anyone who has encountered this particular challenge? A religion teacher would find it helpful to ask his or her students to think about their own experiences of loss when they study suffering and think about how to be helpful to others who are suffering. The teacher finds that when students place these concepts into their own experiences, they have a different attitude to learning about suffering. Recalling how a grandparent faced death or how a close friend struggled with a disabling disease helps them to grapple with issues they might find uninteresting and unimportant otherwise.

Good Pauses Are Often Unpredictable

What do you think? Of the following two options, which is best?

1. Teachers should conduct their classes the same way every time so students know what to expect.
2. Teachers should make changes, keeping their students guessing what will come next.

Of course usually the best answer to this kind of a question is a combination of the two. I was surprised at how many of my colleagues chose option 1. "Keep it the same," they said. One added, "Students need consistency and like to be able to predict what is coming next." It can be true that using a consistent approach to class brings a certain level of comfort to the teachers and the students. It is also the case that when a faculty member is trying something new, it may be wise to suggest for them to use it a number of times to check its effectiveness and efficiency. Faculty developer Kevin Barry states, "I often suggest that instructors start with two or three engagement strategies and use them multiple times so that the overhead of explanation of the process pays off as the students get more and more competent" (K. Barry, personal communication, July 27, 2017).

Cognitive scientists provide some surprising insights on the relationship among change, unpredictability, and learning and suggest that changing things up has real benefits. These researchers tell us option 2 is actually better for learning. Chip and Dan Heath (2007), talking about how to make learning stick, suggest that "the most basic way to get someone's attention is this: Break a pattern. . . . Our brain is designed to be keenly aware of changes. . . . Unexpected ideas are more likely to stick because surprise makes us pay attention and think" (p. 64–65, 68). Bozarth (2011) said the following:

> Several lines of thought converge on the role of surprise in learning. One biological explanation says novel stimuli activate the hippocampus, triggering release of dopamine; another says the brain is a pattern-matching machine, with the basal ganglia jumping to attention when something breaks a pattern. Cognitive psychology recognizes the importance of the "discrepant event": something that has an unexpected outcome engages the brain and encourages problem solving and critical thinking. If you had a good science teacher, I'll bet you remember things such as demonstrations showing that a Styrofoam ball and a metal ball with the same volume will, when dropped, hit the ground at the same time.
>
> When surprised, we jump-to a little, pay more attention, give something some thought. . . . Kathy Sierra, a resident of the brain-as-pattern-matching camp, puts it in simple, commonsense terms when she suggests

that the brain spends far less time processing things that meet expectations than it does on things that don't.

Surprise actually helps us learn. Research reveals that surprise drives the motivation to learn and is an important tool in cognitive development. Surprise brings pleasure, which is associated with the release of dopamine, a chemical that activates reward centers in the brain associated with readiness to learn. This may not be true for all of us, but many do confess that a surprise birthday party is just a little more special than one that was known about all along. Researchers at Emory University who wanted to see if surprise made a difference compared individuals who received squirts of fruit juice into their mouth at predictable intervals versus those who received the squirts randomly. Magnetic resonance imaging scans showed a significant difference between the two groups. Those receiving unexpected squirts were much more delighted than those expecting their reward (Berns, McClure, Pagnoni, & Montague, 2001).

The hippocampus is the brain's novelty detector. When information comes into the brain, the hippocampus notes whether this input is familiar. New material is more stimulating to the hippocampus, which causes the release of dopamine, which results in our creating connections that lead to long-term memory storage, which is why we remember things better in the context of novelty (Fenker & Schütze, 2008; Straker, 2008).

I have flown a lot with Delta Air Lines over the years. I don't know how many times I have seen the short safety video at the beginning of each flight, but I am quite sure that I had it memorized. A couple of years ago, I noticed that the video seemed different. Delta officials know what it takes to get people to pay attention. When something looks the same and sounds the same over and over again, pretty soon people stop paying attention to it. After years and years of playing the same video, Delta administrators finally got smart and changed it. They put some humor into it. We saw identical triplets sitting in the exit row and cartoon characters in the aisles, and the woman in the in-flight safety video who insisted on no smoking was in a different setting than usual. All of a sudden the passengers started watching the screen and listening.

Surprise and unpredictability are important to good pauses. Unfortunately, we professors are known for our tendencies to get into ruts. We find something that works and repeat it over and over, unaware of how boring this can be to our students. Students generally appreciate it when we bring surprise and unpredictability into our pauses. It may be better to skip a pause occasionally than to overuse it. In other words, A Penny for Your Thoughts (CP 59) is only going to be a good closing pause experience for our group once in a while. If we repeat that exact same thing too often, our students will bring less and less creative and critical thinking to the task. During a typical quarter or semester, we should probably not use it too often. There are many other approaches we can take to close a learning session (see Appendix C for ideas). Students will pay more attention to a pause that requires them to think a bit differently than before. The more novel the approach, the more likely students are to find it intriguing, interesting, and likely to promote long-term memory.

Metaphors for Teaching

Unfortunately, it is so easy for us as educators to become extremely focused on the content of our presentation—the lecture, the theory, the information that must be passed on—that we tend to lose sight of the cognitive science that emphasizes the importance of going beyond simple delivery of content to plan how we will help our students learn. We are all guilty of entering the classroom, teaching, and leaving. I am sorry to admit that sometimes my metaphor for teaching and learning has been that of the container. My responsibility as the teacher is thus simply to provide information; everything else is the learner's concern, such as figuring out why the information might be valuable, how it should be used, and if it will be transferred to personal and professional settings outside the lecture hall.

A better metaphor might be something like a gardener or tour guide. Gardeners know they can't simply toss seeds onto the ground and expect results. They carefully prepare the earth, adding nutrients to the soil, before placing seeds into furrows. They don't just leave the seeds there to make do on their own. They water, fertilize, and place soil over the top of those seeds to close them into their protective and ideal environment. Tour guides don't just lecture to individuals at sites of interest. They plan the tour carefully; provide introductory information; and give instructions on how to dress, where to go, and what to do beforehand. They often prepare readings to finish before or after attending the site visit. They do more than just refresh their knowledge in preparing for this learning event; they guide learners through the experience, enhancing every aspect.

Instructors with good metaphors for learning will envision how optimum learning begins and ends. Instructors who motivate students seek ideas on how to prepare the learner, how to make the learner want the learning, how to help the learner understand what the potential value of the learning might be, and how to create curiosity and eagerness for learning.

Additionally these instructors look for ways to finish their lectures well. What do they do at the end besides asking for student questions? How do they encourage learners to pause to look back and see the beauty of what they are learning, to actually do something about what they have just heard? What can the instructor do to increase the likelihood that the students will transfer their learning to practice? What can be said so that learners value this lecture content enough to revisit it, to incorporate it into their lives?

Positive, purposeful, personalized, and unpredictable pauses will help us bring about ideal learning. They provide natural ways to chunk lecture content into reasonably sized memorable learning experiences.

3

STARTING PAUSES FOCUS ATTENTION

If we are not in the habit of starting learning by first pausing to get a sense of where our learners are, it may be with good reason. A number of myths support the concept that good learning requires teachers to do all the talking.

Myths About Teaching Without a Starting Pause

Many instructors would like to start their classes with opening pauses but find that their presuppositions get in the way. Commonly held myths make it hard for us to begin learning with a pause. Following are some of the myths that lead teachers to plunge into their presentation without preparing learners for the content to follow.

Myth 1: Content Must Precede Applications

A common belief of teachers is that students must first hear the facts before they can do anything with a topic. Teachers with this orientation emphasize delivering information as their major role in the classroom. They plan to teach by organizing content, preparing outlines, and delivering the material, and this must happen first. They assume that only after the material is learned can applications and expansions of the content occur. And the only model they have for learning is students listening to the teacher talking.

Pike (2003) discusses three approaches to starting the teaching process. He suggests starting with theory, awareness, or experience to prepare for the other parts of learning. The myth that many teachers hold dear is that you must start with theory, otherwise there is no foundation, no basis for developing awareness or experiencing applications. When we start with a pause, however, we start with an experience, which cognitive science suggests is often a better way to begin learning.

Myth 2: If I Don't Say It, They Won't Learn It

This common educator belief contributes to more wasted classroom time than any other. We can't let go of the idea that we must tell our students everything that is important for them to know; if we don't, we have failed. Probably the biggest source of frustration for faculty members in professional programs is the ever-increasing body of knowledge we wish to convey to our students in what seems to be less and less time. When I have conducted workshops on active learning and the importance of pausing, participants generally are enthusiastic but reluctant because they wonder how they can pause and still cover the content when they will have even less time for teacher talk. In this age of increasing information, it is more necessary than ever for teachers to choose those objectives that are most important and teach them well. It is also essential for instructors to explore alternate ways to teach besides talking. Written handouts, Web-based instruction, case and dilemma discussions, retrieval exercises, and out-of-class activities are obvious examples.

Myth 3: Knowledge Is Received

Many teachers see the learner as a receiver of knowledge and perceive teaching as transferring content. Their task is simply to move information from one location to another. The teacher is the authority; all knowledge comes from the teacher. Instructors who think this way may not be aware of what the learner brings to the teaching-learning process. As a result, they ask for little feedback on how the teaching is meeting the needs of the learner or how the learner will use the provided lecture material.

It is necessary for us to challenge these common ways of thinking to craft effective learning experiences for our students. As long as we believe these myths, we will find it hard to break learning into manageable chunks; we will neglect those important pauses, and learning will suffer as a result.

Characteristics of Good Starting Pauses

Cognitive science research can help us shape learning pauses to maximize the benefits. In the previous chapter we looked at the importance of pauses being positive, metacognitive, memorable, personalized, and unpredictable. In the following, we examine the characteristics of good starting pauses.

Grab Attention, Focus, and Break Preoccupation

The purpose of the starting pause is to grab our students' attention. "The small boys came early to the hanging" is the first sentence in one of my favorite novels, *The Pillars of the Earth* (Follett, 1989, p. 11). Good novelists know something that good teachers also have discovered. First impressions are extremely important, and if we can grab attention at the beginning, we are off to a good start. Our students arrive at our classrooms with many things on their mind—the car that didn't start, the child who seems to be coming down with a cold, the roommate who was in a bad mood, or the student who didn't have time for breakfast and is starving. It goes without saying that it may not be easy for them to switch gears and become engrossed in the topic for our class. And yet we so often lose the power of those first few minutes of class by failing to plan for activities or questions that will break their preoccupation and focus our students' attention.

A faculty member invited me to visit his class to view the way he typically pauses at the beginning. Here is what one of his students said:

> At first I thought it was kind of weird. Dr. Sharp started class by turning the lights down and asking us to close our eyes and concentrate on our breathing. He had us breathe in and out slowly and let go of all of our thoughts. After a while we were ready for class to start. I wondered why we were wasting all of this time, but I think our teacher knew what he was doing. When class started, it really started. I do think I was able to pay attention right from the beginning without all of the distractions that usually slow me down. (Anonymous, personal communication, October 24, 2016)

Sharp teaches a three-hour class once a week in communication science. Regarding his opening pauses, he said,

> I find I can accomplish much more in 160 minutes with that opening time to focus that prepares students to fully immerse themselves in class than I could in 180 minutes without that pause. It is as important for me as it is for the students. It is the time for me to concentrate on how I will proceed with my class plan and what I should focus on, which of the students I especially want to watch for particular signs from, and what cognitive concepts I want to request feedback on. (B. Sharp, personal communication, May 12, 2017)

Although Sharp finds meditation to be a good way to focus his students' attention on learning, Vicki Halsey (2011) starts classes with high-energy creative experiences. Halsey brings an educational psychology background to her work helping trainers to understand how to teach effectively. As she describes it, the initial task of the teacher is to energize the learner. When instructors start with an energizing activity, signals are sent to the brain that this learning has great promise. Attention is focused, and readiness occurs. According to Halsey, "The faster you get your learners talking about relevant interesting topics, the faster you excite them, activate their interest and commitment to your content" (2011, p. 68). It doesn't take these learners long to discover that great learning doesn't start by sitting and listening to a lecturer talk about her PowerPoint slides.

The speed of thought is about six times faster than that of speech (Weaver, 2008). If we instructors are doing all the talking, expecting our students to sit and listen to us speak significantly slower than they can think, it is highly likely their attention is going to begin to wander very quickly, no matter how interesting the topic we are addressing is. So our pauses will be most effective if they are designed to be interesting and capture our students' attention, if they help students focus and break their tendency to allow their minds to wander to things that will break in and distract them from listening to the teacher.

Honeycutt (2016) recognizes the importance of helping students focus at the beginning of learning and offers 50 suggestions, each of which starts with the word *focus*.

Teachers have been known to do pretty hilarious things to grab their students' attention, but we also have to admit that it often works. It may not fit your personality to wear a condom hat to your public health class on family planning methods, but if it does, it will probably pay off with increased student attention from the very beginning.

Generate Curiosity and Anticipation

Those important first few minutes of class can be used to create an expectation of what is to follow, which can have an impact on the rest of the class period. We have long suspected that the element of anticipation or curiosity can enhance learning, but now we have data to confirm this.

A group of University of California, Davis researchers asked 19 individuals to rate how interested they were in more than 100 trivia questions. After indicating how intrigued they were by the questions, the participants were given the answers to all the questions. As might be expected, subjects particularly remembered the answers later to the questions they were curious about. The researchers in this study scanned the subjects' brains using magnetic resonance imaging, which revealed differences in brain activity when positive anticipation was present. The brain actually set up an expectation of reward, related to the release of dopamine, when an answer was eagerly anticipated. This chemical, neurological response seems to ready the brain for enhanced learning and better retention. The researchers concluded that piquing curiosity before learning improves short- and long-term retention (Gruber, Gelman, & Ranganath, 2014; Yuhas, 2014).

Some ideas to help students discover their curiosity about a topic might include the following:

- Provide answers to questions in sealed envelopes either passed out to students or taped to the bottom of some of the chairs. Throughout the learning session, questions could be discussed and then the teacher could ask the student with envelope number 4, for example, to open it and read the answer.
- Bring a brown paper bag or box to the front of the classroom with an object in it that will be used to introduce your topic and objectives; see What's in the Box? (SP 17). An instructor teaching a group of new parents about breastfeeding might have a golf ball in her bag. Most of the new fathers would probably be quick to suggest that the golf ball's connection to new parenting and breastfeeding meant that there would be no more golfing in the foreseeable future for them with a new baby about to arrive. But, in fact, the instructor is using this pause to give the group a vivid lesson on the size of a newborn infant's stomach. The actual amount of food an average newborn can consume in a feeding is about the size of a golf ball.
- Give students a quiz at the beginning of class; see Quiz Time Start—Audience Response System (SP 10) and Quiz Time Start—Color Cards (SP 11). Students who might not have thought they were interested in a topic and guessed the answers for the quiz become curious about how well they answered the questions. They are likely to care more about the topic, having invested themselves into the introductory pause activity, and will find the learning more interesting because the instructor has helped to create curiosity, which research suggests primes the brain for learning and retention.

Activate, Build on Prior Knowledge, and Scaffold

A scaffold is a structure used in building construction to allow workers to reach otherwise inaccessible areas. Scaffolding is a valuable concept in education. When we pause before providing new information to students to explore prior experiences and existing knowledge, we help them to scaffold (Alber, 2011). In other words, we do not want to start on fresh ground if a structure is already present that can be built on (Merrill, 1991). When we take time to help learners discover what they have to build on, we do them a favor. According to Medina (2011), "Information is more readily processed if it can be immediately associated with information already present in the learner's brain" (p. 115). Jensen (2008) suggests that "finding out what students already know, and asking them to make connections to another more accurate model, is how the real learning process begins" (p. 47). And yet, it is so easy to skip this part of planning in our teaching. One of the values of taking time for the pause at the beginning of instruction is to provide learners with the opportunity to explore their earlier experiences with a given topic and find something to which they can attach the new learning.

I have developed an interesting activity to help educators experience the tremendous advantage we give our students when we help them attach new learning to something they already know. I divide the learners into two groups of teachers and learners. They pair up, and each teaches a colleague a set of codes for the numbers one to nine and then administers a short quiz. All the teachers teach the same content and give the same quiz, but they have been given different instructions on how to teach the material. Half the teachers use a sheet with instructions that include Figure 3.1. They teach their learners to memorize these symbols to represent the numbers.

The other teachers have a teaching instruction sheet that looks the same but with the suggestion that it might be easy for the learners if they use the tic-tac-toe model to help them learn the symbols for each number (Figure 3.2).

All the teachers are teaching that number 1 is represented by a symbol that looks like a left-facing *L*, but half of the teachers teach their students to memorize it. The other half of the participants teach it using a tic-tac-toe grid to show a number 1 surrounded by the left-facing *L*, making it quite easy to remember what the symbol for number 1 is. The purpose of the activity is to show that when you teach a new code for the numbers one to nine, if you place them in the nine squares of a tic-tac-toe diagram, it is easy to remember them, as each number's code is the lines surrounding the numbers in the diagram. Using something students already know (tic-tac-toe) allows them to build on preexisting knowledge to make learning new information easy, such as remembering that the symbol for a five is a four-sided box.

As might be expected, those who learned by adding the new information to what they already understood about the tic-tac-toe game quickly learned the codes and aced the quiz. By recalling the simple diagram, they were able to do equally well on a similar quiz months later. Not so for the group that learned the codes for each number using rote memorization. It took this group 10 to 20 times longer to prepare for their quiz, and their long-term retention was

Figure 3.1. Teaching aid for the teaching codes activity.

1		6	
2		7	
3		8	
4		9	
5		10	

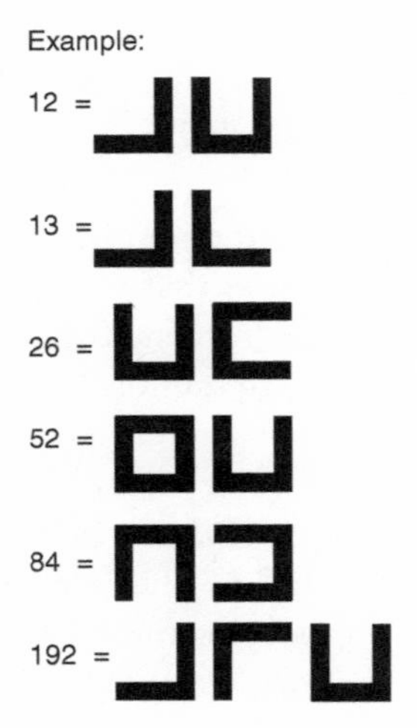

Figure 3.2 Additional teaching aid for the teaching codes activity.

1	2	3
4	5	6
7	8	9

extremely poor because they had no prior knowledge or experience to attach the new learning to.

Using students' prior experience requires several steps, the *first* of which is to activate knowledge or experience. We have more and more evidence that our students will learn better when their prior knowledge has been activated. Ambrose and colleagues (2010) tell us that new knowledge works best when it can attach to old knowledge. Once we get students to acknowledge what they already know and have experienced related to a given topic, then it is important to determine the adequacy and accuracy of that prior experience. We have all run into challenges of assuming solid prior experience that ended up being pretty shaky or worse, insufficient, inaccurate, or inappropriate. Finally, once students identify knowledge and prior experiences, they will be able to build on their knowledge, fill in the gaps where their earlier experiences are inadequate or inaccurate, and work toward stronger learning results.

A number of the starting pauses in Appendix A are specifically designed to activate prior knowledge (see SP 1, SP 2, SP 4, SP 5, and SP 6). Many suggest that students should consider and share their personal experiences, hunches, or ideas about the content under study and connect and relate those experiences to their personal lives. When this occurs, barriers to learning are broken down, and new learning is possible.

Connect to the Topic

A good starting pause is not an icebreaker; even though it may serve to break the ice and connect students to others in the room, it is much more than that. It is an introduction to the concept or topic of the day, so it should be related to that topic. An instructor in a creative writing class might start class with a word puzzle (wuzzle) shown in Figure 3.3.

Figure 3.3 Sample wuzzle to start class.

Cross out six letters to find a common word

SIBXALNEATTNEARS

Figure 3.4 Solution to wuzzle.

~~S~~~~I~~B~~X~~A~~L~~N~~E~~A~~T~~~~T~~N~~E~~A~~R~~~~S~~

The answer to the puzzle is "banana." Solving the wuzzle required removing the words *six letters* and not any six individual letters, as shown in Figure 3.4.

We generally don't associate bananas with creative writing. This instructor might connect the two by telling a story about a monkey that was captured by a trapper who placed a banana inside a cage. The monkey came along and saw the banana in the cage, put its hand into the cage, but couldn't get the banana out because the monkey did not know that it had to turn the banana so that it would pass through the cage wires. The trapper was able to catch the monkey that wouldn't let go of the banana. As it turns out, the monkey that held on to the banana had a lot to do with the creative writing process, as letting go of unnecessary words is an important concept for writers.

Create Community and Connect to Each Other

I attended a one-day seminar in a large conference center close to the airport. I drove to the hotel and parked my car. I picked up my seminar materials and found a seat between two other attendees near the back of the room. The first thing the instructor did was ask us to turn to the person sitting next to us and tell him or her the best thing that had happened to us in the past 24 hours. In a matter of minutes, the energy and enthusiasm in the room totally transformed the large conference center into a warm and comfortable place where no one felt alone or like a stranger. We all had at least one friend in the room, and that seemed to change everything. I don't remember much else about that conference, but I learned a valuable lesson about the power of a positive starting pause that allowed us to meet at least one other person in the room and think of something to be thankful for. This instructor wisely set the tone for the whole day as one of the objectives for the conference was to craft powerful learning environments.

Starting pauses can create a sense of community among learners by creating connections among participants, giving them opportunities to share their insights and encourage each other along the way. When learners feel they have things in common with others, they will find learning much more enjoyable and beneficial.

It is important for starting pauses to connect learners to each other; this creates a safe place for individuals to explore attitudes and possible barriers to learning as well as alternative ways to grow and learn. Students benefit when focusing activities allow students to talk with each other, make new friends, or find out how their thinking may be similar or different from that of others in the room.

This may be even more important when we are teaching a course using the Internet. Our online students often feel remote and alone and benefit when we find ways of connecting them to each other. This may be fairly easy to do through chat rooms and discussion boards or group assignments. But we can also connect our online students to others besides their fellow learners. An ethics instructor teaching a course on health care, humanity, and God asked his students to find administrators in the health care field and interview them about how they bring God and humanity into their professions. When the online students reported their experiences to each other, an extremely rich discussion resulted. Just getting online students away from their computers and talking to others outside the class, as well as inside, can have great benefits.

Exploit Primacy

First impressions are extremely important, and the way learning begins can have a major impact on the learning session. We are often told to pay attention to how we present ourselves in a new situation, as those first impressions could take a very long time to change. Early impressions have a lasting effect, and what is learned early in the session tends to be remembered more than what is presented later. Hunter (1994) stated that "information introduced at the beginning of any sequence is more easily learned and better remembered than equally difficult material encountered later in that same sequence" (p. 27). This concept, referred to as *primacy*, is well recognized by learning theorists. An interesting way to test this is to ask learners to put their pens down while you read a list of 10 numbers out loud. If you ask participants to write down as many of the numbers they can remember after the list is read, nearly every person remembers the first number, even though it was the earliest number given and the farthest from memory.

One of the early studies that called our attention to the importance of primacy reported that student attention rose for about 10 to 15 minutes and then fell dramatically for the rest of the class hour (Stuart & Rutherford, 1978). If our students are paying more attention at the beginning of class, then it may be wise to rethink how we begin our classes. We may want to find a way to take attendance or return assignments or give housekeeping announcements to our students at another time or in another way rather than use these precious early minutes of the class hour for things that have little to do with learning. Some instructors do this during the break or before class begins, sometimes using a running slide show.

Lang (2016a) understands the concept of primacy. When talking about the first five minutes of class, he suggests that in just five minutes we can affect learning for the entire class period. That opening pause before the beginning of the lecture can help prepare students for learning. Asking students to recall what was learned during the previous lecture, asking them to summarize their reading in preparation for the lecture, or asking them to propose a question or two they would like to address during this class period are some ideas to help us get our students thinking during those early prime learning moments of the class period. Some professors have found that they could post these primer questions in PowerPoint slides before class begins. Others place a printed sheet at each student's desk. Some faculty members like to start with a story or a problem and ask students to predict the solution ahead of time. Others find it helpful to project an interesting picture to start students thinking about the topic of the day.

A simple change we can make when we plan our teaching sessions is to reorganize our use of student time, paying particular attention to how we begin our classes. Our students quickly catch on to the fact that important things are happening at the very beginning of class, and they will put more effort into being there on time.

A colleague once asked me why we should do important things at the beginning of class if a number of the students are late. This is a particularly challenging issue for those of us who teach evening graduate classes to health professions students. These students often rush from their afternoon clinics or labs, skip supper, and still are late for their evening class. So what do we do when we want to take advantage of primacy and get our classes off to a great start if a number of the students are not there yet?

The obvious answer to my colleague's question is to ask to have the class scheduled later the next time it is taught to give students more time between finishing patient labs or professional responsibilities and the evening class. Probably the best answer to this frustrating dilemma for the present is to go ahead with the class as if all of them were there. This can be hard to do, but if we don't, we generally compromise the learning experience for those who are there. Frequent latecomers might develop a friendship with someone who has been there from the beginning and get a briefing if there is a break during class. We might plan to use Fresh Person Standing Summary (MP 29), which asks individuals to share what they have learned with each other, when we notice that a number of students have come to class late and would appreciate an opportunity to catch up on what they missed.

Start Learning With an Experience

Kolb (2014) suggested that ideal learning begins with an experience. A starting pause is a good example of an experience or activity to begin learning. This activity does not have to involve physical movement; it could be a reflective exercise, a writing assignment, or watching a video and thinking about a question. In other words, learners who are prepared for learning by an appropriate beginning pause have done more than just hear from the instructor what the learning objectives for the session are. They have had to do something; they have had to think about what they were doing and not sit quietly in their chair with their mind elsewhere.

Starting learning with an experience that helps students set aside everyday concerns and distractions requires careful planning. A physics teacher might create an experience to assist learners to do this by placing a three-inch-by-five-inch card on each chair and giving the following instructions:

> Please write on your card (you can use both sides, if necessary) all the things that are on your mind just now—all the things you are worried about, what you are thinking about as you come into class that might distract you from learning as much as possible today.

Each of the students would then take the cards and place it in a bucket beside the door (see Dump Bucket [SP 16] for more details on this activity). This unusual experience could help students to think about the importance of purposely forgetting distractions that could get in the way of learning. At the end of this class a student might comment, "Thank you for helping me forget my issues and focus on class today, especially when we were dealing with such a challenging topic—the dump bucket was a novel and effective wakeup call for me." Or another one might say, "I got a lot more than usual out of class today—maybe helping me throw my troubles in the bucket had something to do with it. ☺"

Writing about the eight minutes in teaching that matter most, Sztabnik (2015) said, "If a lesson does not start off strong by activating prior knowledge, creating anticipation, or establishing goals, student interest wanes, and you have to do some heavy lifting to get them back." Effective teachers plan the beginning of learning to place the learners at the center of instruction, allowing them to decide what they want to learn, what the learning will do for them, and how they want to go about it.

4

MIDPAUSES REFOCUS ATTENTION

The other teachers in the department snickered when they looked at the list of students who would be taking my graduate course. I soon found out why. I was new in the department, and it wasn't long before I met the least favorite student in the program. Jonathan, a tall blond, blue-eyed, disheveled fellow, arrived about 10 minutes late, entered the classroom, noisily made his way to the one empty chair in the front, sat down, and placed his large briefcase beside his seat. Jonathan was busy taking premed courses along with his master's degree in public health while managing an emergency medical service across the border in nearby Mexico. He introduced himself as having an extreme case of attention deficit hyperactivity disorder, and that was true.

Jonathan would sit there in the front row and watch me with rapt attention as long as I kept him engaged. The minute I failed to interest him, his hand would plunge into that large open briefcase at his feet and out would come one of his projects. At first, I found Jonathan's actions distracting, and I understood my colleagues' frustration in having him in their classrooms. But then I realized what a blessing having Jonathan in my front row could be. He became a barometer for me. Whenever I saw him reach for a project, that was my signal to switch gears. When I lost Jonathan, I was probably losing other students who would not make it so obvious but whose minds were going in other directions nonetheless. One teacher referred to this as the doughnut phase of the lecture hour, when the eyes started to glaze over. I needed to constantly monitor my students for signs of disengagement, and I needed to be ready to pause and let the students do the talking. I needed to have questions ready for the students to consider. I needed to have activities ready to give students opportunities to apply concepts and check their understanding. At the very least, I needed to do something different.

My experience with Jonathan helped me realize that many of our students require more than pausing at the beginning and the end. They need opportunities to continually refocus. We cannot expect to do all the talking and have students pay attention for very long. Researchers tell us the following about today's students:

- Students take better notes at the beginning of the lecture hour than the end (Major, Harris, & Zakrajsek, 2016).
- Students retain more information from the beginning of the lecture than the end (Hartley & Davies, 1978; McKeachie & Svinicki, 2013).
- Student attention drops after the beginning of the lecture (Bligh, 2000).
- Students learn more from a short lecture than a longer lecture (Penner, 1984).
- Students retain more from lectures that include less information than from those that have more (Russell, Hendricson, & Herbert, 1984).
- Pausing every 15 minutes or so essentially begins the lecture again (Major et al., 2016).
- Students need a pause midway through the class hour to reset (Harrington & Zakrajsek, 2017).

They need opportunities to

- refocus and apply,
- review,
- relieve cognitive load,
- retrieve, and
- reenergize and refresh.

Refocus and Apply

Eric Mazur, a Harvard University physics professor, realized that even though his students appreciated him as a good teacher, he was not teaching as well as he could be. He knew that when he was doing all the talking, he was having most of the fun and doing most of the learning. So he decided to give some of the talking and the fun of learning to his students. He initially adopted ConcepTests, a form of peer teaching (Mazur, 2017). He would lecture for 20 minutes or so and then stop for the students to grapple with a challenging question, often asking them to work in small groups to try to come up with an answer (Mazur & Hilborn, 1997).

Mazur and Hilborn (1997) found that this opportunity to teach each other resulted in new energy and focus in the classroom. Students understood course concepts better and improved their exam performance, particularly on difficult problem-solving questions.

The ConcepTest is an excellent way to pause midway through the class. It gives students not only a break from listening to the instructor but also a chance to apply the ideas being presented to solving a problem. Mazur (1977) recommends a form of peer instruction where he first presents the problem, and then, after a period of time, he pairs students up to discuss their answers and come to conclusions. Figure 4.1 is an example of what a ConcepTest question might look like in a geology class, illustrating a thought-provoking issue to debate.

Pausing during the class session gives students opportunities to refocus attention and check their understanding. Research at all levels shows that student learning is enhanced when students are more than lectured to, when they have opportunities to listen and reflect, share ideas, and move (Udvari-Solner & Kluth, 2007).

Figure 4.1 Example of a ConcepTest question.

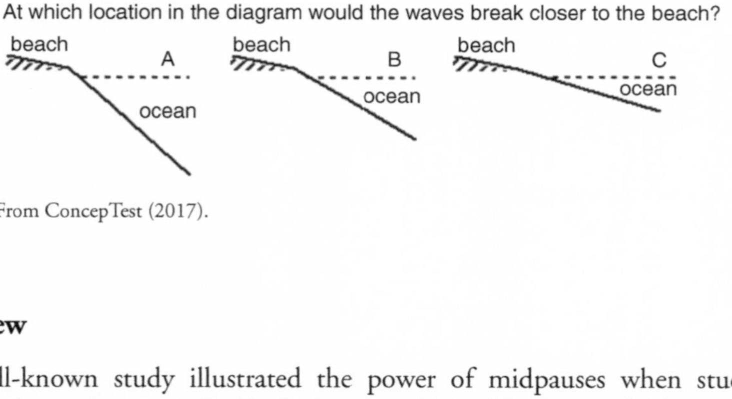

At which location in the diagram would the waves break closer to the beach?

beach A ocean

beach B ocean

beach C ocean

Source: From ConcepTest (2017).

Review

A well-known study illustrated the power of midpauses when students stopped to review periodically during class (Ruhl, Hughes, & Schloss, 1987). This study contrasted two classes in which one group had traditional lectures and the other had three two-minute breaks for students to share their notes with each other. This study didn't require the instructor to design any active learning techniques. The instructor simply stopped talking and asked students to fill in gaps that might exist in their understanding of the concepts presented. They were able to look at each other's notes and explain to each other what the instructor had just talked about. At the end of the five lectures, each of the groups took a multiple-choice examination. The group that had six minutes less lecturing for each of the lectures actually performed better on the exam—nearly a full letter grade better, in fact (Ruhl et al., 1987). So much for the idea that covering more content leads to better learning.

Another study provides further support of the concept that less is more. In this study, medical school professors prepared three different sets of lectures on the same subject—a high-density, medium-density, and a low-density version (Russell et al., 1984). In the high-density lectures, 90% of the sentences contained new information, whereas only 50% of the sentences in the low-density lectures had new information. Students were assigned to the three groups and pretested to show no differences in knowledge base. After they were taught in one of the three methods, they took a posttest immediately after the lecture and then were given an unannounced test 15 days later. The results clearly demonstrated that students learned better when they were taught in a low-density manner. They not only did better on the early test but also improved their longer range retention (Russell et al., 1984). In other words, the students who were given less new information learned more and performed better on tests than those who were given more.

These studies illustrate the limits of the human mind. Our students are only capable of learning so much new information. If we think we can race along with fast-paced lectures that keep pouring information into their open and receptive minds, we are probably fooling ourselves. Students perform better on short-term and long-term performance tests when teachers do less talking. Students learn more when we lecture less, when they do more of the talking, and when we pause to ask them how they are processing what we have tried to tell them.

Relieve Cognitive Load

Gary Larson (1991) designed a cartoon which beautifully illustrates cognitive overload. The student in the cartoon has his hand up, asking to be excused because his brain is full. This is exactly how our students feel when they experience cognitive overload.

Cognitive overload occurs when we overwhelm our students' mental pathways and structures, leading to errors and lack of comprehension. We do this when we provide nonstop information for long periods of time. Without opportunities to stop and check their understanding and apply what we are teaching them, students quickly lose interest. Even the best and most entertaining lecturers begin to lose the attention of their audience within 15 to 20 minutes after beginning (Jensen, 2005). Today's students are so used to fast-changing visual images and media-driven short bites of information that continuous intense attention to oral instruction can only be sustained for 10 minutes or less (Bligh, 2000; Udvari-Solner & Kluth, 2007).

Reducing cognitive load and keeping students' attention requires regular mental breaks (Howard, 1994; Major et al., 2016; Rossi & Nimmons, 1991). Perhaps the student in Larson's cartoon who is asking to leave because his brain is full doesn't really need to leave the classroom; maybe he just needs to pause, as my granddaughter Rosa's variation of the popular cartoon in Figure 4.2 suggests. In Rosa's cartoon, the student with her hand up is asking for the teacher to stop talking for a bit, to pause, and to give the students a chance to process things before continuing

The instructor who pauses during the lecture has learned an important lesson about relieving cognitive overload. When we pause to ask students to think of an example, complete a sentence, finish an activity, explain a concept, predict an outcome, write about their thinking, or solve a dilemma, we reduce the density, minimize cognitive load, and provide the needed break for learning to continue. Pausing the lecture occasionally for student activities such as these will allow us to make learning bite size, thus reducing cognitive overload. Major and colleagues (2016) state that "varying instructional methods, even with a quick 1–3 minute pause every 15–20 minutes can help to reset student attention and thus improve their retention of information" (p. 9).

Figure 4.2. "Teacher, may we pause? My brain is full!"

Note. R. Morel, reprinted with permission.

Retrieve

When we ask students to review and summarize, it is recommended to encourage them to work from their memory rather than looking at notes or references. We have good evidence (Glenn, 2009; Karpicke & Roediger, 2008; Karpicke, 2012; Karpicke & Blunt, 2011) that students remember better when they test themselves and try to remember answers to questions without looking them up. We need to shake up the commonly held metaphor of filling the students as so-called empty receptacles with our knowledge. Instead, when we perceive our role as bringing information out of the student rather than putting it in, we will be more successful at helping students not only learn better but also understand the process of learning.

Nilson (2013) uses a "mind dump" (p. 31) to get students to write down everything they remember. This is a good example of retrieval practice and illustrates getting things out of our students instead of putting things into them. Another good way to help students retrieve information is to ask them to write an exam question and then test their colleagues (see Exam Question Challenge [CP 58]). Certainly retrieval practice improves more than just memory. Research suggests that it improves complex thinking, application skills, and the organization of knowledge as well as the transfer of knowledge to new concepts (Agarwal, 2017).

One of the most exciting findings about the indirect benefits of retrieval practice is referred to as the forward effect of testing. Pastötter and Bäuml (2014) report that

> recall testing of previously studied information can increase long-term retention of subsequently studied new information. The forward effect of testing is particularly striking because it is on learning of information that is not necessarily related to the previously tested material. (para. 1)

It appears, then, that when we ask students to test themselves by using retrieval to recall something they have recently learned, we train them how to relate to new learning challenges and improve retention as a result.

Quizzing provides a good opportunity for retrieval practice. Polling works especially well when pausing to quiz. In fact, using a form of Internet polling may be the ultimate pause technique available to us. When we ask students to take out their phone and text a response to a question, several things happen: We have their attention; they cannot text us and their friend at the same time, they cannot use their phone for e-mail, they cannot surf the Web anymore, they will have to evaluate the question we have posed and select or compose an answer, and they will actually have to think about something related to the class. In addition, they will get to test themselves and discover if they have understood something important, they will see how well they are doing in relation to the rest of the class, and their attention to learning from the teacher will be heightened, simply because they have had to do something and think about what they were doing.

My first experience with polling impressed on me that stopping the lecture for an occasional comprehension check could improve engagement and retention. John Jacobson, Loma Linda University gynecologist, gave a lecture on estrogen and arteries long before we had audience response systems available on the Internet. Everyone in the audience had a drug company's keypad, a little like what the audience uses to vote on the quiz program *Who Wants to Be a Millionaire?* As Jacobson proceeded with his technical lecture, he paused occasionally to project a multiple-choice question on an overhead screen. The audience could respond to the question by pressing a button, and the answers showed up on the screen. As soon as the first question appeared, something interesting happened. I was anxious to be right the next time a question flashed up on the screen, so I took more careful notes and paid closer attention to the lecture. I imagine not everyone is as competitive as I am, but one thing I noticed for sure: Those little question pauses certainly energized me to focus.

It used to be quite complicated to insert public polling into our lecture. If we were using a commercially available program, like TurningPoint polling software, we had to install the software and transfer our slides into the program. We are fortunate now to have much easier (and free) options to poll our students to check for understanding and to increase student engagement. The following are some of the programs currently available:

- Poll Everywhere (polleverywhere.com) is one of the oldest and most popular of the polling programs. It is free for up to 40 respondents. You can keep your questions in your own account on the website. It is easy to set up questions from your phone or laptop and project the responses immediately.
- Polldaddy (Polldaddy.com) is possibly the best known of the polling websites. It is particularly useful for blogs and creates attractive pie charts and bar graphs.
- Kahoot! (kahoot.com) may be the most user-friendly of the polling software. It has a nonacademic look to it so may suit certain audiences particularly well.
- Flisti (flisti.com) is one of the newer polling options. Some like it because you can create a poll almost instantly, and you don't even have to register.

- MicroPoll (micropoll.com) has the advantage of working very well with a learning management system, so it is well suited to online teaching.

Reenergize and Refresh

Physical movement can enhance learning. Medina (2011) devotes an entire chapter to the topic of exercise and learning. Physical movement activates chemicals and neurotransmitters that improve learning. When we combine physical movement with task-related pauses, we add to the good outcomes of the learning task. Students not only bring their personal answers and applications to the concepts presented but also benefit from the increased circulation and improved oxygenation to the brain that accompanies movement. One thing to keep in mind when we plan for an activity that asks students to move about the room is the importance of accommodating students with any mobility challenges. It is important to provide options for any of these participants. A number of the midpauses in Appendix B combine physical movement with the activity.

A colleague on my campus recognized the need for something to energize and awaken his audience during a one-hour presentation. Ernie Medina e-mailed me the following:

> I'm doing a presentation that will have about 100 teachers in it. I want to do an activity that gets them up and moving around the room, possibly in a constant motion, not just standing in one place. I'm trying to think of what we learned in class, what we did, but wanted to ask if you had any suggestions. It could be an educational activity to give them an idea how to incorporate movement into their class lesson. Any thoughts would be welcome. Thanks. (E. Medina, personal communication, June 26, 2016)

I responded that he might want to do something like Musical Concentric Circles (MP 27). About midway through the session, ask everyone to stand. Tell them how simply standing increases blood flow to the brain and helps us all to think more clearly. He might continue with a statement like, "Now that you are standing, I would like you to be ready to share with someone what you have learned in this seminar so far and why you value it." Depending on the space available, ask the group to form two circles, one inside the other and play some lively music while the circles rotate in opposite directions. When the music stops, the person on the inside circle gets to share his ideas with the person standing opposite. The next time the music stops, individuals from the outside circle could share their answers with their new partner.

A few days later, Ernie sent me a short message, saying,

> The overall talk went well. I was tight for time so didn't get to do the full moving around the room activity like I had planned, but I did get them up and doing something mid-way. . . . So, thanks for all the great suggestions. (E. Medina, personal communication, July 15, 2016)

The participants rated his session the highest of all the sessions during the weeklong event. I am certain that his pauses had something to do with the evaluation summaries. Learners appreciate having opportunities to process and personalize what they are learning midstream. Medina's learners especially enjoyed reenergizing and refreshing as well as connecting to others after a long day of sitting through nonstop lectures.

Like Medina, we recognize the importance of allowing those important breaks, but we don't always get around to providing them. Too often we discover the class period is over, and we have done all the talking. Or we may do a bit better than that. We might remember to provide a break or two in our lectures, but, unfortunately, we have gotten into a rut. All our breaks are exactly the same. Students tend to get weary of our breaks if there aren't some new twists, at least once in a while. Students enjoy new challenges and respond well to opportunities to try something different, to present their ideas and receive feedback in varying ways. To ensure that our pauses are effective, it can be quite easy to vary our approaches. We might ask the same question several weeks in a row but have students respond to the question in different ways. This is why it can be very helpful to have them write down ideas and send them around a small group of fellow students one week and then have them post their ideas on sticky notes on the board in the front of the room the next. Another time, students might form small groups and develop an artistic version of a concept they are working on in class.

In Appendix B we present some possibilities for giving students pauses in the middle of a learning session. Even though these breaks take a few minutes of class time, they are worth it. It may help to remind ourselves of the research cited earlier in this chapter. Less may really result in more. Not so dense is better than denser. Leave out some of the extra material. Chunks of learning work better. Take a break. Let students catch a breath. Let's hit pause.

5

CLOSING PAUSES CAPTURE LEARNING

How many times have we attended wonderful lectures, workshops, seminars, or conference presentations that left us convinced that this tremendous learning experience would make a profound difference in our professional lives, only to discover later that we have never looked back at the notes we wrote and we have only a vague recollection of the event? When this happens, it's probably not our fault; it is usually because instructors leave the closing pause out of their presentations. Research indicates that without a proper close, learners can expect to recall less than 15% to 20% of what was presented (Broad & Newstrom, 1992; Kornikau & McElroy, 1975).

Closing Pauses Are Powerful

Because closing pauses allow students time to process the content and decide how to use it, these pauses have the potential to be the most powerful teaching technique available. Closing pauses can help learners retain and transfer knowledge, summarize and prioritize the learning that has occurred, make action plans for the future, and close the learning session so they can attend to new concepts. Good closure is the factor most likely to lead to the learner's remembering anything from the lecture and, most important, doing something about it, that is, actually transferring it to future action.

Closing pauses are powerful, not only because of the tasks they help students accomplish but also because of when they occur. We referred earlier to a numbers activity, where students were able to remember the first number in a series best due to the primacy effect. Psychologists tell us that we also remember better what occurred last because of an effect referred to as *recency*. The closing pause takes advantage of recency, when instructors stop the teacher talk before time is up and allow students to do some thinking about what they have learned and what will they do with it. These last few minutes of learning will be more significant, partly because they are the most recent in learners' experiences. Sousa (2006) stated, "Closure is usually the last opportunity the learner has to attach sense and meaning to new learning" (p. 276).

Closing Pauses Are Rare

Even though the closing pause is a powerful tool for affecting learning, it is often neglected. Jensen (2008) indicated that we fall short of the mark of providing appropriate closure when he said, "Students rarely get training in how to be calm, thoughtful, or reflective, and they are given little time to practice these skills in class" (p. 37). Writing about a pause to close learning, Eggleston and Smith (2002) said that we are giving too little attention to the important task of providing closure at the end of a course or seminar.

As a faculty developer, I have been impressed with the importance of including closing pauses in my lesson plans, and yet I often find myself skipping it when I am out of time and failed to plan carefully to include that closing pause. I have discovered that I am not alone. Sometimes it appears that teachers everywhere have forgotten the importance of closure for individual learning sessions.

I participated in a pilot project designed to ascertain if college professors were actually pausing at the end of class for any kind of reflective activity. We gave the professors a short survey to complete at the end of their class asking, How did you close class? Did you allow students to reflect on the class and consider what they had learned? Nearly all the faculty members said that they did give reflective pauses at the end of their classes.

In the complementary part of the project, graduate assistants, educated to recognize what constitutes a good reflective closing pause, were asked to observe each class to describe how the educators closed their class sessions. The graduate assistants reported a quite different finding than the professors. They said that none of the faculty members provided a truly reflective closing pause. If there was any kind of break before dismissing class, all the instructors did was ask for questions. Apparently, these professors thought that giving an opportunity to ask a question would be sufficient to help the students close their learning session.

We often close our learning sessions by asking if there are any questions. It would make such a difference if instead of asking our students for questions we prepared questions to ask our students. These questions would help learners summarize what they had learned and determine what gaps exist as well as what follow-up actions might be necessary.

Although our pilot project was small and unscientific, if any of us were to sit in on a few of our colleague's classes, we would probably observe something pretty similar. Very few, if any, professors regularly take time to allow students to look back and provide their own summary at the end of class. We just can't shake that commonly held myth about teaching and learning, "If you don't say it, they won't learn it"; we tend to think it's okay if we are saying so many important things that we run out of time and there is no time for student reflection at the end of class (Eggleston & Smith, 2002; Pescosolido, 1999).

The following are some of the reasons we might give for avoiding closing pauses:

- I ran out of time.
- I needed to include as much content as possible.
- I didn't know how important closing pauses are.
- I don't know how to do them.

As a result, for various reasons we think we are doing a pretty good job of closing our classes, but in fact we do little to help our students wrap up the learning session. We do all the talking and assume that when there are no questions, everyone fully understood everything that was discussed. Because we have used all the time, there is none left for our students to do any summarizing, answer any questions, or do any forward planning.

This is a common picture: Class time is up, but the teacher hasn't finished the lecture. Students are restless and anxious to leave, lecturers keep talking more and more rapidly as students begin to gather their materials, and finally things just disintegrate as students vacate and teachers wonder where all the time went and if their students learned anything.

The following are examples of what a good closing pause does *not* look like:

- Dr. Baker is wrapping up the chemistry class when she notices the time is up. She quickly reminds the class of the assignment that is due before class meets again.
- Dr. Crabtree notices there is another minute left for the lecture on health promotion. He takes the minute to summarize for the students what he attempted to do during the lecture hour and invites them to the next lecture, which will follow up on the topic.
- Mr. Anton is so excited about his topic that he keeps on talking long after the session was supposed to be over. Students quietly leave one by one until just a few remain. At that point, he apologizes for getting carried away and thanks the few who remained for staying.

- Well-known speaker Clara Osborne finishes her talk for her organization's annual conference with the words "thank you." After the audience applauds, she asks if there are any questions.

All these educators probably thought they had done a pretty good job of closing up their presentations, with the possible exception of Anton. How sad that much of the potential for real learning was lost because of the poor closings.

When we think about our goals for our students, what we hope they gain from taking a course from us or attending a class we teach is that they will retain what we have taught, they will think and behave differently for having been our students, and what they have learned will be applied appropriately. How sad that more often than not we run out of time before anyone other than ourselves has a chance to speak. Without that closing pause with opportunities for students to think, write, and speak, we have not helped them discover their personal applications and plans. We have thrown away the possibility of affecting the learners' future behavior. We are part of the reason that much of the class session was a waste of time for most of the students.

Characteristics of Good Closing Pauses

Now that we know our closing pause deserves as much attention as the rest of our class session, we would like to know how to plan a good class closure. Has anything changed since we were students? What can we learn from social psychologists, neuroscientists, and learning specialists that will help us to reinforce learning to the maximum? What can cognitive science tell us that might be helpful for capturing those powerful final five minutes of class? To plan for an ideal end to any kind of learning experience, whether a short one-on-one encounter, a one-hour class of more than two dozen students, or a presentation at an international conference to hundreds, it is helpful to consult the literature on what makes a good ending. A good closing pause will

- review content (Halsey, 2011; Jensen, 2008; Lang, 2016a; Lutsky, 2010; Pike, 2003),
- require reflection (Jensen, 2008),
- celebrate accomplishments (Bowman, 2009; Halsey, 2011; Jensen, 2008; Pike, 2003; Solem, 2016),
- motivate students to act (Jensen, 2008; Lutsky, 2010; Pike, 2003), and
- bring full circle and create a bookend (Lang, 2016b; Lutsky, 2010).

Review Content

The most obvious function of a good closing pause is to review the content of the learning (Halsey, 2011; Pike, 2003). It is essential for learners to be given a chance to look over what they learned, which has the advantage of reliving those aha moments, just as viewing a snapshot of yourself sometimes brings back memories with great detail.

Angelo and Cross (1993) encouraged teachers in higher education to slow their teaching so they could assess what was happening with their students. In their classic text they describe the minute paper, which is an excellent closing pause that allows students to take just one minute to write two sentences, the first answering the question, What was this learning session about? and the second, What do you still need clarification about? (Angelo & Cross, 1993). Multiple variations of the minute paper have been widely used by professors as an effective way to help students take those last few minutes of class to look back over the session and try to summarize what was learned (Barkley, 2015). Our version is A Penny for Your Thoughts (CP 59).

There are multiple approaches to reviewing content. Many instructors look for playful ways to review by using games like *Jeopardy*, *Trivial Pursuit*, *Who Wants to Be a Millionaire?* or bingo. These closing activities lend themselves well not only to a single class session but also to closing a workshop, conference, section of the course, or the course itself.

Questions that help students review content include the following:

- What is one thing you learned today?
- What is the most important thing you learned today?
- What concepts and insights will you take away from class today?
- Before class today, what were you beginning to wonder about?
- What is one thing from today's lesson that you would like to know more about?
- How would you compare and contrast what you knew about this topic before class today and what you know now?
- What did you understand better after today's class?
- How does today's class change previous perceptions you had about this topic?
- How would you summarize today's lesson for someone who wasn't here?

Require Reflection

Neuroscientist Terry Sejnowski's idea of a good closing pause is to take a walk after learning to let learning settle in before new learning begins

(Churchland & Sejnowski, 1992). The cartoon in Figure 4.2 illustrates this principle. A student in the classroom and a neuroscientist both recognize the importance of stopping the information flow to allow processing before attempting anything else, particularly trying to learn something new.

Sometimes we think that closure will occur without any help from us. Although our learners consider new ideas, they can at the same time close a learning session by analyzing, sorting, and applying. This is not likely to just happen, however. Research demonstrates that the brain can really focus on just one thing at a time (Medina, 2011). In other words, all students can do at a time is take in new information and nothing beyond that. Students are either listening or they are learning. Rarely are they doing both at the same time. If we talk right up to the end of the class period, it is unlikely that our students can think through their closing questions. Learning is often suspended when someone else is talking.

Multitasking is nearly impossible for most of us, which is illustrated in a YouTube video clip from Simons and Chabris (2010). Viewers are asked to count the number of times players in white shirts pass the basketball while ignoring passes made by players wearing black shirts. During the 30-second flurry of balls flying around, a person in a gorilla suit walks through the middle of the action. The first time viewers see this, 90% or more never notice the gorilla. In fact, they refuse to believe they are watching the same video when they view it a second time and clearly see the gorilla. This video illustrates that when you are totally focused on one thing, you will not be able to notice much else. This may explain why students sometimes tell us with great certainty that we didn't talk about something in class that we clearly did address; they probably missed it while they were checking their e-mails or doing a little Web surfing.

It is becoming increasingly clear that the brain cannot deal with constant input; it needs time for processing (Mednick et al., 2002). Jensen (2008) tells us that "learning can be far more effective when external stimuli are shut down and the brain can pause to link new information to earlier associations, uses, and procedures" (p. 44). We can't do two things at once; either students take in new information or they process that information. They can pay attention to the instructor or they can make meaning, but rarely they can do both at the same time.

What the neuroscientist and the student who needs a pause because his or her brain is full are missing, however, is that learners need more than just time to process new information. They also need some structure that suggests how to think and what to think about. The educator who simply sends the learners on their way, hoping that while taking their walk or hurrying to their next appointment they will be processing the lecture are overly optimistic. It is more likely that other things will press the recent lecture material into the background. Learners need to be given time to consider specifically what they learned and how they will use it. If they don't consider this before they leave the classroom, they most likely won't do it at all.

Celebrate Accomplishments

A number of authors suggest a good closing pause should include an element of celebration (Halsey, 2011; Jensen, 2008; Pike, 2003; Solem, 2016). Many have found that optimism is important when ending learning. Ideally, learners will leave their session, whether it is a workshop, a class session, or a 10-minute therapy conference, with a sense of celebration. Teachers don't want their learners to walk away from the class thinking it was a waste of time, they don't know what to do with this information, or the seminar was a waste of money.

Instead, we hope they feel it was a great learning experience or that they were glad they didn't miss that learning opportunity.

The following are questions to ask at the end of the learning session that help learners celebrate:

- Why are you glad you were here today?
- How will this information help you to achieve your goals?
- What pleased you about this learning session?
- Why do you wish more of your colleagues were here today?
- What would you like to thank the instructor for?

Related to optimism and celebration, a good way to wrap up the learning experience is to help learners focus on how important objectives have been met and how this makes new accomplishments possible. A good learning activity ends with an increased desire to practice new skills (Lutsky, 2010). Celebrating what has been accomplished during the learning time enhances the likelihood that learners will apply the positive experience to their personal and professional lives.

Motivate Students to Act

Students do not want to lose what they have just learned. They want to be able to capitalize on it, develop new skills, and bring it into future practice. For learners to leave a session feeling they have achieved acceptable closure and can safely move on to other tasks without forgetting what they have learned, they must:

- review what they have learned,
- plan how they will continue learning, and
- make specific plans for action and follow-up.

This is particularly valuable when attending a learning experience with a number of components, such as a multi-day conference with back-to-back sessions or an entire course consisting of many classes. Learners typically listen to a speaker, perhaps take some notes, and feel they have learned some important new material. They may be thinking to themselves, "This was really good stuff. I will definitely think more about this topic and try to incorporate some of these ideas." The problem is that often the lecturer has not provided the learners with opportunities to wrap up the session. Learners haven't stopped to think about what they have learned, what is particularly important to them, and what their action plans to move forward are. Without writing down these concepts, without talking about them out loud, without even considering these important ideas, learners rush to their next class or conference session. As a result, learning sessions are stacked one on top of another, pauses are forgotten, and learners are overwhelmed. Attendees are expected to forget all about the session they left 10 minutes ago and be fresh and ready to listen and learn from the next presenter. These learners wonder why it is so hard to give their full attention to the next learning task; they do not realize it is because they did not find adequate closure for what they previously learned.

Learners not only require time and direction to place new learning into the context of why it is valued and how it will be used but also benefit from opportunities to commit to act. Motivational psychologists frequently ask their listeners to write down and speak about their goals. Without expressing a goal, participants are unlikely to reach one. They are more likely to realize a shared commitment than a commitment that is merely thought about.

The following are questions to ask at the end of the learning session that help learners commit to action:

- What will you do with this information?
- What action step will you take?
- How will you proceed with your plans as a result of attending our learning session today?
- What are your next steps?

Although committing to action is not always necessary for a good learning closure, it captures a very positive element, namely, what educators call *transfer of training*. The whole purpose of teaching often comes down to making a difference in the learner's thinking, understanding, attitudes, and behavior. For that to happen, learners must be helped to think about how they want to apply this new learning, what they intend to do with it, and how they plan to act. This is why an essential element in good closure requires sharing—writing it down or talking about it. To tell someone or write down what you will do, you must come to a decision, a commitment to respond to the ideas that have been provided.

Bring Learning Full Circle and Create a Bookend

Full circle learning brings learners back to the objectives set forth at the beginning. A closing pause that circles back to the beginning might review the objectives and ask students to briefly summarize their learning related to those objectives. A good closing pause has integrity. It is meaningfully related to and consistent with what has preceded it (Lutsky, 2010). It ties to promises of the beginning. A good ending is not tacked on but rather pulls together what has come before and helps to make final sense of it all.

It is especially effective to be able to connect the closing pause to the opening pause. Dixie Fisher and I tried this when we taught a conference session on the topic of getting started with classroom research and getting a cool idea off the ground. We began the session with a Hot Potato (CP 50) exercise in which we asked participants to freely associate the first word that came to mind when given the word *research*. The learners wrote down their word, then formed a circle, and passed around a hot potato toy with a built-in timer that we provided for the activity. When the timer went off, whoever was holding the hot potato was asked to say the word he or she had written down. The group had some laughs on discovering that many of the group members had some pretty negative feelings about doing research. This helped us introduce some possible objectives for the session and created a sharing, caring community of learners. At the end of the session, we again passed the hot potato toy. This time learners were asked to name the one most important first action for follow-up they planned to take with the content of the session and to show how this action related to their first impression of the topic. Fisher and I were pleased to hear that learners had changed their opinion and formed definite, concrete plans for getting their cool idea off the ground.

Closure Activities

Books and Internet resources emphasize the importance of specific techniques to close learning. Educators have begun to pay increasing attention to the importance of pausing so students can close learning (Barkley & Major,

2015; Honeycutt, 2016; Lang, 2016b). Lang (2016a, 2016c) writes about the last five minutes of class. Eggleston and Smith (2002) share ideas for closing not only an individual learning session but also an entire learning event, such as a full course.

With few exceptions, nearly everything written for higher education teachers that provides specific suggestions about good closing pauses has appeared since 2015. In contrast, corporate trainers have recognized this need for years (Bowman, 2009; Deck, 1995; Halsey, 2011; Meier, 2000; Pike, Pike, & Busse, 1995).

In addition to books and articles about pausing to close learning, a number of websites suggest specific closing pause ideas that can be adapted to complete good learning experiences in many settings (Finley, 2015; Sipe, n.d.; Wiggins & McTighe, 2005). Rod Lucero (2017) suggests quick closing pauses to "create powerful learning effects at the tail-end of class, something that will reverberate for hours after the lesson is over." Todd Finley (2015) described a good closing pause in the following: "Like contracting your bicep at the top of a dumbbell curl, closure squeezes an extra oomph into a lesson."

Summary

Powerful closing pauses can accomplish a number of important learning objectives. They review content, allow reflection, celebrate what has been accomplished, motivate, and commit to action. Many pauses to close learning are not fancy and do not require special preparation. Asking patients at the end of a doctor's visit what they learned provides a closing pause that allows them to check to see if their perceptions are accurate and to correct misunderstandings. If we didn't have time to plan a closing pause for our lecture, we can always ask students to tell the person sitting closest to them one idea that they found especially helpful from the class. Later, we discuss more examples of how closing pauses affect learning in a number of different settings. In Appendix C we share more formal closing pause ideas that we have used in higher education and health professional education settings and found to be effective in capturing the powerful benefits of looking back at the end of learning.

PART THREE

REASONS FOR PAUSING

6

WHY START WITH A PAUSE

It is not our natural inclination as teachers to begin by pausing. One of my colleagues described herself at the beginning of class as a racehorse entering the starting gate. Another saw himself as a firefighter with a fire hose. We know that we have a lot of teaching to do, and we are anxious to jump in and start covering our content as quickly as possible. If we take time to pause, we will do it at the end after we have met our primary objective of delivering the information. What we might not have considered is the fact that taking time to prepare our learners at the beginning may actually make covering our content easier, more efficient, and more powerful.

The benefit of pausing at the beginning of learning is not a new concept. Years ago Hunter (1994) suggested the importance of the *set,* her word for a starting pause, and Bonwell listed seven activities to do at the beginning of class (Bonwell & Eison, 1991). Mel Silberman (1996) introduced the concept of the active learning pause in his book, *Active Learning: 101 Strategies To Teach Any Subject.* It was aimed at younger students, but he later addressed active learning in higher education. Johnston and Cooper (1997) published their version of pausing instruction with their oft-cited article, "Quick Thinks," which provided many specific suggestions to stop teacher talk and get students participating in their learning. Barbara Millis, a pioneer in the cooperative learning literature, suggested that getting students to take ownership in their learning involves putting their heads together in activities, such as the think-pair-share and its many variations (Millis & Cottell, 1998; Millis, 2010).

Efficient, effective education starts with a focused student. As Heath and Heath (2007) remind us in their valuable text "the first problem of communication is getting people's attention" (p. 64). How to get that attention can be difficult if we don't pause at the beginning to prepare learners. This idea seems to be gaining attention as more and more teachers ask how to begin instruction in the best way. In the past few years, a number of books, articles, and Internet posts have specifically addressed the importance of the opening pause to start learning off right (Honeycutt, 2016; Lang, 2016a).

This starting pause allows learners to take a moment to think about the topic to be considered and prepare themselves for it. The following stories illustrate some of the things a starting pause can do.

Provide an Organizing Theme

A good starting pause could provide an organizing theme for an entire learning session. Emily was planning to teach a group of psychiatric residents about how to evaluate clinical competence. She sent me an e-mail asking what she could do to start her seminar. After thinking about evaluation, I sent her the Pilot Exam (see Table 6.1). This example, contrasting the scores of two pilots on their examination, formed a starting activity that Emily used as her pause to gain attention and focus on the concepts she would be teaching.

After teaching the session, she wrote the following to me:

> Thanks so much for sending the Set [starting pause]. I loved the pilot idea. I went with that theme. We broke up into groups and built small glider planes (which got folks to stop chatting about work/patients). They were all concerned with how their planes were going to be judged (good for later discussion of educational effect of evaluations—they'll be sure to learn what they know will be on the exam). While they built planes I wrote 15 credentials listed in applications for a piloting job onto large papers on wall. Once they were done I made up a story that they were no longer academic psychiatrists. . . . They'd won the lottery, . . . hung up their white coats, . . . purchased their own remote island, [and now] needed a plane to get to and from [the] island. . . . [They] bought a private plane . . . [and] now must hire a pilot. In the small groups they decided which criteria/credentials were most important to them as they sought out the right pilot. The criteria were things like attended 50 hours of lectures about flying, read a classic textbook for beginning pilots, read 15 seminal articles on flying, authored a paper on the history of flying that was published in a prestigious journal, logged 20 hours of solo

TABLE 6.1
Pilot Exam

	Pilot A	**Pilot B**
Takeoff	20	16
Instruments	20	16
Weather	20	16
Navigation	20	16
Landing	0	16
Total	**80**	**80**

> flying time, flew alongside an experienced pilot for 20 hours, passed a flight simulation exam, passed a written pilot exam, passed a practicum (in-flight) exam, and so forth. Each group was given dot stickers and asked to place them next to the most highly valued credentials. As a group we discussed the merits of each credential and why people had chosen which ones. It worked out nicely that they chose mostly the in-flight experiences, leading us into a discussion about outcomes-based education and evaluation versus process-based education and evaluation. . . . All in all we covered more material than I thought we would get through and the faculty stayed more engaged than I had predicted. (E. Doyle, personal communication, December 2, 2012)

Emily's message underscored the importance of planning for more than just the content. As she said, the starting pause not only focused her students at the beginning but also kept them on track throughout the workshop. Notice the comment about covering more material and keeping learners engaged. When Emily decided to start with pilot training, she not only moved quickly to some seminal issues regarding evaluation but also found a theme that unified the entire presentation and kept people more interested than she anticipated.

Introduce Guiding Concepts

Emily's starting pause helped organize a three-hour workshop, but a good starting pause can also introduce guiding concepts for an entire course of study. Vicki Halsey teaches a course in executive leadership, and in her first session, she provides a starting pause for not only that session but also the entire event. To introduce the concept of individual and organizational learning, the instructor asks everyone to think of a good learning experience and then write several descriptive words on sticky notes. After the students bring their notes to the front and place them on a whiteboard, the instructor hands several to each person. Then she asks them to share, use notes still on the whiteboard, trade, or barter until they have three notes with words that describe their ideal learning. Then the students form groups with others who made similar selections and make a poster with only pictures to depict their concepts. Finally, students examine each poster to try to figure out which words were used to build them. This starting pause provides an effective introduction to the course and suggests themes that come up repeatedly (Halsey, 2011).

Induce Learners to Desire Learning

A starting pause can help learners to desire learning. A sociology teacher might devise a pretest for the beginning of class that consists of 10 true-or-false questions. After students complete the quiz, the instructor can proceed with the lecture, answering the questions one by one and using the questions as an outline for the lecture. Students will likely remain interested throughout the hour, as they will be eager to see if they had selected the right answers. Investing themselves in deciding whether the statements were true or not also will increase their willingness to participate in the discussion.

Another way to induce learners to desire learning might be to start with a question. Bain's (2004) "natural critical learning environment" begins with a question and proceeds with the instructor helping students find answers to that question. Bain suggests that instead of helping students find questions they want answers to, we often provide "an answer to a question that no one has raised" (p. 107). Teachers can help learners raise the question that the lecture will answer.

Heath and Heath (2007) describe this as creating a gap. They suggest that a gap in our knowledge is an uncomfortable experience; when our students perceive a gap, they will want it filled. Our job may be, then, to "open gaps before we close them" (Heath & Heath, 2007, p. 85). We do this when we pause early in the instructional period. Rather than tell our students the facts, we highlight some specific knowledge that they're missing. "Sticky learning" occurs when we "think about how to elicit interest rather than force-feeding facts" (Heath & Heath, 2006, p. 86). Starting class with a quiz can be a good way to heighten students' awareness of the questions they don't have answers to, of the gaps they would like to fill. The lecture then clarifies and simplifies complex ideas, giving answers and filling gaps.

Bring Emotion Into the Equation

A good starting pause can do more than help students want information—it may also help them become emotionally involved. When learners care about something, they are much more motivated to learn about it. Creating that caring can be a challenge, but it is often worth it.

Jeanette Norden, who teaches neuroscience at Vanderbilt University School of Medicine, starts her lecture on drugs for patients with Parkinson's disease by bringing an actual patient with Parkinson's disease into the classroom. Dr. Norden asks the patient to skip his usual morning dose of medication before coming. She introduces the patient, asks him to take his medication, and then proceeds to discuss with the patient how the disease has affected his life. Students notice the gradual change brought on by the medication as the speech, gait, and tremors improve. After the patient leaves the classroom, Norden explains how Parkinson's disease medications work. Her students are concerned about the patient they just met and now care a great deal about the side effects of the medications. They listen and learn quite differently because Norden set them up ahead of time to care about the subject. They now know someone whose entire life has been affected by the disease (J. Norden, personal communication, September 10, 2007).

Another example of bringing emotion into the equation is based on the following hypothetical situation. In this scenario, imagine that a faculty member at a major medical school had a personal experience that illustrated the vital role emotion plays in learning. As a young resident, he nearly killed an older, compromised patient in pain. What would normally be an appropriate dose of morphine was too much for this particular patient, and she stopped breathing. He was able to resuscitate the patient, but he never forgot the importance of reducing the dosage of morphine when a patient is an older adult or has a debilitating disease. The emotions evoked during that life-and-death struggle resulted in lifelong learning for him.

This physician, years later, decides to prepare a simulation activity for medical students that duplicates this experience. The students develop a relationship with a technologically advanced, remote-controlled mannequin that talks, breathes, and struggles with severe pain. The students will very likely repeat the mistake the young doctor made years earlier when they assist this elderly, debilitated patient (mannequin). Again, they will also struggle to resuscitate the patient, and, again, they will also learn something in a powerful, long-lasting way. You don't forget nearly killing a patient, even if it is a mannequin. When students experience strong emotions, when they care, they learn, and they remember.

Another Example of Emotions and Learning

A thoughtful starting pause can also help learners acknowledge emotional baggage and face some of the barriers to their learning. For example, Carol Melcher scheduled her yearly visit with the public health nurses who were responsible for the care of drug-abusing pregnant teenagers in the high desert of southern California. The group of six nurses sat in a circle to talk about better ways to help these needy clients. Melcher noticed some formality and stiffness in the group, so she decided to use a creative activity to begin her presentation. She asked the nurses to use a couple of pipe cleaners to create a design that illustrates what it is like to try to make a difference in the outcomes for the mothers and babies to which they were assigned. As the women showed their designs to each other and described the tremendous challenges they faced in their jobs on a day-to-day basis, Melcher noted a change in the group's demeanor (C. Melcher, personal communication, October 6, 2006).

One nurse used her pipe cleaners to form the shapes of two women, one with a large tummy, sitting on the other's lap. The nurse said she was the one holding the pregnant teen and wishing that she could be the mother this young woman had never had and would never be. As the women around the circle took turns telling their stories, tears began to flow and arms went around each other. This starting pause created a sense of trust, common ground, and safety and prepared the learners for the discussion that followed. At the end of their time together, Melcher asked each of the participants to write down one thing they planned to do immediately with what they had learned from the session. The women around the circle wrote and spoke of the ideas they found helpful and would implement. During the next few weeks, Melcher's e-mail inbox was filled with stories of the outcomes of the learning session. Melcher's teaching included more than the simple update of information. Because it provided preparation for learning and for future planning, the time the nurses spent together increased their openness to new possibilities and follow-up actions (C. Melcher, personal communication, October 6, 2006).

Create a Safe Environment

Learners need to identify their concerns and sometimes their emotions before they are ready to learn, and they also fare better when they feel they are in a safe place for sharing and growing. A good starting pause can help learners achieve this. We can establish a good environment for learning when we invite our students to interact with the person sitting next to them, when they share humorous moments, or when we foster a sense of community through solving a puzzle together or telling something about ourselves to others.

Michele Deck knows how to set the stage for good learning. I first heard Deck speak at a childbirth education conference, and I remember things she taught us 30 years later. The first thing Deck does to get her learners' attention is to ask them to stand and move away from their chairs. The next thing she does is get them talking to someone they did not know prior to coming to the seminar. Then she moves them into a group in a new part of the room. After a few minutes, the entire atmosphere of the room is changed. Instead of a tense, nervous hall filled with strangers, the room becomes warm and comfortable. Participants have been listened to. In addition, the presenter has been able to get some good ideas of what the participants expect to learn and is able to reassure them that it will be a positive learning experience, focused on their needs, and not a boring, stagnant ordeal where only the teacher will be talking.

Create Interest

A good starting pause can increase student interest where little previously existed. Imagine two chemistry laboratories. In each lab the students are going to conduct an experiment to determine the chemical compound present in a drinking glass. The instructor decides to experiment with a starting pause to see if he could create interest by telling a story to begin the lab. He tells one of his groups, "The glass in front of you was discovered with a dead body." This intrigues the students, and because now they want to find out how the woman died, they see that completing the assignment will help them solve a mystery. Bain (2004) suggests that "people learn most when they are . . . trying to solve problems . . . that they find intriguing, beautiful, or important" (p. 109). The instructor would likely notice a big difference between the two lab groups. The group working on a solution to an important problem would likely be full of energy and anticipation and accomplish the task more quickly and accurately than the group that didn't have a starting pause at the beginning of the lab. This instructor would have discovered that pausing at the beginning of the session to tell a story creates a desire for discovery and improves the students' experience.

It is our responsibility to create interest and help our students understand the potential value of a learning experience during the starting pause. It is easy for us to assume that students can make connections between what we are teaching them and occupational success, but students often need our help. Before physical therapy students hear a lecture on muscles used in walking, they may need to pause first to appreciate how knowing about the physiology of gait will assist them when they evaluate their next patient. This knowledge will enable them to prevent injury and promote health and well-being. Realizing this, the student will listen carefully, focus, and ask appropriate questions. When we skip the focusing pause, however, it is possible that a number of the students will see the connection too late for them to learn what they need to know.

Motivate to Action

Sometimes providing information is enough to help learners solve problems, explain mysteries, or answer important questions. But when we need to motivate our learners to action, we may find that information alone does not do the trick.

As a faculty developer, I have taught about active learning, student engagement, chunking, and the importance of pausing for learning. In the past, I enthusiastically began my workshops by describing and demonstrating many ways teachers could pause to break up teaching into chunks and engage students. My efforts met with varying results. Usually the workshops were reviewed positively, but I wondered what difference the workshops actually made in teacher behavior, especially when I read a comment such as the following:

> Thanks for an engaging and enjoyable workshop, *but* there is no way I could use these ideas in my class. I already have too much content to cover and not enough time—why should I try to pause and cover even less?

I realized that a powerful starting pause in my own lesson was necessary if my learners were going to change anything they were doing. I was presently showing them different ways to teach, but I wasn't making them want to teach differently. Could I do anything to increase the effectiveness of my seminars? I worked for some time on a new way to introduce the concepts, a way to stop them long enough to help them question what they were presently doing. I developed a one-way and two-way communication game using matching dominos on trays. Participants sat in pairs, back to back. One person made a pattern with the dominos on the tray and tried to explain to the other one how to duplicate the pattern. They were to do it in a series of rounds, starting with one-way communication, in which only the person making the pattern could talk, and eventually using two-way communication, which allowed all participants to chime in. I asked them to contrast the differences between creating and duplicating domino patterns when communication was only one-way compared to when it was two-way. Their summary is shown in Table 6.2.

After playing the game and analyzing the results, educators were very quick to see the point. Although two-way communication had real advantages over one way, almost all their classes consisted of teacher talk and very little, if any, student talk. With one-way communication, students were probably confused, frustrated, unmotivated, and learning very little. The starting pause activity helped the teachers want to answer questions such as the following:

- How can I do less lecturing (one-way communication) in my classes?
- How can I still cover the lecture content yet get students to interact with the ideas?
- How can I find the time for pauses at the start and the close of class?
- Are there quick ways to pause that won't take too much time away from my lecture?
- How can I increase two-way communication in my classes?
- How can I get a 9 or 10 for my lecture, instead of a 3 on a scale of 1 to 10?

Before the seminar with the starting pause domino game, the participants enjoyed the pause ideas but were skeptical about actually using them in their own teaching. After I changed the way the workshop began, I received different comments in their e-mails, such as the following:

I would love to show you how I am using the ideas you presented at our workshop in my teaching.

My student evaluations have really improved since I have started using the techniques that you showed us.

I always thought that good teachers were born—and I just wasn't born to be good. Now I know that I can learn to be a good teacher. Thanks for helping me to improve my teaching in ways that are really making a difference.

TABLE 6.2
Learners' Descriptions of Differences in One- and Two-Way Communication

One-Way Communication	Two-Way Communication
Frustrating	Motivating
Confusing	Empowering, supportive
Unmotivating	Confidence building
Inaccurate (average score 3 out of 10)	Accurate (average score 9 out of 10)
Ineffective	Effective

Enhance the Power of the Lesson

In addition to motivating learners to action, a good starting pause can enhance the power of the lesson. Tim Floyd (2014) gave a talk about the importance of diversity. He instructed the first section of the audience to snap their fingers, the second section to clap their hands on their thighs, and the third section to stomp their feet on the ground. He said that when we all did this at the same time, we were going to create a rather convincing thunderstorm. He walked across the front of the room, asking each section to either increase or decrease the sounds they were making. The resulting noise was amazingly like that of a bona fide thunderstorm, complete with rain and wind. He said that just as our thunderstorm was more real because of our diverse contributions, our effectiveness as team workers could be more authentic because of the unique differences each of us brought to the task. And because we are not the same, that impact is even stronger—we wouldn't have had that powerful experience if we hadn't been doing different things. His short talk on the value of diversity concluded with the comment that we are better because of our diversity. We can be united, but we cannot be uniform. We can take our snaps, stomps, and knee claps and make a wonderful impact when we are together. His lesson was so much more powerful and memorable because of the pause he planned at the beginning of his short presentation. The memory of the vivid storm we experienced helped us remember the message about diversity (Floyd, 2014).

Introduce Process as Well as Content

Most starting pauses introduce the topic, but occasionally a starting pause might have more to do with process than content. Teachers using team-based learning introduce their course with team-building pauses, which increase student commitment to working with the group rather than focusing on their individual accomplishments. A survival activity or other team-building activity can be a powerful reminder to independent students who prefer to work alone that their performance might be improved if they were working with a team.

To help students understand how to participate in discussions, an instructor could ask students to form a circle and toss a ball of yarn back and forth. When the instructor starts the toss, she holds one end of the yarn. Each person who catches the ball holds a string of the yarn snugly before tossing the yarn ball to another individual so that a sort of spiderweb forms as the ball crisscrosses around the circle. The ball reaches the final class member, and the professor suggests to the students that the design represents a well-balanced class discussion. Students notice how nice their design looks when everyone participates equally. Then the instructor asks one of the students to reach forward to pull as much of the web toward herself as she can. The instructor might suggest that this is how a discussion looks when one person is dominating it. Then she asks a couple at the far side of the circle to let go of their yarn to show what it looks like when individuals choose not to participate. As they roll the yarn back into a ball, each student could state a personal objective for the class and would likely now be ready to participate in the discussion.

Teach the Entire Lesson

Sometimes the starting pause can constitute a major part of the day's lesson. This is what happens when Desmyrna Taylor teaches a group of allied health students about caring for older patients. The students are asked to wrap cardboard around their knees and elbows, put Vaseline on their glasses, or wrap strips of wax paper around their head to cover their eyes. They place cotton balls in their ears and strong-smelling ointment in their noses. They put a large towel in their pants. Now they are old; that is, they don't see or hear or taste or smell as well as usual, and their mobility is limited. Then they go through a list of tasks—find a classroom, use a key to open a mailbox, get in and out of a car in the parking lot, use the restroom, and identify smells and tastes.

After experiencing what it can be like for some in old age, these students are now ready to discuss health care for older adults. They are eager to know how the changes of advancing age affect their role as health professional caregivers. How should they adapt their expectations to accommodate the needs of the older population? The experience of trying to get into an automobile with a knee that won't bend heightens their sensitivity to what their patients might be undergoing in their activities of daily living. Now they care (D. Taylor, personal communication, December 10, 2004).

At the end of the session, Taylor asked the students to pause to reflect on the workshop. Students had comments like, "I will never forget the frustration of not being able to unlock my car. My rheumatoid-stiffened hand would not work right. Thank you for this experience." Another said, "I will never rush an old person again." It's difficult to imagine this happening after a lecture on aging that didn't include the carefully planned beginning pause. Taylor has found a successful way to help students experience and care about the changes that growing old involves and how these changes affect the way they will work with their elderly patients (D. Taylor, personal communication, December 10, 2004).

Occasionally, as in this example on aging, the starting pause and ensuing discussion are so powerful that little teacher talk is necessary. Planning a powerful starting pause followed by class discussion can be an effective way to teach and can leave lessons never forgotten. I remember one of the first times I learned this way. I was a graduate student quite confident in my ability to accomplish tasks on my own. One of the objectives for a course in educational leadership was to prepare students for group work. The class started with a survival exercise involving surviving an unexpected plane crash, first individually and then as a group. We were asked to rank a number of items according to their value in helping us live through the experience. It was an important learning moment for me when my survival score was significantly lower than our group's survival score. Perhaps I wasn't as self-sufficient as I thought. Maybe I could benefit from listening to and working with others. The class starting pause taught me a lesson I would not have picked up from a lecture. I became a better team member as a result.

7

WHY CLOSE WITH A PAUSE

A closing pause allows students time to process what they have learned; they can decide how it will benefit them and how they will use it.

Closure brings the major ideas in the lesson into a sharper focus. It provides time for the student to gel the learning. It might be as simple as asking students to explain the major ideas in a lesson or as complex as having students argue the value of what was learned. Closing pauses are all about checking for understanding and knowing the end result. Brian Sztabnik (2015) draws our attention to the importance of the closing pause when he says, "If we don't know the end result, we risk moving haphazardly from one activity to the next. Every moment in a lesson plan should tell. . . . If it [the lesson] fails to check for understanding, you will never know if the lesson's goal was attained."

In Chapter 5 we examined the characteristics of good closing pauses. The following examples illustrate how closing pauses can help students achieve important objectives.

A Closing Pause That Reviews and Celebrates

A closing pause can review content and celebrate learning. A professor who teaches a course on underrepresented populations in French literature gave each student a large sheet of paper and some colored markers toward the end of the semester. She instructed them to choose a passage from any of their readings and list five important terms or key phrases to describe the passage they had chosen. On the back of their sheet they wrote the title of the work that contained the passage.

The students posted their sheet of five phrases on the wall of the classroom, then walked around the room in pairs, and wrote down their guesses for the titles that the phrases on each of the other sheets provided clues for without peeking at the answer on the back of the sheet. After each of the students revealed their mystery literary work for each of the posted sheets, the instructor awarded prizes to the student pairs with the correct identification (A. Rice, personal communication, May 14, 2017).

A Closing Pause That Wraps Up

A closing pause can effectively close a session. Imagine the following hypothetical scenario: A group of faculty developers started their session at a conference on higher education with an activity using various pictures of pennies (Common Cents, 1998). They asked their learners to select which of the 12 pictures accurately depicted a real penny. The educators wanted their participants to consider how much detail we remember about a common object. More than half the participants could not pick the right picture. Surprised at how little they really knew about something they had experienced many times, the learners considered possible explanations. After pausing to heighten their awareness, learners were then curious and wanted to learn more about the topic, one they might have thought they already knew a lot about but may have missed some important details.

As a closing pause for the session that started with identifying the accurate penny, these hypothetical faculty developers asked their learners to think about the penny exercise and summarize what they had learned on a three-inch-by-five-inch card under the title "A Penny for Your Thoughts" (CP 59). The participants told each other what they had written down, what they had learned, and how it related to the opening pause.

By taking learners back to the beginning of the session, these educators were able to provide a bookend for the learning period. The stops they provided at the beginning and the end separated the learning session from the rest of the day. The penny exercise at the beginning helped the students set aside what they had been thinking about prior to attending the session, and the closing pause helped them look back and finalize their takeaway concepts and action plans. Having written their summary down on their penny cards, learners knew they didn't have to try to keep this in their minds during the next conference session. They had their cards to refer to at a later time.

So often we leave a learning activity trying to keep in our minds the lessons we have learned but find that other things quickly crowd them out, and we forget them. The beauty of a closing pause that provides the opportunity to summarize and jot down anything that we want to remember is that we can keep the notes we wrote during the pause and refer to them without trying to remember them.

A Closing Pause That Applies

A closing pause can help students analyze and apply learning concepts. An instructor might say the following:

> We have finished discussing the effects of the Industrial Revolution on men and women. . . . I am going to ask you a question. Think to yourself and be prepared to defend your answers in about 30 seconds. No hands, I'll randomly invite responses. Given what you know about the Industrial Revolution, can we assume it is over? If yes, what proof do you have? If no, what proof do you have? (Hunter, 1994)

This pause was intriguing for two reasons. It required deep thought and could not be answered with one or two words. The teacher not only carefully planned a question that required high-level thinking but also used a technique that is very likely to foster high levels of engagement for all students. She used the Pause Procedure Question (MP 26) when she said, "I'll randomly invite responses." Adding this phrase increased the pressure on students who might otherwise sit back and wait for someone else to answer the question. Students do not want to appear dumb to their peers; they are likely to think carefully about how they might respond when the instructor says, "I will call on one of you."

A Closing Pause That Commits to Action

Faculty members at the University of Southern California School of Medicine developed the Commitment to Action (CTA) Closing Pause (CP 46) to plan future actions. (D. Fisher, personal communication, March 10, 2013). Based on the commitment to change model (Prochaska & DiClemente, 1984), teachers ask learners at the conclusion of the lecture to state what they will do with the new information. Most CTA statements have three components: specific context (when practice can occur), target action, and frequency of the action.

A CTA closure might sound something like, "I will take a complete history about anticoagulation including bleeding and bruising in the evaluation of every patient I admit to the acute stroke care unit." Another CTA statement might be, "I will bring the journal article about the use of checklists prior to surgery at the operating room team meeting next week." A CTA closure after a half-day seminar on interdisciplinary education and the importance of using numerous resources in a health care facility might result in the following statements:

> I will always consider what resources, beyond the physicians, might be able to help me achieve more comprehensive care of my patients.
>
> I am committed to increase my awareness of the potential contributions of all of the health care providers available to the patient and will look for ways to incorporate the possibilities in my care planning.

CTA closing pauses are not restricted to the health sciences. After a presentation on ethical standards for business practices, students might respond, "I will always think of my clients' needs first when financial planning," and "Clients' financial interests must always take precedence over my own when making decisions about investing money."

A Closing Pause That Engages, Energizes, and Encourages

Audience response systems offer a way to wrap up a learning session in an energizing and engaging manner. Kroski (2014) used polling to see how well students could use library indexes and databases after her lecture. One of her questions was, "My paper is on protest music about the Vietnam War. What databases should I use?" Students then responded in teams to the multiple-choice questions on the screen, and she gave out prizes to each of the teams that had correct answers. Kroski said, "The class was a huge success—not only did my students have a great time, but they demonstrated to me that they had actually retained one of the more critical lessons of the semester" (Kroski, 2014, para. 2).

A Closing Pause That Makes Connections

English professor James Lang (2016a) talks about closing his class session on Browning's monologues by telling students they had the last five minutes to make five connections between what they discussed and what is happening in the world around them, such as listing five popular songs in which the speaker clearly does not represent the voice of the singer. He describes how quickly the students can focus when this is all that stands between them and lunch. Lang's closing pause goes a step further than helping students review content. It moves them up Bloom's (1956) cognitive domain from simply summarizing material to applying it in contemporary contexts. A number of the closing pauses in Appendix C suggest ways to review content and make connections.

Figure 7.1. Closing pause mnemonic.

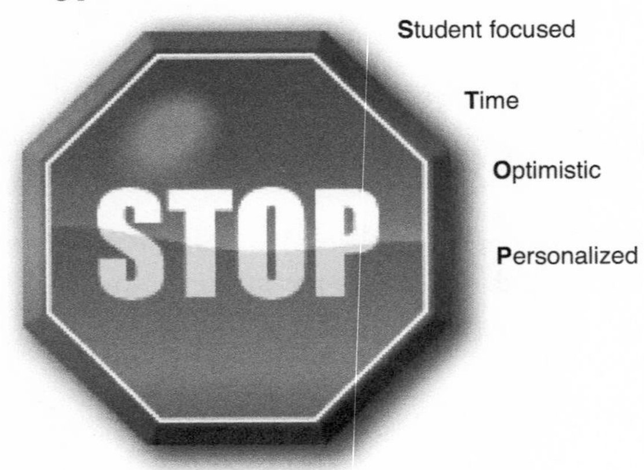

A Closure Memory Aid

A simple STOP mnemonic (Figure 7.1) may help you remember four important principles of good closing pauses: student focused, time, optimistic, and personalized.

Student Focused

It is essential for the summaries to come from the learning participants and not from the teacher. What the student thinks happened during the class is what is really important. Meier (2000) said, "What the learner thinks and says and does is more important than what the instructor thinks and says and does" (p. 91). Imagine two fellows standing in front of a bird cage. One says to the other, "I thought you said you taught the bird to talk?" The other replies, "I told you that I taught him to speak, I didn't say that he learned to speak." We care about the end result. The teacher may think a great deal of learning occurred during the lecture, but it is possible that very little actually took place. What is important here is what the students demonstrate.

Many educators feel it is our responsibility to do the teaching, the talking, and the review. The common assumption is that a good presentation includes telling students what you are going to tell them, telling them, and then telling them what you told them. This implies that only the teacher summarizes; the learner has no responsibility for reviewing content. The instructor's review may or may not be the learner's review, however. Wise educators have discovered that because personalization is essential for a good close, this review will be most valuable if it is the learner's review. According to Pike (2003), "Adults don't argue with their own data" (pp. 3–4).

When they close a learning session, teachers are often surprised when learners identify the most valuable thing they learned. Fifty attendees may well indicate 50 different most important learning ideas from the presentation, which is why the learner's review is more important than the instructor's. What really matters is what the learner says matters. Because they bring different backgrounds and different expectations to the experience, learners value lessons learned that relate to them. Closing pauses that allow learners to look over the content and decide for themselves what they learned and what they personally value will help with retention and transfer.

When analyzing what the students say about the class hour, or what the patient states was transferred during the conference, teachers and physicians can assess how effective they were in meeting their objectives and what strategies were most effective. If none of the summaries of the learning session mentioned what the instructor planned as the major objective, then the instructor should reevaluate his or her plan for the next session, revisit the point that was missed, and seek more effective ways to communicate.

Time

Good closing pauses take time. Closure will happen only during the learning session. It won't happen after the class time is up, no matter how wonderful the lecture was. For closure to be effective, it must occur before the session is supposed to be over. Stopping the lecture a few minutes early is not easy, but the effort is worth it. Wise instructors realize that without a closing pause students are likely to forget most of what was discussed almost immediately, and they are unlikely to transfer much of what was taught to life outside the classroom.

Optimistic

Teachers hope students leave the classroom, lab, or clinic feeling good about the learning session. In addition, when asked optimistic questions, students are more likely to value the class and teachers' efforts on their behalf. Teachers might include questions like the following in their closing pauses:

- Why are you glad you were here today?
- What was useful to you in today's lecture?
- How will you use the information you learned today in your profession?
- What was most valuable to you from our learning session today?

Learners usually pay a great deal for learning, whether in tuition, workshop fees, or conference registrations, and often make sacrifices in time and travel. After adding up the costs, some may regret the investment made. To avoid this, we should encourage students to focus on the benefits they have received from attending the learning session.

Personalized

At the end of the teaching session, we want to highlight each individual's personal experience. It is important to ask questions like the following:

- What happened for you?
- What did you learn?
- What is your 60-second summary of the learning session?
- What will you do with the information?

Again, what is important is what the student has experienced—not what the teachers thought they taught but what the learner learned, how the learner values that learning, and what the learner plans to do with the information.

Importance of Writing or Speaking About Action Plans

We can help our students retain what they have learned when we plan appropriate closing pauses. We increase the chances that students will actually follow up with their plans when we ask them to write them down and talk about them. Motivational psychologists frequently ask their clients to write down and speak about their goals. Without committing to their goals, the participants are much less likely to reach them. A decision that is shared is more likely to lead to action than one that is merely thought about. In a study at Dominican University of California, 267 adults with very real goals, such as selling a house or getting a contract, were placed into five categories. Participants were asked to plan different ways to reach their goals. After one month, the individuals who wrote down their goals achieved them at a significantly higher rate than those who merely thought about their goals (Matthews, n.d.). Evidently, the act of making a public commitment increases the likelihood of action. Once you have announced or committed to writing a goal, it is human nature that you will be more likely to follow through to attain it.

As educators, we often finish a teaching session hoping that our students will remember and apply what they have learned. How exciting is it to discover that when we take just an extra minute or so to ask our students to compare notes with the person sitting next to them or to write down their action plan, we are so much more likely to make a real difference in their lives. No wonder educators refer to the power of the closing pause.

An Example

Public health students assigned to teach a session on exercise to a group of patients came up with a closing pause that illustrates the STOP mnemonic for getting commitment to action. They asked their participants to address a postcard to themselves. Then they asked them to write down their responses to the following: Why I am glad that I was here for the exercise discussion today? and What I do plan to do in the next few weeks to get more exercise into my daily life? The student instructors collected the cards, discussed with the group what they had written down, and promised to mail back the cards with a personal comment in four to six weeks. (P. Herring, personal communication, n.d.).

This closing pause met the STOP criteria for a good ending. It was focused on the students, the learners. They summarized what they had learned during the session rather than listening to a summary provided by the instructors. The instructors allowed time for this to happen before the learners had to leave. Asking learners why they were glad to be there was optimistic; it emphasized the positive. Finally, each participant wrote down his or her personalized plan for the future. Most important, when the leaders asked the group to commit in writing to a goal, this greatly increased the likelihood that the participants would actually exercise. What particularly impressed the learners was hearing they would get the cards back in a few weeks. They did not want to discover a few weeks from now that they would be reading what they had planned to do and had not yet done.

Teaching experts tell us that small changes in the way instructors say things and how they structure the learning task can have major effects on student learning and transfer (Brown et al., 2014; Lang, 2016c). Why would we ever let students leave a learning session without reinforcing the conviction that what they learned was important, was personally meaningful, and will result in success? It is not enough to plan wonderfully organized, powerfully illustrated, elegantly delivered content. We must design closing pauses that will help learners construct meaning from what they have learned and develop plans to implement their continued learning. Educational psychology and brain science support this. We must pause with our learners.

APPENDIX

PAUSES YOU CAN USE

The pause examples are divided into three appendixes: Appendix A: Starting Pauses, Appendix B: Midpauses, and Appendix C: Closing Pauses. These pauses are specifically designed to incorporate what educational researchers and cognitive scientists have discovered about ideal learning. Some of these pause techniques will be familiar, as we have been using variations of these approaches intuitively for some time. Some we recognize as variations of classroom assessment techniques. For example, A Penny for Your Thoughts (CP 59) is very similar to Angelo and Cross's (1993) famous minute paper.

Faculty members might be comfortable using some of these pauses with certain groups, and others not at all. They may be concerned these activities are too playful or childlike for sophisticated audiences. When we are reluctant to incorporate starting, mid-, and closing pauses into our lecture plans, it might be helpful to remind ourselves of the following:

- Teaching less can lead to more learning (Ruhl et al., 1987).
- "Adults are babies in big bodies" (Pike, 2003, p. 3).
- "Learning is directly proportional to the amount of fun you are having" (Pike, 2003, p. 3).
- Small changes can make powerful differences in student learning (Lang, 2016c).

Trying something new in our teaching requires a willingness to take a risk. Occasionally we are tempted to think that pauses to engage students are a waste of valuable learning time. It is true that pausing takes time, but if we plan a playful method to ask a substantive question, our students generally respond with appreciation for the opportunity to test their knowledge and get feedback. They often don't mind having a little fun in the process.

A while back, a statistics teacher reluctantly decided to try a few of these pause techniques in her class. The first one was the Stand Up, Hand Up, Pair Up (MP 36) for a fairly simple mathematical problem—computing a *t*-test. Later in the same class period, the teacher had students in small groups use a Round Robin (MP 38) pause for a more challenging question requiring interpretation of statistical test results. The closing pause was a 60-second summary of the class. The following are some of the graduate students' comments from the 60-second summary:

> This is the first session in this course that I can truly say I enjoyed. I was always nervous in this class before, but today I relaxed. It was helpful to be able to work together to solve the math problems, as I had a check on my calculations with my partner.
>
> The Round Robin activity was reassuring when we could talk together and use our group consensus to reach a conclusion.
>
> Thanks for your creativity in planning today's class. The time flew. I felt that I really understood the *t*-test calculation and the case we worked on. Hearing others talk was really good.
>
> I really learned a lot in class today. Working in groups is much more reassuring than trying to do math and answering stat questions by yourself. Hope for more classes like this.

The statistics teacher, who was reluctant to change the approach she had been using, was gratified that she gave her students some pauses. As a result of the pauses, students felt more confident about their skills and received feedback about how well prepared they were for their upcoming midterm exam.

Note to Readers

Thank you for starting the journey with me of searching for better ways to teach and learn. I hope that the concepts I have shared in this book will spark a continuing conversation. One of the challenges of developing and compiling teaching strategies involves remembering who should receive credit for initiating the idea. Please visit my website (www.drgailrice.com) and share your experience with pausing. I also welcome reminders of those whom I may have forgotten to credit, so I can correct this in future editions of the book.

APPENDIX A

STARTING PAUSES

STARTING PAUSE 1

K-W-L START

K-W-L Start allows learners to answer two questions at the beginning of the learning and a third question at the end of learning (see K-W-L Closure [CP 43]). The *K* stands for What do you know?; *W* stands for What do you want to know?; and the *L* is for What did you learn?

Settings for Use

- ☑ Small classroom lecture
- ☑ Clinical or laboratory presentation
- ☐ One-on-one session
- ☐ Conference presentation/ in-service education
- ☐ Keynote/large-group presentation
- ☐ Course/unit
- ☑ Online learning module

Characteristics

- ☐ Affirming, positive
- ☐ Physical/movement
- ☑ Activates prior knowledge/ experience
- ☑ Focuses/refocuses
- ☐ Creates community
- ☐ Generates curiosity
- ☑ Metacognitive
- ☑ Reviews
- ☐ Celebrates
- ☐ Commits to action
- ☐ Provides a bookend

Procedure

1. Prepare charts for each student that have four columns and space to write in the columns.
2. Alternatively, project the chart on an overhead screen and ask students to create their own chart in their notebooks or laptops.
3. Use the following column headings: Topic, K: What You Know; W: What You Want to Know; and L: What You Have Learned (Table A.1).
4. At the beginning of the session, introduce the topic, have students write down the topic in the first column, and then give them some time to complete Columns 2 and 3.
5. This activity is suitable for small groups as well as individuals.
6. Ask students to share with the larger group what they have written in their *K* and *W* columns.
7. Adjust the content of the lecture to fit what you have learned from the group sharing.

8. At the end of the learning session, have students complete the final column (CP 43).

TABLE A.1
K-W-L Chart

Topic	K: What You Know	W: What You Want to Know	L: What You Learned

Additional Suggestions

- This activity almost requires using the K-W-L Closure (CP 43) activity, in which learners look back at what they wanted to learn, what they thought they already knew, and what they learned from the session.
- Metacognitive benefits from this final step can be enhanced by asking students how they learned what they learned and if they thought this was an effective way to learn. If not, how could it have been more effective, and what will they do to learn further and remember what they learned?

Online Adaptation

This starting pause works extremely well in an online module. Students can complete the chart at the beginning and the end of the module.

Key References and Resources

Barkley, E. F., & Major, C. H. (2015). *Learning assessment techniques: A handbook for college faculty*. San Francisco, CA: Wiley.

Halsey, V. (2011).*Brilliance by design: Creating learning experiences that connect, inspire, and engage*. San Fransisco, CA: Berrett-Koehler.

K-W-L chart. Retrieved from www.readwritethink.org/classroom-resources/printouts/chart-a-30226.html

Ogle, D. M. (1986). KWL: A teaching model that develops active reading of expository text. *Reading Teacher, 39*, 564–570.

STARTING PAUSE 2

ENTRY TICKET

This starting pause is used to help students and the instructor get a sense of what they already know and what they might still need or want to know. The Entry Ticket is designed to collect specific information about what learners' prior experiences or level of knowledge might be with a particular topic. The tickets are handed to learners as they enter the classroom. Students are instructed to respond to the questions on the ticket and then return the completed ticket to the instructor before class begins. The purpose of this beginning pause is to allow the instructor to quickly look through the tickets before class begins to gain a sense of the most effective starting point and most appropriate level of instruction.

Settings for Use

- ☑ Small classroom lecture
- ☑ Clinical or laboratory presentation
- ☐ One-on-one session
- ☐ Conference presentation/in-service education
- ☐ Keynote/large-group presentation
- ☐ Course/unit
- ☑ Online learning module

Characteristics

- ☐ Affirming/positive
- ☐ Physical/movement
- ☑ Activates prior knowledge/experience
- ☑ Focuses/refocuses
- ☐ Creates community
- ☑ Generates curiosity
- ☐ Metacognitive
- ☐ Reviews
- ☐ Celebrates
- ☐ Commits to action
- ☐ Provides a bookend

Procedure

1. Prepare tickets with no more than two or three questions on them and space for writing answers to hand out to the students as they enter the classroom.
2. Possible questions might be the following:
   a. What do you already know about this topic?
   b. What experiences have you had with this topic?
   c. What would you like to know about the topic?
3. Ask for additional things anyone would like to share with the instructor before the class begins.

4. Instruct learners to complete the tickets immediately.
5. Collect the tickets as soon as most students have arrived.
6. Quickly look through the collected tickets, noting trends and important ideas.
7. Respond to the trends you have noted as you begin class.

Additional Suggestions

- Consider giving this assignment before students arrive to class.
- Hand out tickets at the end of the previous class and make it clear that tickets need to be completed as they will be collected before students enter the class.
- Post the ticket on the course management system with instructions.
- E-mail the ticket to students before class.
- A particularly good closure technique to use with this is Exit Ticket (CP 39).

Online Adaptation

The Entry Ticket works well at the beginning of the online course module. Students click on the activity, and the Entry Ticket comes up. Students respond to the questions on the prepared ticket and submit them. Some instructors find it helpful to require that items in the module are completed in the order they appear. This keeps students from skipping the pauses they may feel are less important than others to their mastery of the module's content.

Key References and Resources

Barkley, E. F., & Major, C. H. (2015). *Learning assessment techniques: A handbook for college faculty*. San Francisco, CA: Wiley.

Barkley, E. F., Major, C. H., & Cross, P. K. (2014). *Collaborative learning techniques: A handbook for college faculty*. San Francisco, CA: Jossey-Bass.

Effective classroom practices. (2017). Retrieved from www.brown.edu/about/administration/sheridan-center/teaching-learning/effective-classroom-practices/entrance-exit-tickets/ accessed2/1/17

Entry ticket. (n.d.). Retrieved from www.theteachertoolkit.com/index.php/tool/entry-ticket/ accessed2/1/17

Marzano, R. J. (2012). Art and science of teaching: The many uses of exit slips. *Educational Leadership, 70*(2), 80–81.

STARTING PAUSE 3

DOT THE OBJECTIVES

This activity asks students to prioritize the instructor's objectives and to decide how they want to learn and what they particularly value. It not only helps students to evaluate their priorities but also helps instructors think about their approaches to their topics and how they will go about their lecture and adjust their topic to fit their students' needs and desires. It may also yield valuable information about what education students may need about the importance of certain objectives.

Settings for Use

- ☑ Small classroom lecture
- ☑ Clinical or laboratory presentation
- ☐ One-on-one session
- ☑ Conference presentation/in-service education
- ☑ Keynote/large-group presentation
- ☑ Course/unit
- ☑ Online learning module

Characteristics

- ☐ Affirming/positive
- ☐ Physical/movement
- ☑ Activates prior knowledge/experience
- ☑ Focuses and refocuses
- ☐ Creates community
- ☑ Generates curiosity
- ☐ Metacognitive
- ☐ Reviews
- ☐ Celebrates
- ☐ Commits to action
- ☐ Provides a bookend

Procedure

1. At the beginning of the learning session, provide the learners with the list of objectives the teacher plans to address. Be sure the number of objectives is not too many for the time allowed (three or four is probably about right for an hour's lecture).
2. Give each student a set of colored dots with sticky backing.
3. Ask the student to place a dot of a particular color (perhaps red) on the objective with their highest priority for coverage during the lecture.
4. Proceed with the colors for ranking the rest of the objectives (e.g., blue for second tier, yellow for third).
5. Ask the students to report to you how they have ranked the objectives.

6. Use the student ranking to order how you proceed with the lecture, beginning with the objective that received the highest ranking from the students.

Additional Suggestions

- Alternatively, project the objectives on an overhead screen and allow students to rank them by
    - show of hands;
    - holding up colored cards; or
    - audience response system, such as Poll Everywhere or Kahoot!
- For the closure, ask students to review the objectives and ask them if you met their objectives. Ask them if their ranking has changed at all or if they still feel the same way about their priorities.

Online Adaptation

This starting pause works well for online courses. Students can provide feedback to the instructor about the online module objectives and how they would prioritize them.

Key References and Resources

Angelo, T. A., & Cross, K. P. (1993). *Classroom assessment techniques: A handbook for college teachers* (2nd ed.). San Francisco, CA: Jossey-Bass.

Barkley, E. F., & Major, C. H. (2015). *Learning assessment techniques: A handbook for college faculty*. San Francisco, CA: Wiley.

STARTING PAUSE 4

COMPLETE A SENTENCE

This is an extremely short and easy way to pause at the beginning of the learning session and ask for a simple answer to one question by completing a sentence. Typically, the sentence they are asked to complete is, Today I want to learn . . . .

Settings for Use

- ☑ Small classroom lecture
- ☑ Clinical or laboratory presentation
- ☑ One-on-one session
- ☑ Conference presentation/ in-service education
- ☐ Keynote/large-group presentation
- ☑ Course/unit
- ☑ Online learning module

Characteristics

- ☐ Affirming/positive
- ☐ Physical/movement
- ☐ Activates prior knowledge/ experience
- ☑ Focuses and refocuses
- ☐ Creates community
- ☑ Generates curiosity
- ☐ Metacognitive
- ☐ Reviews
- ☐ Celebrates
- ☐ Commits to action
- ☑ Provides a bookend

Procedure

1. Before you ask the question, provide some introduction to the topic being addressed.
2. Decide what sentence you would like students to complete. It could be a content-related sentence, but it is usually more effective if it does not have one right answer. In other words, individuals indicate their personal response to the question, such as, What would you most like to learn about this topic? What have you found most puzzling in the past about this topic? Why do people find this topic difficult? or What experiences have blocked you from learning about this topic in the past?
3. Decide how you want students to answer—by writing the answer, telling it to someone sitting close by, posting it on a sticky note, putting it on a three-inch-by-five-inch card, or sending a text or response through an audience response system.

4. Project the sentence needing completion on an overhead screen or prepare cards or half sheets of paper with the partial sentence on it.
5. Give instructions to the students.
6. Allow adequate time for the activity.
7. Conduct a brief large-group discussion on a few of the individual responses.
8. Be sure you have a sense of the groups' responses so that you can address them in the presentation.
9. If students wrote their responses, you might want to collect the cards or half sheets to conduct a more in-depth analysis after the learning session.

Additional Suggestions

- This activity can be particularly helpful in identifying prior experiences with topics that might block openness for new learning. It is nicely complemented with the Complete A Sentence (CP 44) Closing Pause.

Key References and Resources

Barkley, E. F., & Major, C. H. (2015). *Learning assessment techniques: A handbook for college faculty*. San Francisco, CA: Wiley.

Honeycutt, B. (2016). *FLIP the first 5 minutes of class: 50 focusing activities to engage your students.* Retrieved from barbihoneycutt.com/store/home/12-50-proven-activities-ebook.html

STARTING PAUSE 5

FIVE FACTS I KNOW

This pause allows students to focus on what they know about a subject before the class begins. It encourages them to activate their prior knowledge and access their experiences with a topic before learning more about it in the lecture. It also provides the opportunity for a quick review to prepare for the upcoming learning experience.

Settings for Use

- ☑ Small classroom lecture
- ☑ Clinical or laboratory presentation
- ☐ One-on-one session
- ☐ Conference presentation/in-service education
- ☐ Keynote/large-group presentation
- ☑ Course/unit
- ☑ Online learning module

Characteristics

- ☑ Affirming/positive
- ☐ Physical/movement
- ☑ Activates prior knowledge/experience
- ☑ Focuses and refocuses
- ☑ Creates community
- ☐ Generates curiosity
- ☐ Metacognitive
- ☐ Reviews
- ☐ Celebrates
- ☐ Commits to action
- ☑ Provides a bookend

Procedure

1. Ask students to take out a sheet of paper and write the topic at the top of the sheet. Alternatively, hand out three-inch-by-five-inch cards or sheets of paper with the topic written at the top.
2. Have students write the numbers 1 through 5 along the left column of the sheet or card.
3. Explain the rules of the activity to the students. They will write down five different facts or concepts that they know about the topic.
   a. As the instructor you get to determine the rules you would like students to use, in particular, rules about using resources if they do not have five facts readily in mind. For example, can they call a friend? Can they look up the topic on the Internet? Can they consult each other in the room? How much time will they have to write down their five facts?

4. Tell the students to start by simply brainstorming—see what they can come up with as they try to recall what they know about the topic.
5. As the instructor, you can decide to do various things at this point in the introductory activity. Ask students to pair up to see if anything on their cards match the other person's or ask students to turn their cards in so instructors could refer to the information as the lecture proceeds.
6. Plan to celebrate when students find a match, such as applause, small rewards, and so on.

Additional Suggestions

- Instructors can ask students to do this before class begins and print their five facts prior to class.
- Closure idea: The instructor might ask students to check off each item on their card that was addressed in some way during the lecture.

Online Adaptation

At the beginning of the online module, you might ask students to list five things they know about the topic of the module and submit it. Ask them to keep a copy of their five facts so they can revisit them at the end of the module.

At the completion of the module students might return to their original five facts sheet and submit it again, this time with a note after each fact indicating how it relates to a defining question, such as, How does this fact affect the way I . . . (e.g., work with patients with this illness, interpret this literary work, negotiate a leadership objective, solve an algebraic problem, interpret a literary work)?

Key References and Resources

Barkley, E. F., & Major, C. H. (2015). *Learning assessment techniques: A handbook for college caculty*. San Francisco, CA: Wiley.

STARTING PAUSE 6

TRIVIA

This energizing way to focus the learners calls their attention to small but important facts that introduce the topic of the learning session. This activity breaks preoccupation with factors that distract from the learning session and helps learners focus on the topic as well as creates a sense of bonding with others in the room and provides readiness for learning. Learners will not forget the answers to the trivia questions, so choose them carefully.

Settings for Use

- ☑ Small classroom lecture
- ☑ Clinical or laboratory presentation
- ☐ One-on-one session
- ☑ Conference presentation/in-service education
- ☐ Keynote/large-group presentation
- ☐ Course/unit
- ☑ Online learning module

Characteristics

- ☑ Affirming/positive
- ☑ Physical/movement
- ☑ Activates prior knowledge/experience
- ☑ Focuses and refocuses
- ☑ Creates community
- ☑ Generates curiosity
- ☐ Metacognitive
- ☐ Reviews
- ☑ Celebrates
- ☐ Commits to action
- ☑ Provides a bookend

Procedure

1. Develop trivia questions that relate to the topic of the learning session.
2. Ask the students to form groups of five to six and choose a leader.
3. Leaders are to select writers, runners, and point managers.
4. Each group is given a set of five or six sticky notes.
5. Each group is given a group number to write on each of their sticky notes.
6. Teams write their group number for each trivia question, answer it on their sticky note, and run it to the front of the room.
7. The instructor indicates the correct answer and how many points go to each team.

8. After all the questions have been answered, the instructor discusses the relationship among the trivia questions, the objectives for the session, and the topic of the hour.
9. At the end of the learning session, prizes are distributed, with highest-scoring team getting first choice at the prize box.

Additional Suggestions

- Use multiple-choice questions to make the activity a little quicker and easier.
- It is important not to have too many trivia questions, as the pause can take much longer than you want it to. It is a powerful way to begin a session, especially when throughout the class you are able to refer to the opening trivia questions.
- The trivia questions will be long remembered, so you will want to choose carefully. Generally, find questions with specific answers, such as, What metaphor does the author use to begin the essay? or What percentage of homes had televisions in America in 1950?
- Wrap up by asking students to write a Two and Two Closure (CP 62) that ties the trivia with the learning goals and main learning concepts addressed.

Online Adaptation

This pause is a bit challenging to use in an online module. It probably will work best as a brief individual focusing activity rather than an online group experience. You could make the first activity in the module a trivia quiz, using the quiz function of the learning management system.

Key References and Resources

Deck, M. L. (1995). *Instant teaching tools for health care educators*. Maryland Heights, MO: Mosby.

Tomm, T. T. (1999). *Forensic science starters*. Retrieved from sciencespot.net/Pages/classforscistarters.html

STARTING PAUSE 7

WHAT'S IN IT FOR ME?

In this activity, abbreviated WIIFM, each student writes down on a sticky note what would make the session worthwhile for that student and posts the note on the whiteboard at the front of the room. This activity gives students a great feeling of control and assures teachers that they are providing what students are requesting.

Settings for Use

- ☑ Small classroom lecture
- ☑ Clinical or laboratory presentation
- ☑ One-on-one session
- ☑ Conference presentation/ in-service education
- ☐ Keynote/large-group presentation
- ☑ Course/unit
- ☑ Online learning module

Characteristics

- ☐ Affirming/positive
- ☑ Physical/movement
- ☑ Activates prior knowledge/ experience
- ☑ Focuses and refocuses
- ☐ Creates community
- ☐ Generates curiosity
- ☐ Metacognitive
- ☐ Reviews
- ☐ Celebrates
- ☐ Commits to action
- ☑ Provides a bookend

Procedure

1. Ask students to think of "WIIFM?" and list as many things as possible that they would like to learn about the day's topic (objectives).
2. Give students several sticky notes.
3. Have them write only one objective on each sticky note.
4. Ask students to place their sticky notes (objectives, WIIFMs) on the whiteboard at the front of the room.
5. Organize the objectives into categories.
6. Use the organized objectives to plan your presentation.
7. Have students help you evaluate your session at the end of the lecture by looking together at the sticky notes by category.

Additional Suggestions

- Limit students to only one sticky note per person and ask them to indicate their most important objective on that note.
- Instead of organizing the sticky notes yourself, allow the students to come up and organize them into categories for you. I often invite them up after the notes are on the board and let them categorize; they usually do a great job of grouping similar items.
- At the end of class you might have students go over the objectives and ask them if the class provided what they wanted when they decided WIIFM.

Online Adaptation

Ask online students to post their answers to their objectives for the lessons or module. At the end of the module, have them revisit what they listed and respond again based what they learned and make any changes to their answers.

Key References and Resources

Angelo, T. A., & Cross, K. P. (1993). *Classroom assessment techniques: A handbook for college teachers* (2nd ed.). San Francisco, CA: Jossey-Bass.

Barkley, E. F. (2010). *Student engagement techniques: A handbook for college faculty*. San Francisco, CA: Jossey-Bass.

Barkley, E. F., & Major, C. H. (2015). *Learning assessment techniques: A handbook for college faculty*. San Francisco, CA: Wiley.

Ting-A-Kee, M. (n.d.). WIIFM: What's in it for me [Web log post]. Retrieved from rationalized thoughts.blogspot.com/2007/07/wiifm-whats-in-it-for-me.html

STARTING PAUSE 8

STICKY NOTE START

This pause provides an opportunity for the instructor to receive feedback from the learners before beginning the session. The instructor asks the students to write a response to a question on a sticky note. Students bring their sticky note up to the front of the room, where the instructor can quickly organize the responses into categories and report the general trend of the answers to the group. An advantage of this starting pause is that the instructor receives input that may be helpful in adjusting plans for the learning session before beginning instruction.

Settings for Use

- ☑ Small classroom lecture
- ☑ Clinical or laboratory presentation
- ☐ One-on-one session
- ☑ Conference presentation/ in-service education
- ☐ Keynote/large-group presentation
- ☐ Course/unit
- ☐ Online learning module

Characteristics

- ☐ Affirming/positive
- ☑ Physical/movement
- ☑ Activates prior knowledge/ experience
- ☑ Focuses and refocuses
- ☑ Creates community
- ☐ Generates curiosity
- ☐ Metacognitive
- ☐ Reviews
- ☐ Celebrates
- ☐ Commits to action
- ☑ Provides a bookend

Procedure

1. Decide on the question you wish to have answered at the beginning of the session.
2. Provide sticky notepads (or just one sticky note) for each student.
3. Project the question on an overhead screen or clearly state it, and allow students time to think of their response and write it on the sticky note.
4. Ask students to bring their sticky note to the front of the room and place it on the whiteboard or easel, where you can quickly skim over them, perhaps moving them into categories, before reporting what you see to the group.

5. Keep in mind what the learners have expressed as you proceed to teach. You might want to adjust the teaching plan to fit what you have gleaned from your quick perusal of the sticky notes.
6. At the close of learning, refer to the sticky notes and ask students to discuss in small groups how their sticky note message has been addressed.

Additional Suggestions

- A particularly good closure technique to use with this starting pause is Sticky Note Closure (CP 45).

STARTING PAUSE 9

RED LIGHT GREEN LIGHT

This pause is designed to help the instructor tailor the objectives for the upcoming lecture to the audience. Based on the ubiquitous traffic signal system, the audience uses the green light to indicate go, the red light to indicate stop, and a yellow light to indicate maybe for the suggested objectives for the learning session.

Settings for Use

- ☑ Small classroom lecture
- ☑ Clinical or laboratory presentation
- ☐ One-on-one session
- ☑ Conference presentation/in-service education
- ☑ Keynote/large-group presentation
- ☑ Course/unit
- ☐ Online learning module

Characteristics

- ☐ Affirming/positive
- ☐ Physical/movement
- ☐ Activates prior knowledge/experience
- ☑ Focuses and refocuses
- ☐ Creates community
- ☑ Generates curiosity
- ☐ Metacognitive
- ☐ Reviews
- ☐ Celebrates
- ☐ Commits to action
- ☐ Provides a bookend

Procedure

1. Design a set of red, yellow, and green cards for each student.
2. If time permits, cut each card in the form of a traffic signal light. If not, a simple three-inch-by-five-inch card in the appropriate colors will work.
3. Develop more objectives than would likely be covered in the lecture.
4. Explain to learners that they will have the opportunity to assist in determining what will be addressed.
5. Ask them to hold up the green card for an objective they definitely want to have addressed.
6. Ask them to hold up the red card for an objective they do not wish to have addressed.
7. Ask them to hold up the yellow card for an objective they are indifferent about.

8. Explain that they should try to discriminate and not go for all green or all red.
9. As you go through the objectives, assess what the consensus is, and adjust your lecture plan to meet the needs of the majority of the audience.

Additional Suggestions

- This pause technique can be used even if you do not have time to prepare the colored cards ahead of time. You can ask for a show of hands. Simply ask how many give this objective a green light by raising their hand. The colored cards are easier to give an immediate read of the room, but a show of hands can also provide a sense of what your learners want in the way of addressing the objectives.

Key References and Resources

Angelo, T. A., & Cross, K. P. (1993). *Classroom assessment techniques: A handbook for college teachers* (2nd ed.). San Francisco, CA: Jossey-Bass.

Barkley, E. F. (2010). *Student engagement techniques: A handbook for college faculty.* San Francisco, CA: Jossey-Bass.

Barkley, E. F., & Major, C. H. (2015). *Learning assessment techniques: A handbook for college faculty.* San Francisco, CA: Wiley.

STARTING PAUSE 10

QUIZ TIME START—AUDIENCE RESPONSE SYSTEM

This helps students assess their own level of knowledge prior to the lecture. This preclass quiz uses an Internet-based audience response system to allow students to see how their answers compare with the rest of the classes' answers to the questions the instructor poses prior to the beginning of class. The particular value of this pause is that it will help individual students self-assess what they already know and what they may not know. It should increase student interest throughout the class period because they will be listening for the answers to the questions to find out if they know the correct answer.

Settings for Use

- ☑ Small classroom lecture
- ☑ Clinical or laboratory presentation
- ☐ One-on-one session
- ☑ Conference presentation/in-service education
- ☑ Keynote/large-group presentation
- ☑ Course/unit
- ☐ Online learning module

Characteristics

- ☐ Affirming/positive
- ☐ Physical/movement
- ☑ Activates prior knowledge/experience
- ☑ Focuses and refocuses
- ☐ Creates community
- ☑ Generates curiosity
- ☐ Metacognitive
- ☑ Reviews
- ☐ Celebrates
- ☐ Commits to action
- ☐ Provides a bookend

Procedure

1. Create a quiz of 5 to 10 questions centered on the main points you want the students to learn from the lecture. The questions can be true or false, multiple choice, or short answer.
2. Use an online student response program such as Poll Everywhere or Kahoot! or any clicker-based program you and your students have access to.
3. At the beginning of class, explain to students that a nongraded quiz related to that day's topic will precede the lecture. Ask students to respond to the questions, using their clickers, smartphones, or laptops.

4. Use the data you receive to adapt your lecture plan. If you see that nearly 100% of the students know a particular concept, you will not need to spend much, if any, time discussing that concept. If, however very few students answer a question correctly, you may need to spend more time explaining that particular concept in the lecture.
5. Plan to pause midway in the lecture to assess whether the concepts that were initially not understood are now being understood, perhaps with additional questions using your audience response system.
6. If possible, use another audience response system closure assessment at the end of the lecture.

Additional Suggestions

- If your students are tired of technology-based assessment, you might like to take a look at Quiz Time Start—Color Cards (SP 11), a technique that works particularly well with team-based learning group application activities.
- Often, both Quiz Time Start pauses couple well with Quiz Time Closure (CP 48).

Key References and Resources

Barkley, E. F., & Major, C. H. (2015). *Learning assessment techniques: A handbook for college faculty*. San Francisco, CA: Wiley.

Kahoot! (2013). Retrieved from kahoot.com

Poll Everywhere. (2007). Retrieved from www.polleverywhere.com

STARTING PAUSE 11

QUIZ TIME START—COLOR CARDS

This exercise helps students assess their level of knowledge about a topic prior to the lecture. It also increases student interest throughout the class period, as students listen to learn if their answers to the questions were correct. Multiple-choice questions and sets of four different-colored cards (one set for each student) are prepared by the instructor before the class. At the beginning of the class, the color cards are given to the students, and questions are projected onto an overhead screen. Each answer possibility is associated with one of the color cards. For each question, students raise a color card in front of them to indicate their answer choice. The instructor then can have immediate feedback on what the students already know. This type of quizzing has been largely replaced by the audience response system but is sometimes preferred as a less technical form of quizzing. It is particularly well adapted to the team-based-learning setting where teams can use the colored cards (or cards labeled A, B, C, D) rather than an Internet-based response system.

Settings for Use

- ☑ Small classroom lecture
- ☑ Clinical or laboratory presentation
- ☐ One-on-one session
- ☑ Conference presentation/in-service education
- ☐ Keynote/large-group presentation
- ☐ Course/unit
- ☑ Online learning module

Characteristics

- ☐ Affirming/positive
- ☑ Physical/movement
- ☑ Activates prior knowledge/experience
- ☑ Focuses and refocuses
- ☑ Creates community
- ☑ Generates curiosity
- ☑ Metacognitive
- ☑ Reviews
- ☐ Celebrates
- ☐ Commits to action
- ☑ Provides a bookend

Procedure

1. Prepare multiple choice questions (5 to 15, depending on how much time you would like to spend). Some of the questions can be about what students need to know prior to class to understand the upcoming lecture, and the other questions can be related to something that will be taught in the lecture.
2. Plan to set aside 5 to 10 minutes at the beginning of the class for this activity.
3. Explain the activity and give each student a set of 4 color cards.
4. Present the multiple-choice questions one at a time, and give the students 10 to 15 seconds to answer each question by raising the color card corresponding to their answer in front of them.
5. Usually, you will give the answers as you go through the lecture, thus keeping students interested in following the lecture and finding out if they got the right answers.

Additional Suggestions

- Different types of quizzing can be used for this activity. A team quiz where students form teams of two or three to take the quiz before the lecture can be a good alternative to the individual quiz. Various forms of Internet quizzing can also be used, such as a quiz prepared using the course learning management system such as Blackboard or Canvas. This could be done face-to-face at the beginning of class, if students all have access to laptops and wireless Internet; it certainly would be appropriate for an online or a hybrid course. In the case of the hybrid course, one might ask the students to take the quiz just prior to coming to class.
- When using colors, instructors need to be sensitive to the possibility of having students in their class who are color blind. One way to avoid accidentally discriminating against the student might be to label the cards as well as use the color. In this case, all the pink cards would be labeled *A*, all the yellow cards would be labeled *B*, and so on. Another way would be to use shapes along with the colors. All pink cards could be round, all blue cards could be squares. Students would then answer the question by raising the appropriate card, either a pink card, a pink card labeled *A*, or a pink circle.
- Teachers could ask students to rate their answers to the quiz questions, perhaps by putting a plus sign in front of those they are pretty sure they have the right answers to, a minus sign in front of those they

think they missed, and a question mark in front of questions they are unsure of.

- Teachers could also ask students to rank the questions according to how much they want to know the correct answer, with higher numbers indicating the strongest preference.
- You might consider using Quiz Time Closure (CP 48) as a way to end class that used this pause.

Key References and Resources

Barkley, E. F., & Major, C. H. (2015). *Learning assessment techniques: A handbook for college faculty*. San Francisco, CA: Wiley.

STARTING PAUSE 12

MODELING CLAY READY

This starting pause is especially helpful when the topic of the lecture is fraught with emotional issues. Students are asked to think about their feelings about the topic and illustrate them with designs made from colored modeling clay, which is provided by the instructor. After students have designed their illustration of their feelings, they share them with others sitting close to them and finally with the larger group.

Settings for Use

- ☑ Small classroom lecture
- ☑ Clinical or laboratory presentation
- ☑ One-on-one session
- ☑ Conference presentation/ in-service education
- ☐ Keynote/large-group presentation
- ☐ Course/unit
- ☐ Online learning module

Characteristics

- ☑ Affirming/positive
- ☐ Physical/movement
- ☑ Activates prior knowledge/ experience
- ☑ Focuses and refocuses
- ☑ Creates community
- ☐ Generates curiosity
- ☐ Metacognitive
- ☐ Reviews
- ☐ Celebrates
- ☐ Commits to action
- ☐ Provides a bookend

Procedure

1. Pass out modeling clay to each participant in the class, telling them that the clay is theirs to keep, and they can play with it throughout the learning session.
2. Announce the topic of the day and ask participants to think about their feelings about it.
3. Ask learners to illustrate their feelings with the modeling clay. Sometimes it is helpful to provide an example, but it is usually not necessary.
4. After a few minutes have passed and most seem to have finished their creation, ask them to show it to two or three people sitting near them, then ask several class members to show their creations to the larger group.
5. Continue with a discussion of the importance of feelings when dealing with this particular topic and discuss (and perhaps adjust) the learning objectives.

Additional Suggestions

- Any number of creative manipulatives can be used for this activity. Modeling clay packages can be purchased at a local store or on the Internet. Pipe cleaners are often a good tool to use to show feelings or attitudes. Graph paper can be used to ask respondents to show how their ideas have had ups and downs.
- Creative manipulatives are especially helpful when the instructor wants the learners to identify issues that might get in the way of learning. Wise teachers understand that feelings can interfere with learning. High levels of anxiety or tension are known to reduce the ability to learn. Learning is heightened when instructors pause for learners to evaluate their feelings and concerns about issues at the beginning of the session.

Online Adaptation

To use this pause with online students, you might want to adapt it to use something that is readily available, such as paper and pencil. Students might not appreciate suggesting they go buy some modeling clay if they don't happen to have some around the house, but you might ask students to make some at home (give them a recipe) and then form it into something to illustrate their response to the question. Students can submit a picture of their creation, and discussion can take place in the discussion area or the chat room.

STARTING PAUSE 13

GRAFFITI BOARD

This is an extremely short and easy way to pause at the beginning of the learning session and ask for concepts that come to mind regarding a new topic. Students are allowed to jot down extremely short (one- to three-word phrases) ideas that they associate with the topic.

Settings for Use

- ☑ Small classroom lecture
- ☑ Clinical or laboratory presentation
- ☐ One-on-one session
- ☑ Conference presentation/ in-service education
- ☐ Keynote/large-group presentation
- ☐ Course/unit
- ☐ Online learning module

Characteristics

- ☑ Affirming/positive
- ☑ Physical/movement
- ☑ Activates prior knowledge/ experience
- ☑ Focuses and refocuses
- ☑ Creates community
- ☐ Generates curiosity
- ☐ Metacognitive
- ☐ Reviews
- ☐ Celebrates
- ☐ Commits to action
- ☑ Provides a bookend

Procedure

1. Provide a whiteboard or a large easel pad and markers for students to write their responses graffiti style.
2. Explain the topic of the day.
3. Ask students to think of an extremely short, graffiti-style phrase that illustrates their thoughts about the topic.
4. Encourage them to form small groups and brainstorm together.
5. Invite them to write their graffiti on the board or easel pad.
6. Depending on the size of the class, ask groups to explain their graffiti to the rest.

Additional Suggestions

- This activity can be particularly helpful in identifying prior experiences with topics that might block students' openness for new learning.
- Students tend to be quite creative with this beginning pause and often use graffiti-like lettering.

- Leaving the graffiti up during the lecture provides nice reminders through the class session of the students' concepts introduced at the beginning of the class, and the instructor can refer to these concepts as the class proceeds. The visual reminders can be powerful additions to what may be discussed.

Key References and Resources

Bennett, B., & Rolheiser, C. (2001). *Beyond Monet: The artful science of instructional intelligence*. Toronto, Ontario, Canada: Bookstation.

Egawa, K. (2004). *Sharing from graffiti boards*. Retrieved from www.readwritethink.org/files/resources/lesson_images/lesson305/graffiti-sharing.pdf

Halsey, V. (2011). *Brilliance by design: Creating learning experiences that connect, inspire, and engage*. San Fransisco, CA: Berrett-Koehler.

Workshop.on.ca. (2006). *Grafitti*. Retrieved from www.eworkshop.on.ca/edu/pdf/Mod36_coop_graffiti.pdf

STARTING PAUSE 14

BAG OF GOODIES

This pause focuses learners by asking them to make connections among common objects and the topic for the session. Participants choose an object from a brown paper bag or from the table in the front of the room and then describe their sense of what this object has to do with the topic.

Settings for Use

- ☑ Small classroom lecture
- ☑ Clinical or laboratory presentation
- ☐ One-on-one session
- ☑ Conference presentation/ in-service education
- ☐ Keynote/large-group presentation
- ☐ Course/unit
- ☑ Online learning module

Characteristics

- ☑ Affirming/positive
- ☑ Physical/movement
- ☑ Activates prior knowledge/ experience
- ☑ Focuses and refocuses
- ☑ Creates community
- ☑ Generates curiosity
- ☐ Metacognitive
- ☐ Reviews
- ☐ Celebrates
- ☐ Commits to action
- ☐ Provides a bookend

Procedure

1. Gather three to six common household objects and place them in a bag or on a table in plain sight.
2. Begin the session by introducing the session's topic and telling students they will have an opportunity to see a number of common objects, each of which has a relationship to the topic.
3. Assign a number to each student and draw numbers to select who will come to the front of the room.
4. Allow those individuals to select two helpers to join them to take something out of the bag and say how that item relates to the topic.
5. Continue until the bag is empty or all the items have been described.
6. Share your learning objectives with the group and adjust the session as needed.

Additional Suggestions

- Alternatively, place all the objects on a table in plain sight. Select individuals to pick up any object from the table and suggest a connection between that object and the class topic. Continue until all the objects have been addressed.
- How participants associate a particular item with a topic can be extremely revealing. In an example of this pause in Chapter 3 (p. 42), the topic was breastfeeding, and one of the items in the bag was a golf ball. The father-to-be associated the golf ball and breastfeeding with the fact that he would never be able to play golf again. The instructor intended to use the golf ball to show the size of a newborn's stomach and how much milk it could typically hold. You can imagine that the lesson was not forgotten—neither what the new parents were in for nor that a newborn may not need to eat very much to feel full.

Online Adaptation

A brief starting pause in the online course might be a single matching quiz, in which participants match images of the common objects with associated concepts.

STARTING PAUSE 15

ONE, TWO, BUCKLE MY SHOE

This exercise enables the instructor to get a quick sense of what students think they know about a subject and what they would like to learn about it. At the beginning of class, students are given a note card with the following questions:

1. What is one thing you know about the topic?
2. What are two things you would like to learn about the topic?

The instructor then collects the cards and scans them quickly to make adjustments in the upcoming lecture if necessary.

Settings for Use

- ☑ Small classroom lecture
- ☑ Clinical or laboratory presentation
- ☑ One-on-one session
- ☑ Conference presentation/in-service education
- ☐ Keynote/large-group presentation
- ☐ Course/unit
- ☑ Online learning module

Characteristics

- ☐ Affirming/positive
- ☐ Physical/movement
- ☑ Activates prior knowledge/experience
- ☑ Focuses and refocuses
- ☑ Creates community
- ☑ Generates curiosity
- ☐ Metacognitive
- ☐ Reviews
- ☐ Celebrates
- ☐ Commits to action
- ☐ Provides a bookend

Procedure

1. Cut note cards into the shape of a shoe. At the top write "One, Two, Buckle My Shoe." Underneath, write the topic for the class session. Write the two questions on the card.
   a. What is one thing you know about the topic?
   b. What are two things you would like to learn about the topic?
2. As students enter the classroom, give them the cards with instructions on how to complete them.
3. Have students share with each other in small groups. You might ask how many found a match to anything they wrote.
4. Collect the completed cards and scan them quickly.

5. Discuss planned objectives and possible revisions, based on the input received.
6. Adjust the planned presentation to avoid lecturing on already known material and to be sure to address the issues students have requested.

Additional Suggestions

- The beauty of this exercise is that it requires students to contemplate before lecture their own readiness for the topic, which in itself can enhance their interest and awareness of their need to know the content.
- Sometimes instructors are concerned that an activity may seem too childish for a sophisticated audience. My experience has been that all adults, no matter how learned or experienced, enjoy some playfulness in their lives. The shoe cutout and the catchy title seem to work for most groups. But the activity could be adapted to simply request responses to the two questions without the shoe analogy or the preparation of the cards.
- The two suggested questions could be changed to other questions such as Why is this a difficult topic? or How important do you perceive this topic to be? or How does today's topic relate to what we studied last week?

Online Adaptation

Students complete a form with the questions on it and submit it at the beginning of the module. The instructor can decide whether to use the shoe design.

Key References and Resources

Angelo, T. A., & Cross, K. P. (1993). *Classroom assessment techniques: A handbook for college teachers* (2nd ed.). San Francisco, CA: Jossey-Bass.

Barkley, E. F., & Major, C. H. (2015). *Learning assessment techniques: A handbook for college faculty*. San Francisco, CA: Wiley.

STARTING PAUSE 16

DUMP BUCKET

This opener draws student attention to the importance of leaving behind all their concerns and distractions before entering class. As they enter the classroom, students are given a three-inch-by-five-inch card to write down what they are thinking about and what they want to forget about while they are in class. Then they are asked to drop their cards into a bucket or box by the door before class starts.

Settings for Use

- ☑ Small classroom lecture
- ☑ Clinical or laboratory presentation
- ☐ One-on-one session
- ☑ Conference presentation/ in-service education
- ☐ Keynote/large-group presentation
- ☐ Course/unit
- ☑ Online learning module

Characteristics

- ☐ Affirming/positive
- ☑ Physical/movement
- ☐ Activates prior knowledge/ experience
- ☑ Focuses and refocuses
- ☑ Creates community
- ☐ Generates curiosity
- ☐ Metacognitive
- ☐ Reviews
- ☐ Celebrates
- ☐ Commits to action
- ☐ Provides a bookend

Procedure

1. Hand students a three-inch-by-five-inch card as they enter class.
2. Place a bucket by the door students use to enter the room. I use a child's bright yellow sand pail for this activity, but a shoebox or any container would work fine.
3. Write the following instructions on the board or project them on a screen at the front of the room.

   Before you sit down, please write on the card whatever is likely to keep your mind from fully focusing on the topic of class today, for example,

   - Worries/concerns
   - Tasks you are facing
   - Other classes you are thinking about
   - Family pressures/responsibilities

4. Ask students to take their cards and throw them into the bucket next to the door.
5. Now they can take their seats where they will find another three-inch-by-five-inch card. Ask them to write down one thing they would like to learn from class this session and share it with a person sitting next to them.

Additional Suggestions

- It might be easier to pass the bucket around the room for students to drop their cards in than have them leave their seats to go to the door where the bucket is located.
- A closure idea that might be particularly useful for this starting pause could be the following: The instructor might ask students to look at the cards they have kept at their desk that say what they wanted to learn. Ask them to turn again to the same neighbor they spoke with at the beginning of class and tell each other how they view the topic now after the class session and if they met their objective.
- A humorous addition: If they want to, students can look for their card in the bucket on the way out in case they forgot what they needed to be worried about.

Online Adaptation

This starting pause can work nicely for the online module. The bucket (a forum) can be created at the beginning of the module, and online students can write down what they want to set aside so they can fully focus on learning. The concept of a dump bucket reminds students and instructors that learning is best when our attention is totally focused on the topic at hand and that their personal stuff can wait.

STARTING PAUSE 17

WHAT'S IN THE BOX?

This activity allows teachers to use curiosity and anticipation to enhance learning in their learning environments. This pause starts with a large box or bag sitting in a prominent place at the front of the classroom. The instructor has placed an item in the box or bag that will be used to introduce the topic of the day. Students try to guess what the object is.

Settings for Use

- ☑ Small classroom lecture
- ☑ Clinical or laboratory presentation
- ☐ One-on-one session
- ☑ Conference presentation/in-service education
- ☐ Keynote/large-group presentation
- ☐ Course/unit
- ☑ Online learning module

Characteristics

- ☑ Affirming/positive
- ☑ Physical/movement
- ☐ Activates prior knowledge/experience
- ☑ Focuses and refocuses
- ☑ Creates community
- ☑ Generates curiosity
- ☐ Metacognitive
- ☐ Reviews
- ☐ Celebrates
- ☐ Commits to action
- ☑ Provides a bookend

Procedure

1. Prominently place a box or bag at the front of the classroom.
2. Project on an overhead screen or write on the board, "What's in the box [bag]?"
3. Tell students you have placed an item in the box or bag that will help introduce an important concept or the topic for the session.
4. Allow students to try to guess what is in the bag or box. Plan to give some clues if necessary.
5. Select a student to come and remove the object. Cheer and applaud if the object is what the students guessed it would be.
6. Ask students why you selected this object to introduce the day's topic.
7. Expand on their answers to introduce your topic.
8. Include your objectives for the session and allow students to give input on the objectives.
9. Leave the object clearly displayed during the class session.

Additional Suggestions

- Ask students to write down on a card or sticky note why they think you chose this object to introduce your topic and bring the card to the front of the room.
- Ask students to write their responses on a Twitter feed or a polling website such as Poll Everywhere or Kahoot!
- A closure idea that might be particularly useful for this starting pause could be the following: The instructor might tell students to keep their cards and ask them to suggest a different object to introduce the topic and add why they chose that object. Cards would be turned in with names and the instructor might promise to announce the winning ideas at the beginning of the next class.

Online Adaptation

The online module could start with a mystery object. Students guess what the object is by providing them with a series of clues until the object is revealed. This could be done interactively with students submitting guesses or simply encouraging them to be thinking about their guess.

Another idea is a 20-questions model, where students could ask questions such as, Is it an animal, mineral, vegetable? and so on at the beginning of the module. Instruction would proceed with the introduction and explanation of objectives.

STARTING PAUSE 18

TWITTER START

This exercise has the particular advantage of allowing students to share their ideas in a public setting, which can add to students' seriousness about their task. The instructor writes the opening question on the board with the hashtag (#) for the lesson that will group their responses together. Students send their responses using Twitter, a popular form of social media, and view all the other answers projected on an overhead screen. Instructors can use the hashtag to instantly review all the student responses and immediately get a sense of where to start the class and what to include or exclude.

Settings for Use

- ☑ Small classroom lecture
- ☑ Clinical or laboratory presentation
- ☐ One-on-one session
- ☑ Conference presentation/in-service education
- ☑ Keynote/large-group presentation
- ☑ Course/unit
- ☑ Online learning module

Characteristics

- ☐ Affirming/positive
- ☐ Physical/movement
- ☑ Activates prior knowledge/experience
- ☑ Focuses and refocuses
- ☑ Creates community
- ☐ Generates curiosity
- ☐ Metacognitive
- ☐ Reviews
- ☐ Celebrates
- ☐ Commits to action
- ☐ Provides a bookend

Procedure

1. Set up your own Twitter account and determine the hashtag for the intended question.
2. Set up the projector to project the responses, if you wish to use this option.
3. Write the question on the board with the Twitter hashtag or project it on the screen.
4. Ask students to respond to the question, using their Twitter accounts (see Additional Suggestions).
5. As the responses show up on screen, you can note the trends.
6. After most of the responses are received, ask for additional responses or clarifying information from the group.
7. Adapt the objectives for the class session.

Additional Suggestions

- If you plan to use this pause, you might alert students ahead of time and invite them to create Twitter accounts. It is likely that many already have one, but possible that several may not. If, at the time you are ready to do the activity, some students still do not have their own Twitter account, encourage them to partner up with someone in the class who does have an account.
- Other forms of social media can be used for this beginning pause.
- Projection on the screen is not necessary for this pause. The instructor can simply report to the group what the answers are as they appear.
- The question used for this activity could be a about content from an earlier class period or the required reading for the day.

Online Adaptation

The online module can begin with requesting students to send their Twitter response to the question the instructor has posted. Although the responses will not be synchronous, this can still provide helpful information to the online instructor that can lead to variations in the assignments and materials posted on the module.

Key References and Resources

Angelo, T. A., & Cross, K. P. (1993). *Classroom assessment techniques: A handbook for college teachers* (2nd ed.). San Francisco, CA: Jossey-Bass.

Miller, S. (2017). *50 ways to use Twitter in the classroom*. Retrieved from www.teachhub.com/50-ways-use-twitter-classroom

STARTING PAUSE 19

PAIR STUMP

This starting technique quickly focuses and energizes students. Individuals are instructed to develop an exam question, a puzzle or word puzzle (wuzzle), or begin a concept map or partially filled-in diagram. After they have had a few minutes to create their stumper, they are asked to pair up with someone and see if their partner can solve the puzzle; correctly answer the question; or complete the incomplete statement, concept map, or diagram. Have students vote on the top stumpers.

Settings for Use

- ☑ Small classroom lecture
- ☑ Clinical or laboratory presentation
- ☐ One-on-one session
- ☐ Conference presentation/in-service education
- ☐ Keynote/large-group presentation
- ☐ Course/unit
- ☐ Online learning module

Characteristics

- ☑ Affirming/positive
- ☑ Physical/movement
- ☑ Activates prior knowledge/experience
- ☑ Focuses and refocuses
- ☑ Creates community
- ☑ Generates curiosity
- ☐ Metacognitive
- ☐ Reviews
- ☐ Celebrates
- ☐ Commits to action
- ☐ Provides a bookend

Procedure

1. Explain to the students that their task is to develop an exam question, incomplete diagram, or puzzle that relates to the day's content. Tell them there will be a vote to determine the most creative, helpful, or clever item.
2. Allow enough time. Usually three or four minutes will be enough, but do your best to help them quickly accomplish their task, perhaps by using a timer on an overhead screen.
3. Ask students to pair up with someone from another part of the classroom. You can pair them up in some kind of playful way to ensure their roommate isn't sitting beside them. For example, place matching numbers under each desk and ask students to find their match. You could ask them to pair with someone wearing the same color clothes. If you have name tags for the participants, you could put an animal sticker, colored

dot, or a number on their name tag and ask them to go around the room looking for students whose name tags have a matching sticker or number.

4. Have students exchange their stumper with each other and see how quickly they can complete the task. Give them a little time to help their partner accomplish the task if necessary. Using a timer countdown on the overhead screen will create a sense of urgency and help them focus without wasting too much time.
5. At the end of the class session, allow a few of the individuals to submit their partner's stumper for a class vote. They need to show the item, telling the class why it was particularly good. Allow the class to vote on the winner. If possible, provide some kind of prize to the winning duo.

Additional Suggestions

- This pause has the potential to take a great deal of time; it is important to emphasize that these stumpers need to be short. A great alternative to taking time at the beginning of class to develop the stumper is to introduce the concept in the previous class and ask students to come prepared to stump a partner. In this case, students may appreciate the references in Key References and Resources at the end of this pause to develop more sophisticated stumpers.
- This generally works best if participants' stumpers require paper and a pencil, which are easy to take across the room. A laptop or tablet, however, might also work.
- The Puzzle Games Daily website offers 100 puzzles and games, and students might find one here ready to go, or they can design their own, using one of the provided templates. The Quiz website provides free templates on which to develop quizzes and activities. Qzzr is a free website where you can create your own quizzes. Alternatively, you may find something already created that fits your course.

Key References and Resources

Cuseo, J. B. (2002). *Igniting student involvement, peer interaction, and teamwork: A taxonomy of specific cooperative learning structures and collaborative learning strategies*. Stillwater, OK: New Forums Press.

Puzzle games daily. (n.d.). Retrieved from free.puzzlegamesdaily.com/index.jhtml?partner=^BK8^xdm002&k_clickid=_kenshoo_clickid_&gclid=CK-N78rWxNECFd6IswodJwg-GbA

Quiz. (n.d.). Retrieved from www.quiz.com/en

Qzzr. (n.d.). Retrieved from www.qzzr.com

WordSearch.com. (n.d.). Retrieved from thewordsearch.com/cat/good-to-know

STARTING PAUSE 20

YOUTUBE STORY START

Starting the class with a short video clip or a story is often a powerful way to begin learning. YouTube can be a very helpful resource for faculty members looking for a way to capture student attention and focus them on the topic for the class session. If you are drawing a blank on what to do to start learning in a positive and upbeat way, you will probably not have to look too far with YouTube.

Settings for Use

- ☑ Small classroom lecture
- ☑ Clinical or laboratory presentation
- ☐ One-on-one session
- ☑ Conference presentation/in-service education
- ☑ Keynote/large-group presentation
- ☑ Course/unit
- ☑ Online learning module

Characteristics

- ☐ Affirming/positive
- ☐ Physical/movement
- ☐ Activates prior knowledge/experience
- ☑ Focuses and refocuses
- ☐ Creates community
- ☑ Generates curiosity
- ☐ Metacognitive
- ☐ Reviews
- ☐ Celebrates
- ☐ Commits to action
- ☑ Provides a bookend

Procedure

1. Craft your introductory story or find your video clip. Usually something that relates to your topic will emerge when you search YouTube or 100 Best Video Sites for Educators (see Key References and Resources at the end of this pause).
2. Determine whether you want to introduce the clip. If so, you can tell students if there is something you especially want them to watch for or if there is a particular question they need to address after viewing the video. However, just starting the video without any introduction quickly catches attention—students will settle down and stop talking very quickly if a video is playing on the overhead screen.
3. After showing the video, discuss it with the students.
4. Tie the introductory clip in to the class session by sharing the objectives and asking for help in ranking or adjusting the objectives.

Additional Suggestions

- Telling a story can be just as effective as showing a film clip. Well-told stories engage students and help them focus on the importance of the class topic.
- A closure idea that might be particularly useful for this starting pause could be the following: A wonderful way to close a class that started with a story or video clip is to return to the story at the end and finish the story, thus providing a bookend to the class.

Online Adaptation

It is extremely easy to embed video clips into course learning management systems. Most have a YouTube icon at the top of each module, which allows the instructors to simply click the icon, search for the clip, and insert it with a keyboard click. It is very important to include a response to an activity involving video or stories in the online course. To ensure that the busy online student doesn't skip over the assignment, place some kind of response activity with the video, such as asking for a reaction and response or using a fill-in-the blank form on the content.

Key References and Resources

Barkley, E. F., & Major, C. H. (2015). *Learning assessment techniques: A handbook for college faculty.* San Francisco, CA: Wiley.

Dunn, J. (2012). *The 100 best video sites for educators.* Retrieved from www.edudemic.com/best-video-sites-for-teachers

YouTube. (2017). Retrieved from www.youtube.com

STARTING PAUSE 21

FILL IN THE BLANKS

This is a quick and easy way to pause at the beginning of the learning session. Learners are asked to simply fill in the blanks in a prepared sentence or short paragraph. A typical fill-in opening pause might include sentences like, Today's topic is ______________, Here is one thing I know about this topic____________________, and Here is one thing I hope I leave with today ______________.

Settings for Use

- ☑ Small classroom lecture
- ☑ Clinical or laboratory presentation
- ☐ One-on-one session
- ☑ Conference presentation/ in-service education
- ☑ Keynote/large-group presentation
- ☑ Course/unit
- ☑ Online learning module

Characteristics

- ☑ Affirming/positive
- ☐ Physical/movement
- ☐ Activates prior knowledge/ experience
- ☑ Focuses and refocuses
- ☑ Creates community
- ☑ Generates curiosity
- ☐ Metacognitive
- ☐ Reviews
- ☐ Celebrates
- ☐ Commits to action
- ☐ Provides a bookend

Procedure

1. Decide if you want this activity to be a free-standing opening activity or if you want to use it as the first part of an outline for the lecture. If you will be using fill-in-the-blanks for more than just the opening pause, you may want to simply have the opening pause activity at the top of the day's outline. Otherwise, you can prepare a card or half a sheet of paper to hand out to students with the sentences and blanks already written on it.
2. Decide what best fits the day's topic, such as, What would you most like to learn about this topic? or What have you found most puzzling in the past about this topic? or Why is this an important topic for people interested in linguistics, or physics, or medicine? or Why do people find this topic difficult? or What experiences have blocked you from learning about this topic in the past?

3. Prepare three-inch-by-five-inch cards or half sheets of paper containing the questions and the blanks to be filled in.
4. Hand out the materials and ask the students to fill in the blanks telling them there are no right or wrong answers to most of the questions.
5. Ask students to share their cards with two or three people sitting near them.
6. Have a short large-group discussion about learners' individual answers. It might be interesting to ask how many found similarities in their answers they shared with others.
7. Check your sense of the groups' responses so that you can address them in the session.
8. Collect responses or instruct the group about what to do with their cards or half sheets.

Additional Suggestions

- Many faculty members like to project the fill-in statements on an overhead screen and ask students to jot down their responses on a piece of scratch paper or on their laptops. In this case, the faculty member will not be able to collect individual sheets of paper, so collating would not be possible.
- This activity lends itself very well to an audience response system with the fill-in option for students to type in their responses. Programs such as Poll Everywhere or Kahoot! project each response and even allow space to quickly summarize the group's responses.
- This opening pause works well with an outline with occasional blanks to be filled in from the session.

Online Adaptation

The online module can begin with the blanks to be filled in and submitted or shared in a pop-up interactive format, a chat or discussion assignment, or an e-mail.

Key References and Resources

Angelo, T. A., & Cross, K. P. (1993). *Classroom assessment techniques: A handbook for college teachers* (2nd ed.). San Francisco, CA: Jossey-Bass.

Barkley, E. F., & Major, C. H. (2015). *Learning assessment techniques: A handbook for college faculty*. San Francisco, CA: Wiley.

STARTING PAUSE 22

WUZZLE START

Using a word puzzle (wuzzle) can be an excellent way to start a class session. It is one of the quickest ways to focus students at the beginning of a class, so it is particularly useful when you have less time than you would like for the class session. The puzzle to be solved is posted as students enter the classroom. It might be a word with letters missing or any number of word puzzles that relate to the topic of the day. Students are encouraged to work with those sitting near them to see how quickly they can find the hidden word or solve the wuzzle. An added bonus is earned when students can explain how the wuzzle relates to the class topic.

Settings for Use

- ☑ Small classroom lecture
- ☑ Clinical or laboratory presentation
- ☐ One-on-one session
- ☑ Conference presentation/in-service education
- ☑ Keynote/large-group presentation
- ☑ Course/unit
- ☑ Online learning module

Characteristics

- ☑ Affirming/positive
- ☐ Physical/movement
- ☑ Activates prior knowledge/experience
- ☑ Focuses and refocuses
- ☑ Creates community
- ☑ Generates curiosity
- ☐ Metacognitive
- ☐ Reviews
- ☐ Celebrates
- ☐ Commits to action
- ☑ Provides a bookend

Procedure

1. Determine what key concepts or words will be highlighted during the class session.
2. Decide what kind of puzzle you want to use to get students to focus.
3. Prepare your wuzzle. You might use one of the free websites in Key References and Resources at the end of this pause to help you put your key words into a word search or a crossword puzzle. You might simply have them guess the letters in one word (similar to the TV game *Wheel of Fortune* or the old-fashioned game of Hangman), or you might use an application to develop another type of word puzzle.
4. Project the puzzle on the overhead screen along with instructions to go to a particular website, or provide printed puzzles at each student's seat.

5. Encourage students to work with those sitting nearby to see how quickly they can complete the puzzle.
6. Acknowledge solving a puzzle with applause or by passing out rewards to the group.
7. During the group discussion, ask students why the word or words were chosen and why are they important to the day's topic.
8. Provide the session objectives and ask if they want to suggest adaptations.

Additional Suggestions

- If the puzzle is a Hangman-style game, let the students guess letters one by one until they solve the puzzle.
- The time it takes to solve the puzzle will vary according to the complexity of the challenge. The pause will probably be short if it involves a puzzle based on *Wheel of Fortune*, whereas a crossword or word search might take longer.

Online Adaptation

Paste your selected puzzle into the course module, or direct students to the link that takes them to the activity. To ensure this is truly a beginning pause, you can set up the module so that students cannot start another activity until the beginning activity is completed.

Key References and Resources

Puzzle games daily. (n.d.). Retrieved from free.puzzlegamesdaily.com/index.jhtml?partner=^BK8^xdm002&k_clickid=_kenshoo_clickid_&gclid=CK-N78rWxNECFd6IswodJwg-GbA

Quia. (2017). Retrieved from www.quia.com

Qzzr. (n.d.). Retrieved from www.qzzr.com

WordSearch.com. (n.d.). Retrieved from thewordsearch.com/cat/good-to-know

FIND A MATCH

This pause allows students to focus on what they know about a subject before the class begins. It encourages them to activate their prior knowledge and access the experiences they have had with a topic before learning more about it in the lecture. It also provides them with the opportunity to move about the room as they talk to their classmates to see if anyone matches their response.

Settings for Use

- ☑ Small classroom lecture
- ☑ Clinical or laboratory presentation
- ☐ One-on-one session
- ☑ Conference presentation/in-service education
- ☐ Keynote/large-group presentation
- ☑ Course/unit
- ☑ Online learning module

Characteristics

- ☑ Affirming/positive
- ☑ Physical/movement
- ☑ Activates prior knowledge/experience
- ☑ Focuses and refocuses
- ☑ Creates community
- ☐ Generates curiosity
- ☐ Metacognitive
- ☐ Reviews
- ☐ Celebrates
- ☐ Commits to action
- ☑ Provides a bookend

Procedure

1. Ask students to take out a sheet of paper and write the topic on the top of the sheet. Alternatively, hand out a three-inch-by-five-inch card or sheet of paper with the topic printed at the top.
2. Give the students your question to be answered before the class begins.
3. You could suggest that they write down one thing they know for sure about this topic or the first thing they think about when they hear this topic mentioned.
4. Tell the students to start brainstorming to see what they can come up with as they try to recall what they know about the topic; if more than one thing comes to mind, tell them to use the first thing that came to mind.
5. Instruct them to see how quickly they can find someone with the same thing written on their card.

6. Offer a prize to the first couple to find a match and raise their hands if you wish. Generally, the prize should be something that you eventually give to everyone, such as low-cost trinkets or candies, in addition to the first couple to put their hands in the air.
7. Allow the activity to continue while you look for the largest group of individuals who match. It is possible that several students will come up with the same thing.
8. Ask the students to tell the whole group what they have written, and then compare and contrast the first things that came to their minds.

Additional Suggestions

- Instructors can decide to do various things at this point in the introductory activity. They might ask students to keep their cards to see if what they have written comes up in the lecture. They might ask students to turn their cards in so the instructor can refer to them as the lecture proceeds.
- Any number of different questions could be addressed in this activity, such as,
  - What would you like to learn about this topic?
  - Why is this an important topic for this course?
  - What makes this a difficult topic for some learners?
- A closure idea that might be particularly useful for this starting pause could be the following: The instructor might ask students to keep their cards or sheets and ask them to indicate additional things they have they learned about the topic or perhaps add an application idea for each thing.

Online Adaptation

At the beginning of the online module, you might ask students to list one thing they know about the topic of the module.

At the completion of the online module, students might return to their original item and submit it again, this time adding all the additional facts addressed during the module they felt were important.

Key References and Resources

Barkley, E. F., & Major, C. H. (2015). *Learning assessment techniques: A handbook for college faculty*. San Francisco, CA: Wiley.

APPENDIX B

MIDPAUSES

MIDPAUSE 24

SHORT WRITE

This quick way to pause during the lecture allows learners to respond to a question by writing down their response. The instructor simply pauses the lecture and asks students to respond to a question by writing their response on a piece of paper or on their electronic devices. If the instructor has provided a written handout, there is usually a boxed area on the handout where the learner can write the response to the question. The instructor may ask students to share their responses in some form of discussion following their short write.

Settings for Use

- ☑ Small classroom lecture
- ☑ Clinical or laboratory presentation
- ☑ One-on-one session
- ☑ Conference presentation/ in-service education
- ☑ Keynote/large-group presentation
- ☑ Course/unit
- ☐ Online learning module

Characteristics

- ☐ Affirming/positive
- ☐ Physical/movement
- ☐ Activates prior knowledge/ experience
- ☑ Focuses/refocuses
- ☐ Creates community
- ☐ Generates curiosity
- ☑ Metacognitive
- ☐ Reviews
- ☐ Celebrates
- ☐ Commits to action
- ☐ Provides a bookend

Procedure

1. This activity can be easily used any time instructors have an important concept or question they want every student to engage with.
2. Most instructors find it helpful to plan for questions ahead of time by posting possible questions in the right-hand margin of their lecture notes, ready to be used whenever it appears that students need a break from hearing the instructor talk.
3. It is a good idea to not overuse this technique—probably no more than one an hour. Short Write can easily mix with the Pause Procedure Question (MP 26) or Think-Pair-Share (MP 25) as well as with other midpause techniques.

4. When you sense that students are getting restless and a pause is needed, inform them that you are going to ask a question and that you would like them to take out their pens or pencils and think of a response and then write it in the box on the handout or on a half sheet of paper that you have prepared or on a piece of scratch paper.
5. Ask the question you have planned ahead of time.
6. Be sure to allow adequate time for students to respond.
7. At this point, you will want to use a variety of approaches. Sometimes you might ask for several students to share what they have written with the large group. Other times you might ask students to share with those sitting nearby, followed by several sharing with the large group. Occasionally you might ask someone to tell the group what someone else shared.
8. A final step is to ask students to look at the answers they wrote and analyze the process they took to reach their conclusion and how they might have followed a different approach.

Additional Suggestions

- This technique is one of three essential midpauses. The other two are Think-Pair-Share (MP 25) and Pause Procedure Question (MP 26). Short Write (MP 24) has the advantage over Think-Pair-Share (MP 25) of being a quiet, active learning break. The room does not become chaotic with everyone talking animatedly. Although energy is not generated in so obvious a manner as it might be with Think-Pair-Share (MP 25) some faculty find this method preferable because it feels more manageable, especially with large groups. Many faculty members have found these simple midlectures pause techniques—Pause Procedure Question (MP 26), Short Write (MP 24), and Think-Pair-Share (MP 25)—to be very effective active learning strategies to reenergize the class, helping students to refocus on the lecture and listen more carefully, take better notes, and improve retention.

Key References and Resources

Angelo, T. A., & Cross, K. P. (1993). *Classroom assessment techniques: A handbook for college teachers* (2nd ed.). San Francisco, CA: Jossey-Bass.

Barkley, E. F., & Major, C. H. (2015). *Learning assessment techniques: A handbook for college faculty*. San Francisco, CA: Wiley.

Briggs, S. (2014). *20 simple assessment strategies you can use every day*. Retrieved from www.teachthought.com/pedagogy/assessment/20-simple-assessment-strategies-can-use-every-day/#

Millis, B. J. (2010). *Cooperative learning in higher education: Across the disciplines, across the academy*. Sterling, VA: Stylus.

University of Nebraska–Lincoln Office of Graduate Studies. (2017). *Quick tips for teaching*. Retrieved from www.unl.edu/gradstudies/current/teaching/tips

Ward, T. (2017). *On course workshop: Six ways to use quick writes to promote learning forum*. Retrieved from oncourseworkshop.com/life-long-learning/six-ways-use-quick-writes-promote-learning

MIDPAUSE 25

THINK-PAIR-SHARE

One of the most popular ways to pause the lecture, *Think-Pair-Share* is known by many names and is used with many variations. It is sometimes called a Buzz Group. It has also been called Pair Share, Timed Pair Share, Triad Team, Turn and Talk, or a Turn to Your Neighbor or Partner. So many have used it in their teaching and so many have described it in the literature that it is hard to appropriately credit it. According to Hassard (1996), Spencer Kagan may have originated the term. Essentially, we pause the lecture and ask the learners to think about a particular question or issue and then turn to the person sitting next to them and discuss it. I have found it helpful to use the phrase "in groups of two or three." By saying this, we let everyone know that someone sitting on the end of a row could be left out if a dyad forms next to the individual on the end, or if the person on either side turns in the opposite direction to find someone to talk to.

Settings for Use

- ☑ Small classroom lecture
- ☑ Clinical or laboratory presentation
- ☐ One-on-one session
- ☑ Conference presentation/in-service education
- ☑ Keynote/large group presentation
- ☑ Course/unit
- ☐ Online learning module

Characteristics

- ☐ Affirming/positive
- ☐ Physical/movement
- ☐ Activates prior knowledge/experience
- ☑ Focuses/refocuses
- ☑ Creates community
- ☐ Generates curiosity
- ☐ Metacognitive
- ☐ Reviews
- ☐ Celebrates
- ☐ Commits to action
- ☐ Provides a bookend

Procedure

1. Post possible questions in the right-hand margin of your lecture notes so they are ready to be used at approximately 15 to 20 minute intervals or whenever it appears that students need a break from hearing the instructor talk.

2. It is a good idea not to overuse this technique, probably no more than one an hour. Think-Pair-Share questions can easily mix with Pause Procedure Question (MP 26) or Short Write (MP 24).
3. When you sense that students are getting restless and a pause is needed, inform them that you are going to ask a question or pose a dilemma and that they should think about for a few moments. Then ask them to turn to their neighbor in groups of two and (no more than) three and come up with an answer to the question or discuss the dilemma for a prescribed amount of time—usually no more than two or three minutes.
4. Ask the question that was planned ahead of time, ask for silence for thinking time, and then indicate when it is time to turn to the neighbor.
5. When it appears that enough time has elapsed for discussion, silence them. Often, we can do this by simply saying into the microphone that conversation should finish soon. If the group is large, we may want to plan a stop talking signal before beginning the activity. This could involve holding your hands up in the air, ringing a bell, or giving another signal.
6. Getting some feedback from the large group is often a helpful way to move forward from this point.

Additional Suggestions

- The Think-Pair-Share activity is highly energizing and can be counted on to awaken even the least engaged members of our classroom. Many of us use this method quite successfully to help students realize that concepts that can seem quite remote and complicated when explained to them by the instructor are not so dense when the students explain to their seatmates something about the concept. Teaching each other helps them understand so much better. It not only improves their understanding but also helps reduce the cognitive overload of keeping so much information, and it allows them to free up some brain space so they are ready for new information. Many faculty members have found these simple midpause techniques—Pause Procedure Question (MP 26), Short Write (MP 24), and Think-Pair-Share (MP 25)—to be very effective active learning strategies to reenergize the class, helping students to refocus on the lecture and listen more carefully with improved retention.

- It is important to keep the groups small. Only allow a triad if you have an uneven number of participants; this allows time for individuals to talk, especially within a limited time frame.

Key References and Resources

Barkley, E. F., & Major, C. H. (2015). *Learning assessment techniques: A handbook for college faculty*. San Francisco, CA: Wiley.

Barkley, E. F., Major, C. H., & Cross, P. K. (2014). *Collaborative learning techniques: A handbook for college faculty*. San Francisco, CA: Jossey-Bass.

Brookfield, S. D., & Preskill, S. (2005). *Discussion as a way of teaching: Tools and techniques for democratic classrooms* (2nd ed.). San Francisco, CA: Jossey-Bass.

Hassard, J. (1996). *Using cooperative learning to enhance your science instruction (grades 6–12): Resource handbook*. Bellevue, WA: Bureau of Education and Research.

King, A. (1993). From sage on the stage to guide on the side. *College Teaching, 41*, 30–35. doi:10.1080/87567555.1993.9926781

Lyman, F. (1987). Think-pair-share: An expanding teaching technique. *MAA-CIE Cooperative News, 1*(1), 1–2.

McKeachie, W. J. (1994). *Teaching tips: Strategies, research, and theory for college & universisty teachers* (9th ed.). Lexington, MA: D. C. Heath.

Millis, B. J. (2010). *Cooperative learning in higher education: Across the disciplines, across the academy*. Sterling, VA: Stylus.

Starting Point. (2017). *Think-pair-share*. Retrieved from serc.carleton.edu/introgeo/interactive/tpshare.html

Yee, K. *Interactive techniques*. Retrieved from www.usf.edu/atle/documents/handout-interactive-techniques.pdf

PAUSE PROCEDURE QUESTION

This is a simple way of pausing during the lecture to ask a question in a way that requires all learners to be prepared to answer the question. The technique raises tension in the room and uses wait time. The instructor needs to phrase the question something like this, "I am going to ask a question, and I want to ask that no one answer the question out loud until I call on someone to answer it." Often when the lecturer asks a question, just a few students answer the questions quickly. The majority of the group gets to relax and tries not to respond or even think of responses, knowing that the quick responders will take care of answering for the group. In contrast, when instructors use the Pause Procedure Question technique, tension rises for all learners because no one can be sure of not being called on. This increases the likelihood of increased engagement and interest on the part of the majority of learners in the class.

Settings for Use

- ☑ Small classroom lecture
- ☑ Clinical or laboratory presentation
- ☑ One-on-one session
- ☑ Conference presentation/ in-service education
- ☑ Keynote/large group presentation
- ☐ Course/unit
- ☐ Online learning module

Characteristics

- ☑ Affirming/positive
- ☐ Physical/movement
- ☐ Activates prior knowledge/ experience
- ☑ Focuses/refocuses
- ☑ Creates community
- ☐ Generates curiosity
- ☐ Metacognitive
- ☐ Reviews
- ☐ Celebrates
- ☐ Commits to action
- ☐ Provides a bookend

Procedure

1. Most instructors find it helpful to plan ahead of time by posting possible questions in the right-hand margin of their lecture notes so they are ready to use.
2. When you plan for a midpause, tell students you are going to ask a question and no one may answer until you call on someone.
3. Ask the question you have planned ahead of time.

4. Be sure to wait an adequate length of time. Research suggests a minimum of two to five seconds.
5. At this point, you may want to use a variety of approaches. Sometimes you may ask for a show of hands and then call on someone who seems to really want to answer the question. At other times, you may want to use a random approach for calling on someone, such as using a random number generator and then calling the student whose number is generated. You could randomly select a student to pick a number between one and the total number of students in the class and then allow the individual who has that number to answer. You might also pull a name from your hat of student names.
6. Occasionally you might ask several students to respond to the question, for a show of hands indicating how many essentially agree, or how many see a slightly different answer to the question.

Additional Suggestions

- This technique is one of the three essential midpauses (the other two are Short Write [MP 24] and Think-Pair-Share [MP 25]). Many faculty members have found these simple techniques to be very effective active learning strategies to reenergize the class, helping students to refocus on the lecture and listen more carefully, take better notes, and improve retention. See Chapter 7, p. 84, for an example of a Pause Procedure Question.

Key References and Resources

Brookfield, S. D., & Preskill, S. (2005). *Discussion as a way of teaching: Tools and techniques for democratic classrooms* (2nd ed.). San Francisco, CA: Jossey-Bass.

Ruhl, K. L., Hughes, C. A., & Schloss, P. J. (1987). Using the pause procedure to enhance lecture recall. *Teacher Education and Special Education, 10*(1), 14–18. doi:10.1177/088840648701000103

MIDPAUSE 27

MUSICAL CONCENTRIC CIRCLES

This activity combines physical movement with retrieval practice and is an excellent refocusing activity during a high-density lecture. It works particularly well when the room has enough space for participants to form two circles around the perimeter of the room.

Settings for Use

- ☑ Small classroom lecture
- ☑ Clinical or laboratory presentation
- ☐ One-on-one session
- ☑ Conference presentation/ in-service education
- ☐ Keynote/large group presentation
- ☐ Course/unit
- ☐ Online learning module

Characteristics

- ☑ Affirming/positive
- ☑ Physical/movement
- ☑ Activates prior knowledge/ experience
- ☑ Focuses/refocuses
- ☑ Creates community
- ☐ Generates curiosity
- ☐ Metacognitive
- ☐ Reviews
- ☐ Celebrates
- ☐ Commits to action
- ☐ Provides a bookend

Procedure

1. Assign each student either the number one or number two. Ask the ones to form the outer circle and the twos to form the inner circle. Explain to them that they are going to move briskly around the room in a circle in opposite directions when the music plays. When the music stops, they will stop moving and talk to the person standing opposite to them.
2. The students are most likely already aware of this but it is good to remind them that the simple act of standing after sitting increases blood flow and oxygen to the brain by 15% to 20% (Sousa, 2006). Walking at a good pace will increase this oxygen flow even more. Accordingly, this exercise will also increase students' capacity to think by at least 20%. We want to capitalize on their improved brain function (thanks to the physical movement) by asking them to give their

partners a short verbal summary of what they have learned from the lecture so far.

3. Proceed to play some lively music for a short while, enough to get pulses up a bit. Then stop the music and instruct someone from either the inner or outer circle to do the summary.
4. After a couple of minutes, start the music again and ask the circles to move again. When you stop the music, ask someone in the opposite circle to do the explaining.
5. Have students return to their seats and jot down a few notes from the activity before you proceed.
6. Always allow for variations when asking students to move about the room, in case there may be students present with physical limitations.

Additional Suggestions

- If you don't have room for the concentric circles, you can simply have students stand and then give their summaries to someone standing near them.
- Another alternative is to ask students to wander around the room until the music stops and then talk to the person standing closest to them.
- You can allow the partners to give a summary to each other when the music stops.
- If you don't have access to music, you can use another signal, like a school bell or a marimba to signal when to partner up.
- An example of this pause is provided in Chapter 4 (see pp. 57–58).

Key References and Resources

Bowman, S. (2009). *Training from the back of the room.* San Diego, CA: Pfeiffer.

Inside/outside circles. (2006). Retrieved from carla.umn.edu/articulation/polia/pdf_files/insideoutsidecircles.pdf

Inside/outside circles. (n.d.). Retrieved from www.theteachertoolkit.com/index.php/tool/inside-outside-circles

MIDPAUSE 28

NOTE SHARE

Note Share is one of the earliest midpauses described in the literature (Ruhl, Hughes, & Schloss, 1987). The instructor stops the lecture and asks students to turn to the person sitting next to them and share their notes with each other. The pause usually lasts about two minutes and allows students to fill in gaps in their notes and to ask each other questions or explain something to their seatmate. Note Share is particularly effective if there is no lecture handout or when the instructor's handout has blanks to be completed. The beauty of this pause procedure is that it allows students to revisit and review, possibly even do a little teaching when they explain something, thus increasing the likelihood of retention.

Settings for Use

- ☑ Small classroom lecture
- ☑ Clinical or laboratory presentation
- ☐ One-on-one session
- ☑ Conference presentation/ in-service education
- ☐ Keynote/large group presentation
- ☐ Course/unit
- ☐ Online learning module

Characteristics

- ☑ Affirming/positive
- ☐ Physical/movement
- ☐ Activates prior knowledge/ experience
- ☑ Focuses/refocuses
- ☑ Creates community
- ☐ Generates curiosity
- ☐ Metacognitive
- ☑ Reviews
- ☐ Celebrates
- ☐ Commits to action
- ☐ Provides a bookend

Procedure

1. Tell students early in the session that you will have a two-minute break for them midway through the lecture for them to share their notes and ask questions.
2. When you want to have the pause activity, explain the process to the students. Tell them they will have a two- or three-minute pause so they can look back over their notes from the first half of the class and fill in any blanks or additional ideas they didn't have time to write down earlier.
3. Explain that during this time they can also ask questions, share answers, and consult with the people sitting close to them. It may be

helpful to suggest that they do this in groups of two or three, which helps avoid having an individual left out at the end of the row or the two people on either side of a student looking the other way.

4. While students are note sharing, it may be helpful to listen in on some of the groups to get an idea of what questions are coming up.
5. After about two minutes, ask the group if there are any unresolved questions for the instructor before proceeding.

Additional Suggestions

- Any number of assignments can be given that relate to note sharing. Students could be asked to study their partner's notes and look for gaps or missing items. Students might quiz each other from their own notes to check for understanding.
- Sometimes instructors ask students to go back over their notes in silence, without talking to their neighbors. After a minute or two for study and reflection, the instructor may ask for a group discussion or a Short Write (MP 24) activity.

Online Adaptation

We can call this adapted midpause A Minute to Think Back. Partway through the online module, some instructors purposely post a regular feature called Stop and Review, or something similar, that asks several review questions. For example, students may be asked to write down three important concepts they have gleaned from the module so far without looking back—just by remembering as much as possible—perhaps posting the reflection on the discussion or in the chat room or sending it as a short assignment to the instructor. Students may be asked to post a question they hope will be answered before they complete the module.

Key References and Resources

Johnson, D. W., Johnson, R. T., & Smith, K. A. (1998). *Active learning: Cooperation in the college classroom*. Retrived from ERIC database. (ED449714)

Nilson, L. (2013). *Creating self-regulated learners: Strategies to strengthen self-awareness and learning skills*. Sterling, VA: Stylus.

Ruhl, K. L., Hughes, C. A., & Schloss, P. J. (1987). Using the pause procedure to enhance lecture recall. *Teacher Education and Special Education, 10*(1), 14–18. doi:10.1177/088840648701000103

MIDPAUSE 29

FRESH PERSON STANDING SUMMARY

Fresh Person Standing Summary is a good example of a midpause that incorporates physical movement to increase its value. Students stand midway through the class and think for a short while about what they have learned so far in this class session. Students then wander around to find someone they have not met before to exchange their thoughts. After thanking their partner, students return to their seats. Class discussion includes asking a few individuals to describe how their partners summarized class so far.

Settings for Use

- ☑ Small classroom lecture
- ☑ Clinical or laboratory presentation
- ☐ One-on-one session
- ☑ Conference presentation/ in-service education
- ☐ Keynote/large group presentation
- ☐ Course/unit
- ☐ Online learning module

Characteristics:

- ☑ Affirming/positive
- ☑ Physical/movement
- ☐ Activates prior knowledge/ experience
- ☑ Focuses/refocuses
- ☑ Creates community
- ☐ Generates curiosity
- ☐ Metacognitive
- ☐ Reviews
- ☐ Celebrates
- ☐ Commits to action
- ☐ Provides a bookend

Procedure

1. When you reach a point in the learning session when you want to use this pause, stop the instruction for a few minutes to allow students to participate in a standing summary exercise.
2. Ask all the students to stand at their seat. You might want to remind them that by standing their brains are getting extra oxygen from the increased blood flow, so they will be thinking especially well for this activity.
3. Ask them to think back and summarize in their minds what they have learned since class began without looking at their notes or handouts.

4. Wait until they have had a little time to think, then ask each person to look around the room and see if they can find a *fresh person*, someone they have not had an opportunity to get well acquainted with prior to class.
5. Ask them to pair up with this fresh person and exchange their summaries within a set amount of time.
6. After time is up, ask them to thank their colleague and return to their seat.
7. When students have returned to their seats, ask a few of them to identify their fresh person and tell the class what their colleagues said they had learned in the first half of the class.

Additional Suggestions

- If you have a large group with tight auditorium-style seating that makes moving about the room difficult, you may need to change this to a two- or three-person standing activity with students who are sitting near each other. The fresh person concept has several advantages, however, that may be lost if students stay close to their seats. Students are likely to be sitting close to their friends, so asking them to find someone else to talk with means they will be more likely to take the activity seriously if they must talk with someone they haven't met before. Moving to another part of the room also increases the physical activity and thus the energizing and refocusing aspects of the experience.
- Always allow for variations when asking students to move about the room, in case there may be students present with physical limitations.

Online Adaptation

This midpause works well in an online module, with some adaptations. If you would like to include the physical activity part, you can ask your students to stand and stretch while they think about what they have learned so far in the module. You could ask them to take a two-minute walk around the room; you might ask them to do some kind of physical exercise (maybe insert some great exercise music right there in your module). Tell them to think while they are moving. For the fresh person aspect of this activity, ask them to provide their summary in an interactive post, perhaps on a discussion area or in a chat room with a small group. They can also send the summary directly to the instructor through an interactive pop-up or e-mail.

Key References and Resources

Barkley, E. F., & Major, C. H. (2015). *Learning assessment techniques: A handbook for college faculty*. San Francisco, CA: Wiley.

MIDPAUSE 30

RECALL SHARE

This pause trains students to listen, practice retrieval, and develop organizing skills. The instructor provides no handout and asks the students to listen carefully to the lecture without writing down any notes. After a certain amount of time, the instructor pauses for students to write down everything they can recall about the lecture.

Settings for Use

- ☑ Small classroom lecture
- ☐ Clinical or laboratory presentation
- ☑ One-on-one session
- ☑ Conference presentation/ in-service education
- ☑ Keynote/large group presentation
- ☐ Course/unit
- ☑ Online learning module

Characteristics

- ☐ Affirming/positive
- ☐ Physical/movement
- ☐ Activates prior knowledge/ experience
- ☑ Focuses/refocuses
- ☑ Creates community
- ☐ Generates curiosity
- ☑ Metacognitive
- ☑ Reviews
- ☐ Celebrates
- ☐ Commits to action
- ☐ Provides a bookend

Procedure

1. Explain to your students before the lecture begins that you are asking them to practice their listening or attending skills without writing anything down and to remember what they have learned.
2. Fifteen or 20 minutes later, pause to allow students to write down a summary of what was presented.
3. Have them share their summaries in small groups with those sitting around them so they can fill in gaps and help each other flesh out their outlines and summaries.
4. You might then hand out an outline that shows the main points that have been covered up to the pause. The outline allows students to compare what they have written with the outline you have been teaching from.

Additional Suggestions

- Some instructors allow students to write their outlines or summaries on their laptops or electronic pads instead of handwriting them. Research suggests there are benefits from handwriting rather than recording electronically. It might be worthwhile to ask students to handwrite their summaries and explain the reason for doing it this way.
- Instead of asking students to write down their own outline or summary, providing them with a partially completed outline with blanks to be filled in may also work well.
- Another way to do this activity is to explain to students that they will be allowed to take notes, but partway through the session they will be asked to put away their notes and summarize the important points of the lecture.
- Interesting research could be conducted by doing the following:
  - Instruct only half the class to refrain from note-taking. After the mini lecture, give students a fill-in-the-blanks exercise and compare scores between those who took notes and those who didn't.
  - Have all students take notes, and give them a fill-in-the-blank exercise after the 20-minute mini lecture. Instruct students to turn in their notes and the quizzes to determine if those who took better notes did better on the quiz.

Online Adaptation

Tell students at the beginning of the module that midway through they will be asked to write a summary of the first half of the readings and activities. The module can be set up so that students cannot proceed with the module activities until they have submitted their summaries.

Students can be encouraged to submit two versions, the first, written from memory without checking notes, and the second, after looking back through the materials, written to be more complete and accurate.

Key References and Resources

Barkley, E. F., & Major, C. H. (2015). *Learning assessment techniques: A handbook for college faculty*. San Francisco, CA: Wiley.

Bonwell, C. C., & Eison, J. A. (1991). *Active learning: Creating excitement in the classroom.* Retrieved from ERIC database. (ED336049)

Nilson, L. (2013). *Creating self-regulated learners: Strategies to strengthen self-awareness and learning skills*. Sterling, VA: Stylus.

MIDPAUSE 31

WRITE A SUMMARY

With this pause, the instructor stops the lecture and asks students to take out a piece of paper and write a summary. This is done midway through the class session, not at the end when we usually expect to summarize. Research has shown that the act of writing a summary has a major effect on retention.

Settings for Use

- ☑ Small classroom lecture
- ☑ Clinical or laboratory presentation
- ☐ One-on-one session
- ☑ Conference presentation/in-service education
- ☑ Keynote/large group presentation
- ☑ Course/unit
- ☐ Online learning module

Characteristics

- ☐ Affirming/positive
- ☐ Physical/movement
- ☐ Activates prior knowledge/experience
- ☑ Focuses/refocuses
- ☑ Creates community
- ☐ Generates curiosity
- ☐ Metacognitive
- ☑ Reviews
- ☐ Celebrates
- ☐ Commits to action
- ☐ Provides a bookend

Procedure

1. Tell students early in the session that they will have a five-minute break midway through the lecture for them to do some summarizing of what they have been learning. Tell the students what they will do with their written summary when they are through writing (e.g., turn them in, keep them for reference, compare them with others).
2. At the midpoint, tell the students they will have several minutes to write a summary of the class so far.
3. Encourage them to write their summaries from memory, not from looking at their notes. You might tell them they will remember much more if they dig down into their memory and pull out what they can recall without jogging their memories from their notes. Tell them it is worth the effort to do this, even though it would be easier to write the summary while looking over notes they have written or a handout they have been given.

4. Ask the students to hold their summaries and turn them in to the instructor at the end of class.
5. Consider asking students to add to their summaries with a closing pause that revisits their preliminary summary and adds to it.

Additional Suggestions

- If students prefer to write on their laptop or notepad, they can do that and send it to the instructor through the course learning management system or by e-mail.
- There are a number of alternatives to having the students turn their summaries in to the instructor. You may want them to keep their summaries for review later in the course or have students pair up after writing their summaries and share them with a partner.
- The instructor can distribute three-inch-by-five-inch cards or sheets of paper for students to use to write their summaries.

Online Adaptation

This is an excellent pause activity for the online module. Students simply pause midway through the module and write their summary. This may be followed by an additional end-of-unit summary and then submitted at the end of the module.

Key References and Resources

Agarwal, P. K. (2017). *Retrieval practice.* Retrieved from www.retrievalpractice.org

Barkley, E. F., & Major, C. H. (2015). *Learning assessment techniques: A handbook for college faculty*. San Francisco, CA: Wiley.

Davis, M., & Hult, R. E. (1997). Effects of writing summaries as a generative learning activity during note taking. *Teaching of Psychology, 24*(1), 47–50.

Nilsen, C., Odahlen, B., Geller, L., Hintz, K., & Borden-King, L. (2011, February). *Fifty ways to teach your students*. Paper presented at the the 30th Annual Conference on the First Year Experience, Minot, ND. Retrieved from www.minotstateu.edu/cetl/_documents/50Ways toTeachYourStudents.pdf

MIDPAUSE 32

MIDWAY SUMMARY CHECK

This pause allows students to think back on what they have learned so far in the class session and discuss it with a partner who may provide corrections or additions. For this activity, only one partner summarizes; the other partner responds with clarifications or expansions. This pause allows students to revisit and review, possibly even teach when they explain something, thus increasing the likelihood of retention.

Settings for Use

- ☑ Small classroom lecture
- ☑ Clinical or laboratory presentation
- ☐ One-on-one session
- ☑ Conference presentation/in-service education
- ☐ Keynote/large group presentation
- ☐ Course/unit
- ☐ Online learning module

Characteristics

- ☑ Affirming/positive
- ☑ Physical/movement
- ☐ Activates prior knowledge/experience
- ☑ Focuses/refocuses
- ☑ Creates community
- ☐ Generates curiosity
- ☐ Metacognitive
- ☐ Reviews
- ☐ Celebrates
- ☐ Commits to action
- ☑ Provides a bookend

Procedure

1. Tell students early in the session that each individual will have an opportunity later in the class to provide a summary of what has been taught and that this will be done without using notes.
2. When it appears that students need a pause to refresh them, give them a signal, such as ringing a bell, striking a xylophone with a mallet, or simply announcing that it is time for the Midway Summary Check.
3. Ask class members to stand, leave their notes at their places, and pair up with someone from another part of the room if possible.
4. Explain to them that they will have different roles, and it is important to determine which person will play each role. During this three-minute break, ask the pairs to determine who will lead off. You might suggest selecting the person who is wearing the most colorful shoes (or socks) as the lead or the person who is shorter or who has the longest hair, and so on.

5. Remind everyone that they are doing this exercise cold and should try to do the best they can without looking at any notes or handouts. Instruct the lead person to summarize the important class concepts covered so far. His or her partner will then respond by clarifying or adding to the summary.
6. Depending on the lecture topic, you might want to allow the pairs to answer additional questions such as, How do you see this as applicable to your work or life? or How important is this information to the issues this course addresses?
7. As the students return to their seats, tell them they will regroup in the same pairs toward the end of the class session and reverse roles.

Additional Suggestions

- Instead of making this a two-part activity, you might simply have one individual share and the other add to the summary by trying to see how many additional ideas might be helpful.
- A playful concept might be to score the partner's summary by holding up a number card or a color card, indicating level of proficiency.

Online Adaptation

If students are online, ask them to pair up in chat rooms and decide which role they will take. They discuss their module summary midway and might be asked to return later for another midway summary check.

Key References and Resources

Barkley, E. F., & Major, C. H. (2015). *Learning assessment techniques: A handbook for college faculty*. San Francisco, CA: Wiley.

Cuseo, J. B. (2002). *Igniting student involvement, peer interaction, and teamwork: A taxonomy of specific cooperative learning structures and collaborative learning strategies*. Stillwater, OK: New Forums Press.

Kagan, S., & Kagan, M. (2009). *Kagan cooperative learning*. San Clemente, CA: Author.

Nilson, L. (2013). *Creating self-regulated learners: Strategies to strengthen self-awareness and learning skills*. Sterling, VA: Stylus.

MAKE IT RIGHT

This activity generates a high level of energy. It is usually a very short break that can be inserted midway through a class period or even a short instructional event. Participants are invited to analyze something that contains an error, identify what the error is, and correct it.

Settings for Use

- ☑ Small classroom lecture
- ☑ Clinical or laboratory presentation
- ☑ One-on-one session
- ☑ Conference presentation/ in-service education
- ☑ Keynote/large group presentation
- ☐ Course/unit
- ☑ Online learning module

Characteristics:

- ☐ Affirming/positive
- ☑ Physical/movement
- ☐ Activates prior knowledge/ experience
- ☑ Focuses/refocuses
- ☐ Creates community
- ☐ Generates curiosity
- ☐ Metacognitive
- ☐ Reviews
- ☐ Celebrates
- ☐ Commits to action
- ☑ Provides a bookend

Procedure

1. Prepare your item that contains an error (that you created on purpose) on three-inch-by-five-inch cards; it could be a diagram, a sentence, an equation, a prediction, or a picture that contains the error.
2. At the appropriate time, tell students they will be receiving something that has an error in it. Their task will be to discover where the error is and if it is a computation error; an error in the statement, diagram, or visual representation; or a logical error.
3. Give the students the cards containing the error and have them write their name on their card.
4. Ask them to identify the error and write the correction on the card.
5. Have them run their card to the front as soon as they are finished. Let them know that the quicker their response, the higher their scores.
6. Give points for an accurate correction as well as bonus points for being one of the first to submit.

7. If you see that many of the students are not making acceptable corrections to the error card, you may want to return the cards to the students and give them an opportunity to add additional information, as well as a reference or further information to defend their correction.
8. Collect the cards at the end of class and post the points everyone earned.

Additional Suggestions

- This activity can be repeated more than once during a course. Students tend to find this exciting, challenging, and an excellent review of important material.
- Certain courses lend themselves very well to this activity. It can be challenging to create the error cards, but students' learning and enthusiasm seem to be greatly enhanced. The pause that students experience is often short, but intense, with a quick return of focus and attention to the learning task. Competition can enhance the value as well.
- Make It Right can be done electronically. The error can be sent to each student, and the student can send the corrected error back to the instructor. The advantage of electronic submissions is that students are used to this way of communicating and are comfortable with it. Also, they can learn more from each other as responses can be posted as they come in. The advantage to doing this face-to-face in a classroom is that physical activity is involved, creating the most effective midpauses, which involve physiologic responses to movement.
- If the group is too large to have everyone run to the front of the room, consider an electronic option.
- This activity could be done as a one-on-one, in which case learners would simply try to identify the error.

Online Adaptation

This pause can easily be done as a module activity in the online course. Students could send their response to the instructor through any number of mechanisms.

Key References and Resources

Barkley, E. F. (2010). *Student engagement techniques: A handbook for college faculty*. San Francisco, CA: Jossey-Bass.

Barkley, E. F., Major, C. H., & Cross, P. K. (2014). *Collaborative learning techniques: A handbook for college faculty*. San Francisco, CA: Jossey-Bass.

Johnston, S., & Cooper, J. (1997). Quick-thinks: The interactive lecture. *Cooperative Learning and College Teaching, 8*(1).

Kagan, S. (1992). *Cooperative learning* (2nd ed.). San Juan Capistrano, CA: Resources for Teachers.

Millis, B. J., & Cottell, P. G. (1998). *Cooperative learning for higher education faculty*. Phoenix, AZ: Oryx Press.

MIDPAUSE 34

QUIZ, QUIZ, TRADE

This pause generates high energy levels. Students are given quiz cards or are asked to develop their own quiz card with the answer written on the back. Students find a partner to show their quiz card to. After the partner answers the question, the one holding the card provides praise, encouragement, and additional helpful information if necessary. The partners switch roles. After quizzing each other, they trade quiz cards and find another partner to repeat the process.

Settings for Use

- ☑ Small classroom lecture
- ☑ Clinical or laboratory presentation
- ☐ One-on-one session
- ☐ Conference presentation/ in-service education
- ☐ Keynote/large group presentation
- ☐ Course/unit
- ☐ Online learning module

Characteristics:

- ☑ Affirming/positive
- ☑ Physical/movement
- ☐ Activates prior knowledge/ experience
- ☑ Focuses/refocuses
- ☑ Creates community
- ☐ Generates curiosity
- ☐ Metacognitive
- ☑ Reviews
- ☑ Celebrates
- ☐ Commits to action
- ☐ Provides a bookend

Procedure

1. Hand a blank three-inch-by-five-inch card to all students and ask them to reflect on the class content so far.
2. Tell them to develop a question from notes taken during class.
3. Ask students to find partners.
4. Partner One asks Partner Two the question on the card. Partner Two answers (or admits not knowing the answer). Partner One acknowledges the correct answer or gives the answer depending on Partner Two's response.
5. The process reverses with Partner Two asking the question.
6. After both questions have been asked, the partners switch cards, find new partners, and the process begins again.

Additional Suggestions

- Instead of asking students to write their questions, the teacher can prepare question cards ahead of time and give them to the students. This can be a good choice when certain critical elements need to be reviewed before class can continue.
- A good way to facilitate finding partners quickly is to use Stand Up, Hand Up, Pair Up (MP 36). When a couple is through questioning each other, they put up a hand and walk around the room looking for someone else who is holding up a hand to be their next partner.

Key References and Resources

Clowes, G. (2017). *The essential 5: A starting point for Kagan Cooperative Learning.* Retrieved from www.kaganonline.com/free_articles/research_and_rationale/330/The-Essential-5-A-Starting-Point-for-Kagan-Cooperative-Learning

Howard, B. (2017). *Cooperative learning structures improve performance and attitudes of high school journalism students.* Retrieved from www.kaganonline.com/free_articles/research_and_rationale/312/Cooperative-Learning-Structures-Improve-Performance-and-Attitudes-of-High-School-Journalism-Students

Lynette, R. (2012). *Quiz, quiz, trade.* Retrieved from minds-in-bloom.com/quiz-quiz-trade

MIDPAUSE 35

BEAT THE CLOCK

This requires students to complete a short matching quiz in small groups. In this timed activity, groups open an envelope that contains paper strips that are to be placed on a card. The paper strips are created by printing two columns of matching items and then cutting each item from the two columns into a paper strip. After students have completed the matching quiz, tell them to put all the paper strips back in the envelope and repeat the activity to see if they can do it quicker the second time, thus beating the clock.

Settings for Use

- ☑ Small classroom lecture
- ☑ Clinical or laboratory presentation
- ☐ One-on-one session
- ☑ Conference presentation/ in-service education
- ☐ Keynote/large group presentation
- ☐ Course/unit
- ☑ Online learning module

Characteristics

- ☐ Affirming/positive
- ☐ Physical/movement
- ☐ Activates prior knowledge/ experience
- ☑ Focuses/refocuses
- ☑ Creates community
- ☐ Generates curiosity
- ☐ Metacognitive
- ☑ Reviews
- ☐ Celebrates
- ☐ Commits to action
- ☐ Provides a bookend

Procedure

1. Tell your students you are giving them a break to review some content that is related to the topic of the day.
2. Tell them they will solve a short matching quiz in groups of three to six.
3. Prepare each envelope in the following way:
   a. Construct your short matching quiz; it is best to have no more than four to six items in Column A and a few additional items (distractors) for Column B.
   b. Make a base card containing the headings and blanks where each of the strips will be placed.
   c. Cut each of the items for Columns A and B into small strips of paper.
   d. Include a piece of paper with the answers. Fold it and put a note on it that it is the answer key and cannot be opened until students are instructed to do so.

4. Give each group an envelope, and give the go signal for groups to open the envelope and complete the matching quiz.
5. Instruct groups to time themselves while solving the quiz and to check their answers with the key included in each envelope.
6. Ask groups to put all the pieces back into the envelope.
7. When each groups' time in solving the quiz and replacing their paper strips in the envelopes has been recorded, surprise them with an invitation to do it all again, this time trying to see if they can beat their original time.
8. It is very rare for a group to fail to beat the clock when repeating the exercise.

Additional Suggestions

- This activity can be done electronically as well as with paper strips, and if your class is large, it will be much easier to use an electronic version of this activity. You can still have them work in small groups or individually, and tell them it will not be graded, it is just done for review and fun.
- This activity can work for a large variety of course topics. For a course in literature, it could be a review of authors and works or authors and quotes. A course in microbiology might use a review of pathogens and descriptions of each. A teacher who has described a technique with numbered steps might use a matching quiz that asks for each step in order with a description of what happens at each phase.

Online Adaptation

To do this activity online, ask students midway through the course module to go to the activity. Quiz systems with matching question-and-answer templates are readily available in your course learning management system. Allow students to submit their answers and get their score. Select the multiple submissions accepted option when developing the quiz and provide the score immediately.

Ask students to complete the quiz. Have them make their matches and time themselves. Many quizzes in online courses have a built-in timing function, so this step might not be necessary. Invite students to repeat the activity; see if they can improve their accuracy, find out if they missed anything the first time around, and beat the clock this time by doing it faster.

Key References and Resources

Deck, M. L. (1995). *Instant teaching tools for health care educators.* Maryland Heights, MO: Mosby.

STAND UP, HAND UP, PAIR UP

This technique can be used often without getting old. It provides a quick way to put students into pairs for an activity. Students are asked to stand, put a hand in the air, and begin walking around the room until a signal is given, at which time they are to find a partner. They can choose anyone who still has his or her hand up. The advantages of this technique are that it inserts physical activity, which is energizing; it requires individuals to move about, thus increasing the chances that their partner will be from a different part of the room and someone they are not too familiar with; and it is quick and effective.

Settings for Use

- ☑ Small classroom lecture
- ☑ Clinical or laboratory presentation
- ☐ One-on-one session
- ☑ Conference presentation/in-service education
- ☐ Keynote/large group presentation
- ☐ Course/unit
- ☐ Online learning module

Characteristics

- ☐ Affirming/positive
- ☑ Physical/movement
- ☐ Activates prior knowledge/experience
- ☑ Focuses/refocuses
- ☑ Creates community
- ☐ Generates curiosity
- ☐ Metacognitive
- ☑ Reviews
- ☑ Celebrates
- ☐ Commits to action
- ☐ Provides a bookend

Procedure

1. The teacher gives students the task or question to answer or discuss.
2. Students are given some time to think.
3. Students stand and put a hand in the air—this allows them to identify those who do not yet have a partner.
4. Teacher asks students to roam around the room.
5. When the signal is given, students find a partner from among those standing near them who still has a hand up. They put their hands down when they have found a partner.
6. If anyone is left with his or her hand up, the instructor can ask that student to join a group of two, making one triad in the room.

7. Students spend the allotted amount of time sharing answers with each other.
8. Students are encouraged to congratulate each other for their good ideas and then return to their seats.

Additional Suggestions

- This activity works equally well without asking participants to put their hand in the air. It may seem more dignified to simply ask individuals to stand and move around until the signal is given and then to find a partner who is standing close by.
- Ideally, you will have an even number of students. If there is an odd number, the teacher can match with a student, or the teacher might allow one triad to work together.
- This technique is simply a way to pair students when pairing or sharing is a component of any pause you might be using.

Key References and Resources

Howard, B. (2017). *Cooperative learning structures improve performance and attitudes of high school journalism students*. Retrieved from www.kaganonline.com/free_articles/research_and_rationale/312/Cooperative-Learning-Structures-Improve-Performance-and-Attitudes-of-High-School-Journalism-Students

Kagan, S., Kagan, M., & Kagan, L. (2015). *59 Kagan structures: Proven engagement structures*. San Clemente: CA: Author.

Lee, G. [Lee RebelTech]. (2013, October 31). *Kagan structure: Stand up, hand up, pair up* [Video file]. Retrieved from https://www.youtube.com/watch?v=7rCTJoTSTJc

McIntyre, G. (2013, February 4). Stand up, hand up, pair up [Video file]. Retrieved from https://www.youtube.com/watch?v=NoUxq_clsEA

MIDPAUSE 37

RALLY COACH

This technique pairs students and trains them to coach each other. The pair receives a set of problems to solve, and they take turns solving problems or answering questions. This technique can be used for any number of problem-solving activities that can be coached by a partner, such as solving a matching problem, reviewing definitions, or selecting an appropriate statistical test for a particular problem. This can be an excellent approach for skills practice as well, where one student performs a laboratory experiment or a clinical skill while the partner gives feedback and assistance as necessary before reversing roles. There are a number of benefits from this activity, including the fact that students will all receive immediate and specific feedback, rarely possible in a large classroom where students are working individually.

Settings for Use

- ☑ Small classroom lecture
- ☑ Clinical or laboratory presentation
- ☐ One-on-one session
- ☑ Conference presentation/in-service education
- ☐ Keynote/large group presentation
- ☐ Course/unit
- ☐ Online learning module

Characteristics

- ☑ Affirming/positive
- ☐ Physical/movement
- ☐ Activates prior knowledge/experience
- ☑ Focuses/refocuses
- ☑ Creates community
- ☐ Generates curiosity
- ☐ Metacognitive
- ☑ Reviews
- ☑ Celebrates
- ☐ Commits to action
- ☐ Provides a bookend

Procedure

1. The teacher gives students the task or question to answer, the concept to discuss, or the skill or experiment to perform.
2. Each pair receives only one pen or pencil and one worksheet or piece of paper to work on.
3. One of the partners solves the first problem, describing what he or she doing.
4. The second partner watches closely and provides support, encouragement, correction, or praise accordingly.

5. They reverse roles.
6. The activity continues if there are additional questions to address.

Additional Suggestions

- This technique is particularly valuable for a quick review of simple concepts. Pairs can work at their own pace, which is an additional benefit.

Key References and Resources

Clowes, G. (2017). *The essential 5: A starting point for Kagan Cooperative Learning.* Retrieved from www.kaganonline.com/free_articles/research_and_rationale/330/The-Essential-5-A-Starting-Point-for-Kagan-Cooperative-Learning

Kagan. [Kaganvideo]. (2014, June 12). *What is Kagan?* [Video file]. Retrieved from youtube/D-yzgJtgVrg

Kagan, S., Kagan, M., & Kagan, L. (2015). *59 Kagan structures: Proven engagement structures.* San Clemente: CA: Author.

McIntyre, G. (2013, January 25). *Rally coach* [Video file]. Retrieved from youtu.be/mNvAHN_x1hY

MIDPAUSE 38

ROUND ROBIN

This small-group technique requires students to form a circle and take turns giving answers to a question or solutions to a problem. It works best when students are sitting around a table, but the circle can also be formed by pulling a few chairs together. This powerful cooperative learning pause builds community and reviews content while allowing everyone to have a voice.

Settings for Use

- ☑ Small classroom lecture
- ☑ Clinical or laboratory presentation
- ☑ One-on-one session
- ☑ Conference presentation/in-service education
- ☐ Keynote/large group presentation
- ☐ Course/unit
- ☐ Online learning module

Characteristics

- ☑ Affirming/positive
- ☐ Physical/movement
- ☐ Activates prior knowledge/experience
- ☑ Focuses/refocuses
- ☑ Creates community
- ☐ Generates curiosity
- ☐ Metacognitive
- ☑ Reviews
- ☑ Celebrates
- ☐ Commits to action
- ☐ Provides a bookend

Procedure

1. Organize students into small groups and have them assign themselves numbers within a specified range (i.e., one through four).
2. The teacher gives students the task or question to answer or the concept to discuss. Ideally, there should be many possible good answers.
3. The teacher gives them a short time for thinking about their answer to the question.
4. The teacher randomly suggests a number to start the Round Robin and tells students which direction to proceed around the circle starting from the student whose number was called.

Additional Suggestions

- This pause can comprise a single turn around the circle, as described here, or it can be a continuous round robin, where the conversation continues around the circle more than once.
- A commonly used variation involves participants writing an answer on a sheet of paper that is passed around the group.
- Another variation is the All-Write Round Robin in which each small group has several questions written on different pieces of paper. All students work on their sheet at the same time and then pass the sheet around the circle.

Key References and Resources

Clowes, G. (2017). *The essential 5: A starting point for Kagan Cooperative Learning.* Retrieved from www.kaganonline.com/free_articles/research_and_rationale/330/The-Essential-5-A-Starting-Point-for-Kagan-Cooperative-Learning

Kagan, S., & Kagan, M. (2009). *Kagan cooperative learning.* San Clemente, CA: Author.

Kagan, S., Kagan, M., & Kagan, L. (2015). *59 Kagan structures: Proven engagement structures.* San Clemente: CA: Author.

Kaplan, J. (2014). *Round robin.* Retrieved from www.betterevaluation.org/en/evaluation-options/roundrobin

Millis, B. J. (2010). *Cooperative learning in higher education: Across the disciplines, across the academy.* Sterling, VA: Stylus.

APPENDIX C

CLOSING PAUSES

CLOSING PAUSE 39

EXIT TICKET

This closing pause technique is used to help students and the instructor get a sense of what they have accomplished during the learning period. The tickets, usually three-inch-by-five-inch cards or half sheets of paper, are handed to learners before the end of the learning session. Students are instructed to respond to the questions on the ticket and then return the completed ticket to the instructor before leaving the classroom. The purpose of this closing pause is for the students to look back over their notes from the learning session, answer the questions on the ticket, jot down their responses, discuss their answers with their classmates and the instructor, and then hand their ticket to the instructor as they exit the classroom.

Settings for Use

- ☑ Small classroom lecture
- ☑ Clinical or laboratory presentation
- ☐ One-on-one session
- ☑ Conference presentation/in-service education
- ☐ Keynote/large-group presentation
- ☑ Course/unit
- ☑ Online learning module

Characteristics

- ☑ Affirming/positive
- ☐ Physical/movement
- ☐ Activates prior knowledge/experience
- ☐ Focuses/refocuses
- ☑ Creates community
- ☐ Generates curiosity
- ☑ Metacognitive
- ☑ Reviews
- ☑ Celebrates
- ☑ Commits to action
- ☑ Provides a bookend

Procedure

1. Prepare tickets to hand out to the students before the end of the class session with two or three questions on them with space to write answers. Half sheets of paper or five-inch-by-seven-inch or three-inch-by-five-inch cards usually work well.
2. Possible questions to consider might include the following:
   a. What do you feel that you learned in this class session?
   b. What contributed most to your learning today?
   c. How well do you feel you met the class objectives for today?
   d. What is the most important thing you will remember from today's class?

   e. What action will you take as a result of class today?
   f. What are you motivated to study more now?
3. Instruct learners to complete the tickets immediately and then discuss them with those sitting nearby.
4. Conduct a large-group discussion.
5. Collect the tickets from the students as they leave the room. Plan to give positive reinforcement to students when collecting each ticket. You might do one of the following:
   a. Thank students with a positive comment.
   b. Hand them a small reward, such as a pack of gum or a writing pen.
   c. Hand them a preprepared note of encouragement.
6. Take note of the trends and concepts and adjust teaching plans accordingly.

Additional Suggestions

- The following are additional questions you might consider for your exit ticket (see Key References and Resources at the end of this pause).
  - One thing you learned is . . .
  - You have a question about . . .
  - What from today's lesson will you try to apply to your learning?
  - What was helpful?
  - What did you think was accomplished by the small-group activity we did today?
  - What was a light bulb moment?
  - What was a struggle to understand?
  - What do you think you would be able to teach to your classmates?
  - Today's lesson had three objectives (which should have been shared at the beginning of class and made available for referral). Which of the three do you think was most successfully reached? Explain. Or, which was not attained? Why do you think it was not?
  - One of the goals of this class is to have all participants contribute to the seminar. How well do you think this was achieved today?
  - Which of the readings you did for class today was most helpful in preparing you for the lesson? Why?
- A particularly good starting pause to use with this is Entry Ticket (SP 2).

Online Adaptation

Place the exit ticket in the online module with a submission requirement.

Key References and Resources

Barkley, E. F., Major, C. H., & Cross, P. K. (2014). *Collaborative learning techniques: A handbook for college faculty* (2nd ed.). San Francisco, CA: Jossey-Bass.

Exit tickets: Checking for understanding. (2015). Retrieved from www.edutopia.org/practice/exit-tickets-checking-understanding

Stewart, R. (2015, March 13). Using exit tickets as an assessment tool [Web log post]. Retrieved from www.scholastic.com/teachers/blog-posts/rhonda-stewart/using-exit-tickets-assessment-tool

Wakeford, L. (2017). *Sample exit tickets*. Retrieved from www.brown.edu/about/administration/sheridan-center/teaching-learning/effective-classroom-practices/entrance-exit-tickets/sample

CLOSING PAUSE 40

FOUR SQUARE FEEDBACK

This pause allows faculty members to receive feedback from students about what and how they are learning. It helps students think about the value of what they are learning as well as what they feel is especially important about what they have learned. Additionally, it allows some action planning. Students draw a table divided into four parts on three-inch-by-five-inch cards or sheets of paper addressing four aspects of the learning task. The instructor might have the students keep them, or the instructor may collect them and then give them back to students for a second look and a chance for additional input at a later time.

Settings for Use

- ☑ Small classroom lecture
- ☑ Clinical or laboratory presentation
- ☑ One-on-one session
- ☑ Conference presentation/in-service education
- ☐ Keynote/large-group presentation
- ☑ Course/unit
- ☑ Online learning module

Characteristics

- ☐ Affirming/positive
- ☐ Physical/movement
- ☑ Activates prior knowledge/experience
- ☐ Focuses/refocuses
- ☐ Creates community
- ☐ Generates curiosity
- ☑ Metacognitive
- ☑ Reviews
- ☑ Celebrates
- ☐ Commits to action
- ☑ Provides a bookend

Procedure

1. Instruct students to take a card or half sheet of paper and draw intersecting lines, creating four boxes to fill in, as shown in Figure C.1.
2. Create four questions you would like students to answer. (The questions in Figure C.1 are only suggestions.)
3. Ask students to supply answers to the four questions in the boxes at the end of the class session.
4. Optional: Ask them to sign their cards and tell them that they will have a chance to add more ideas later in the course.
5. Optional: Collect the cards and use the data to plan for next steps in the teaching.

6. Optional: Allow students to keep their cards and add to them, eventually turning them in to the instructor.

Figure C.1. Four square feedback.

What did I learn that is really important?	How did I learn? What contributed to my learning?
How will this class make me a more effective professional?	What will my next steps be? Name ____________________

Additional Suggestions

- Many instructors prefer to have students complete this activity using their electronic devices instead of writing on cards. In this case, you would provide a template using spreadsheet software.
- If you ask the students to sign their names on the cards when they turn them in, you can give them back at the final class, let them add additional comments, and ask them to turn them in again for additional feedback.
- This version is designed to be an independent activity, with students working by themselves and sharing directly with the instructor without peer input. A good alternative to consider would be to have them compare and contrast their answers in small groups.

Online Adaptation

Post the table on the online course and ask students to complete the table and submit it to the instructor.

Key References and Resources

Barkley, E. F. (2010) *Student engagement techniques: A handbook for college faculty*. San Francisco, CA: Jossey-Bass.

Barkley, E. F., & Major, C. H. (2015). *Learning assessment techniques: A handbook for college faculty*. San Francisco, CA: Wiley.

Four square feedback. (n.d.). Retrieved from wvde.state.wv.us/abe/file-cabinet/Core_Sessions/Four_Square_Feedback.doc

CLOSING PAUSE 41

THREE-TWO-ONE

In this activity participants are asked to write three answers, two answers, or one answer to any set of questions (usually a set of three questions) designed by the instructor to fit the learning session. Typically, learners write their responses to the questions on three-inch-by-five-inch cards and turn the cards in to the instructor at the end of the session. The instructor analyzes the responses, summarizes them at the next meeting, and makes adjustments in future planning for teaching based on the analysis. Questions are often based on the following: things learned, things participants want to know more about, things they now understand better, things on which they want to take action, things on which to follow up, immediate action to take, corrective action to take, and so on.

Settings for Use

- ☑ Small classroom lecture
- ☑ Clinical or laboratory presentation
- ☐ One-on-one session
- ☑ Conference presentation/ in-service education
- ☑ Keynote/large-group presentation
- ☐ Course/unit
- ☑ Online learning module

Characteristics

- ☐ Affirming/positive
- ☐ Physical/movement
- ☐ Activates prior knowledge/ experience
- ☐ Focuses/refocuses
- ☑ Creates community
- ☐ Generates curiosity
- ☐ Metacognitive
- ☑ Reviews
- ☐ Celebrates
- ☑ Commits to action
- ☐ Provides a bookend

Procedure

1. Begin by deciding which three questions you want students to answer.
2. Decide which question will ask for three responses, which question will ask for two responses, and which question will ask for a single response.
3. Pass out the cards with the questions written on them, leaving room for students to write responses.
4. Alternatively, project the questions on an overhead screen.
5. If you are not using cards, ask learners to write their answers on a piece of paper or on their lecture handout.
6. Encourage sharing. They may start by talking with someone sitting beside them or talking with those in their group if they are sitting at tables, followed by a few individuals speaking to the larger group.

7. Have students turn in their cards if you wish to collect them. You may wish to have them keep their responses, particularly if the questions address follow-up actions or commitments to future behavior.

Online Application

Prepare your document and post it on the online course. Have students submit their answers in the online module.

Key References and Resources

3-2-1. (n.d.). Retrieved from www.theteachertoolkit.com/index.php/tool/3-2-1

3-2-1. (2016). Retrieved from www.facinghistory.org/resource-library/teaching-strategies/3-2-1

Kagan, S., & Kagan, M. (2009a). *Kagan cooperative learning.* San Clemente, CA: Author.

Riche, R. (2015). *3 2 1 performance feedback method.* Retrieved from www.linkedin.com/pulse/3-2-1-performance-feedback-method-richard-riche

CLOSING PAUSE 42

SUCCESS STORIES

Most closing pauses occur during the last five minutes of the learning session. This closing pause is a little unusual as it occurs after the learning session is completed. It works well after a one-day workshop or seminar. It can also occur at the end of the course. Each participant in the class, workshop, or seminar tells a success story in which they describe something that worked for them following the learning activity. Participants are each assigned a due date for their stories, and the teacher usually posts one story each week from a participant for the rest of the class. Tell the people in the class that they can expect to receive as many weeks of success stories as there are class participants. Expectations are high as everyone looks forward to hearing ideas of how the learning from the class has affected the others in the group.

Settings for Use

- ☑ Small classroom lecture
- ☑ Clinical or laboratory presentation
- ☐ One-on-one session
- ☑ Conference presentation/in-service education
- ☐ Keynote/large-group presentation
- ☑ Course/unit
- ☐ Online learning module

Characteristics

- ☑ Affirming/positive
- ☐ Physical/movement
- ☐ Activates prior knowledge/experience
- ☐ Focuses/refocuses
- ☑ Creates community
- ☐ Generates curiosity
- ☐ Metacognitive
- ☑ Reviews
- ☑ Celebrates
- ☑ Commits to action
- ☐ Provides a bookend

Procedure

1. Make a list of all class participants in random order.
2. Assign each a due date—one each week for as many weeks as the number of participants.
3. Give a copy of the list of participants with their due dates to everyone.
4. Ask participants to write their success story based on the class content. They can write anything they would like to share with the rest of the group about how something they learned in class has worked for them.
5. Request all participants e-mail you their success stories by their specific due date.

6. Send one success story a week by e-mail to all class participants.
7. Add your own comments, if you would like to, and any additional resources.

Additional Suggestions

- Class participants could be assigned their due date, or they could be allowed to choose a date. You may provide some examples of success stories before they are asked to write their own.
- Instead of asking for successes, the instructor might ask for other types of learnings, such as baby steps, which might be less threatening than the concept of success.
- If participants can use their new content right away, they are more likely to strengthen new behaviors and changed attitudes. Ask participants to share with you how they have used the learning from the course and what results have they received. These simple success stories will inspire the writer and the receivers. In addition, knowing that a success story is due in a few weeks will be a tremendous motivator for participants to look for ways to use new learning and to look for results.

References and Resources

Angelo, T. A., & Cross, K. P. (1993). *Classroom assessment techniques: A handbook for college teachers* (2nd ed.). San Francisco, CA: Jossey-Bass.

Halsey, V. (2011). *Brilliance by design: Creating learning experiences that connect, inspire, and engage*. San Francisco, CA: Berrett-Koehler.

CLOSING PAUSE 43

K-W-L CLOSURE

The K-W-L Closure is the closing pause to be used if the K-W-L Start (SP 1) was used as the starting pause for the class. In this activity, learners answer the third question on the K-W-L chart that they started at the beginning of the learning session with the K-W-L Start. The final question is, What have you learned?

Settings for Use

- ☑ Small classroom lecture
- ☑ Clinical or laboratory presentation
- ☐ One-on-one session
- ☐ Conference presentation/ in-service education
- ☐ Keynote/large-group presentation
- ☐ Course/unit
- ☐ Online learning module

Characteristics

- ☐ Affirming/positive
- ☐ Physical/movement
- ☑ Activates prior knowledge/ experience
- ☑ Focuses/refocuses
- ☐ Creates community
- ☐ Generates curiosity
- ☐ Metacognitive
- ☑ Reviews
- ☑ Celebrates
- ☐ Commits to action
- ☑ Provides a bookend

Procedure

1. Prepare charts for each student that have four columns and space to write in the columns.
2. Alternatively, project the chart on an overhead screen and ask students to create their own chart in their notebooks or laptops, or provide a template using spreadsheet software for laptops.
3. Use the following column headings: Topic, K: What You Knew, W: What You Wanted to Know, and L: What You Have Learned (see example in Table C.1).
4. At the end of the session, have students write the topic in the first column, and then give them some time to complete the rest of the table.
5. Assuming that the students have completed the first three columns before the learning session began, you will want to allow some time at the end of the class period for students to summarize the final column—what they have learned.

6. It may be helpful to collect the charts to determine if your objectives met those of the students, what prior knowledge and experiences they brought to the session, and what they felt they had learned from the session.

TABLE C.1
K-W-L Chart

Topic	K: What You Knew	W: What You Wanted to Know	L: What You Learned

Additional Suggestions

- This closure has the particular advantage of helping students reflect on different ways to connect to prior experiences, define personal objectives regarding desired learning, and summarize what was learned.

Key Reference and Resources

Barkley, E. F., & Major, C. H. (2015). *Learning assessment techniques: A handbook for college faculty*. San Francisco, CA: Wiley.

Fletcher, J., Najarro, A., & Yelland, H. (2015). *Fostering habits of mind in today's students*. Sterling, VA: Stylus.

Grundy, L. (2015). *9 high-yield instructional strategies by Robert J. Marzano*. Retrieved from www.3plearning.com/9-high-yield-strategies-robert-j-marzano

Halsey, V. (2011). *Brilliance by design: Creating learning experiences that connect, inspire, and engage*. San Francisco, CA: Berrett-Koehler.

National Education Association. (2017). *K-W-L (know, want to know, learned)*. Retrieved from www.nea.org/tools/k-w-l-know-want-to-know-learned.html

Ogle, D. M. (1986). K-W-L: A teaching model that develops active reading of expository text. *Reading Teacher, 39*, 564–570.

CLOSING PAUSE 44

COMPLETE A SENTENCE

This extremely short and easy way to pause at the end of the learning session asks for a simple answer to one question. Learners are asked to complete a sentence such as, Today I learned . . .

Settings for Use

- ☑ Small classroom lecture
- ☑ Clinical or laboratory presentation
- ☑ One-on-one session
- ☑ Conference presentation/ in-service education
- ☑ Keynote/large-group presentation
- ☐ Course/unit
- ☐ Online learning module

Characteristics

- ☐ Affirming/positive
- ☑ Physical/movement
- ☐ Activates prior knowledge/ experience
- ☐ Focuses/refocuses
- ☑ Creates community
- ☐ Generates curiosity
- ☑ Metacognitive
- ☑ Reviews
- ☑ Celebrates
- ☑ Commits to action
- ☑ Provides a bookend

Procedure

1. As always, be sure to stop delivering content before the session has concluded.
2. Decide what sentence you would like students to complete. It could be a content-related sentence, but usually it is more effective if it does not have just one right answer. In other words, individuals would provide a personal response to the question such as, What was most important to them? or What did they learn? or What was new to them? or What was surprising to them?
3. Decide how you want them to answer—by writing the answer, telling it to someone sitting next to them, posting it on a sticky note, putting it on a card, and so on.
4. Decide if you want students to keep their answer or turn it in.
5. Prepare three-inch-by-five-inch cards or half sheets of paper or hand out sticky notes.
6. Give instructions to the students.

7. This one of the quickest closing pauses. Often it can be accomplished in just a couple of minutes, but it is still important to allow adequate time.
8. Ask students to find someone to share their answers with. Often the Stand Up, Hand Up, Pair Up (MP 36) is a great way to avoid overusing the Think-Pair-Share (MP 25) method.
9. Allow a brief large-group discussion on a few of the individual responses.
10. Collect responses.

Additional Suggestions

- This is an easy activity to add to a lecture at the last minute if you forget to plan ahead of time for a closing pause. It can lead to a rich discussion and a powerful final few minutes of class—a nice complement to Complete a Sentence (SP 4).
- Following are some more ideas for sentences to complete:
  - I learned . . .
  - I want to learn . . .
  - I was surprised to learn . . .
  - I thought I already knew . . .
  - I would like to know more about . . .
  - I am glad I learned . . .
  - The thing I value most about what I learned today is . . .
  - The one thing I hope I never forget is . . .

Online Adaptation

This pause is concise and simple for the online module. You could use a template for each module and include the starting and closing pauses in the template and insert it into the closing pause.

CLOSING PAUSE 45

STICKY NOTE CLOSURE

This pause provides an opportunity for the instructor to receive feedback from the learners at the end of the learning session. The instructor asks the students to write a response to a question about the class on a sticky note. Questions about the lecture or learning might be selected from the following:

- What do you most want to remember from our class today?
- What are the three most important concepts from class?
- Why are you glad you were here today?
- How will this course make you a more successful professional?
- What one action will you take as a result of class today?

Students bring their sticky notes to the front of the room, where the instructor can quickly organize the responses and report the general trend of the answers to the group. An advantage of this pause is that the instructor receives input that may be helpful to determine what the students have valued about their learning and what they have felt confident about.

Settings for Use

- ☑ Small classroom lecture
- ☑ Clinical or laboratory presentation
- ☐ One-on-one session
- ☑ Conference presentation/in-service education
- ☐ Keynote/large-group presentation
- ☐ Course/unit
- ☐ Online learning module

Characteristics

- ☑ Affirming/positive
- ☑ Physical/movement
- ☐ Activates prior knowledge/experience
- ☐ Focuses/refocuses
- ☐ Creates community
- ☐ Generates curiosity
- ☐ Metacognitive
- ☑ Reviews
- ☑ Celebrates
- ☑ Commits to action
- ☑ Provides a bookend

Procedure

1. Decide which question you wish to have answered at the end of the session.
2. Provide sticky notepads (or just one sticky note) for each student.

3. Project the question on an overhead screen, or clearly state it, and allow students time to think of their response and write it on their sticky notes.
4. Ask students to bring their sticky notes to the front of the room and place them on the whiteboard or easel, where you can quickly skim over them, perhaps move them into categories, before reporting what you see to the group.
5. You might summarize for the group what you have found. You might also suggest that the students walk by the front of the room on their way out and notice what the others have written. Some instructors will take a photo to organize their next lecture based on what the students have reported from the present lecture.

Additional Suggestions

- A particularly good technique to use with this is Sticky Note Start (SP 8). When using sticky notes for the starting and closing pauses, be sure to take slightly different approaches. For example, if you summarized the responses at the beginning of class, then you might want to allow students to organize the responses at the end of class.
- Consider using an app that will let you digitalize sticky notes (see Burns, 2012, in Key References and Resources at the end of this pause).

Online Adaptation

You can paste a picture of a sticky note in the closing pauses section of the online module. Using a sticky notes app will also provide opportunities for pauses.

Key References and Resources

Barkley, E. F., Major, C. H., & Cross, P. K. (2014). *Collaborative learning techniques: A handbook for college faculty.* San Francisco, CA: Jossey-Bass.

Burns, M. (2012). *Class tech tips.* Retrieved from classtechtips.com/2012/08/23/sticky-notes-for-a-tech-friendly-classroom

Johnson, B. (2012). *Tools for teaching: The amazing sticky note.* Retrieved from www.edutopia.org/blog/sticky-note-teaching-tool-ben-johnson

Kagan, S., & Kagan, M. (2009a). *Kagan cooperative learning.* San Clemente, CA: Author.

CLOSING PAUSE 46

COMMITMENT TO ACTION

This pause builds on Prochaska's (Prochaska & DiClemente, 1984) work on commitment to change. It provides an excellent way to close a lecture when a specific application is required. Participants complete a statement on a three-inch-by-five-inch card, which might include three parts: specific context (when the practice can occur), target action, and the frequency of behavior (when applicable). The cards are then taken by the participant to use in a way that reinforces the desired action. This pause capitalizes on the power of psychology to increase the likelihood of transfer of new information to the practice setting. Writing down what they will do increases the chances that the participants will actually do the new behavior.

Settings for Use

- ☑ Small classroom lecture
- ☑ Clinical or laboratory presentation
- ☑ One-on-one session
- ☑ Conference presentation/in-service education
- ☑ Keynote/large-group presentation
- ☑ Course/unit
- ☑ Online learning module

Characteristics:

- ☐ Affirming/positive
- ☐ Physical/movement
- ☐ Activates prior knowledge/experience
- ☐ Focuses/refocuses
- ☐ Creates community
- ☐ Generates curiosity
- ☐ Metacognitive
- ☑ Reviews
- ☐ Celebrates
- ☑ Commits to action
- ☐ Provides a bookend

Procedure

1. Prepare the cards with the three components clearly indicated: specific context, target action, and frequency of the action.
2. Allow time at the end of the lecture (usually three to four minutes) for participants to complete the cards. Provide an example of a completed card if this is a new concept to your audience.
3. Ask participants to share their statements with each other, first in small groups, then in the larger group.
4. Instruct participants to take their cards with them and place them in a readily visible location, where they will be reminded of their new intended behavior.

Additional Suggestions

- This closure technique works particularly well with medical students. The following examples illustrate some Commitment to Action statements in these settings:
  - After a lecture on the care of stroke patients: "I will take a complete history about anticoagulation, including bleeding and bruising, in the evaluation of the next patient I admit to the acute stroke care unit."
  - After a lecture on stress management: "I will identify a person with signs of stress and use the technique described to intervene within the next two weeks."
  - After a simulation experience with overdosing a patient: "I will always think about possible factors that might require a smaller than usual dose of potentially life-threatening medications for a patient."
  - After a lecture on a particular medication: "Every time I prescribe this medication I will review the black box warning to be aware of its potential side effects."

Online Adaptation

Cards to be completed by online students are easily placed in the closing pause section of a course module. Students can submit their completed cards, and instructors can post these for all to see. Another option would be to create a word cloud from the submitted closure (see Word Cloud Closure, CP 47).

Key References and Resources

Prochaska, J. O., & DiClemente, C. C. (1984). *The transtheoretical approach: Crossing traditional boundaries of therapy*. Homewood, IL: Dow Jones-Irwin.

WORD CLOUD CLOSURE

In this pause, students respond to a question about the content they have just learned and then see those responses projected in an artistic design. Students either text their responses using their cellular phones or e-mail their responses using their computers. The responses are collected and placed into an Internet program that generates a word cloud (Figure C.2). The clouds give greater prominence to words that appear more frequently in the source text. The word cloud can be projected for immediate impact, posted to the online course, or printed on the course syllabus.

Settings for Use

- ☑ Small classroom lecture
- ☐ Clinical or laboratory presentation
- ☐ One-on-one session
- ☑ Conference presentation/in-service education
- ☑ Keynote/large-group presentation
- ☑ Course/unit
- ☐ Online learning module

Characteristics

- ☐ Affirming/positive
- ☐ Physical/movement
- ☐ Activates prior knowledge/experience
- ☐ Focuses/refocuses
- ☑ Creates community
- ☐ Generates curiosity
- ☐ Metacognitive
- ☑ Reviews
- ☑ Celebrates
- ☐ Commits to action
- ☑ Provides a bookend

Figure C.2. Sample word cloud.

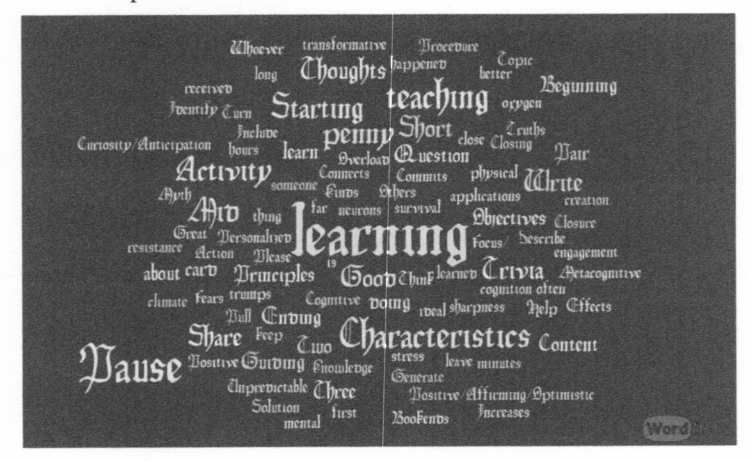

Procedure

1. Decide what you want students to address. For example, say, "In a few words, describe the most important thing you learned in our session today."
2. At the end of the learning session, provide instructions on how you want students to respond (i.e., what platform; Poll Everywhere, Kahoot!, Poll Daddy, or other platform that you have chosen and set up in advance). Responses will start streaming on the screen.
3. After responses have been received, use the polling system's word cloud generator or go to a word cloud website, such as Wordle, paste your content, and generate your word cloud.
4. Allow students to talk about their impressions and what they see in the art.

Additional Suggestions

- This pause works particularly well for the end of a course or the end of a conference or large gathering. For example, at the end of a conference I attended in Atlanta, Georgia, the presidential address concluded with a word cloud. Participants were asked to text their ideas about how faculty in higher education could work better together and collaborate to improve teaching in their institutions of higher learning. The group of about 600 began seeing their texts appearing on the screen.

Key References and Resources

Barkley, E. F., & Major, C. H. (2015). *Learning assessment techniques: A handbook for college faculty*. San Francisco, CA: Wiley.

Barkley, E. F., Major, C. H., & Cross, P. K. (2014). *Collaborative learning techniques: A handbook for college faculty*. San Francisco, CA: Jossey-Bass.

Feinberg, J. (2014). Wordle. Retrieved from www.wordle.net

Flisti (n.d.). Retrieved from flisti.com

Kahoot! (2013). Retrieved from kahoot.com

MicroPoll. (2017). Retrieved from www.micropoll.com

Millis, B. J. (2010). *Cooperative learning in higher education: Across the disciplines, across the academy*. Sterling, VA: Stylus.

Polldaddy. (n.d.). Retrieved from polldaddy.com

Poll Everywhere. (2007). Retrieved from https://www.polleverywhere.com

CLOSING PAUSE 48

QUIZ TIME CLOSURE

Quiz Time helps students assess their own level of knowledge about a topic after the lecture. This closing ungraded quiz might be a repeat of a quiz given earlier in the session, a different version of the quiz, or an entirely new quiz. Students find it gratifying to check how well they are mastering concepts, and faculty members find it helpful to receive specific feedback on how well students are learning.

Settings for Use

- ☑ Small classroom lecture
- ☑ Clinical or laboratory presentation
- ☐ One-on-one session
- ☑ Conference presentation/in-service education
- ☐ Keynote/large-group presentation
- ☐ Course/unit
- ☑ Online learning module

Characteristics

- ☐ Affirming/positive
- ☐ Physical/movement
- ☐ Activates prior knowledge/experience
- ☐ Focuses/refocuses
- ☑ Creates community
- ☐ Generates curiosity
- ☐ Metacognitive
- ☑ Reviews
- ☑ Celebrates
- ☐ Commits to action
- ☑ Provides a bookend

Procedure

1. Create a 5- to 10-question quiz centered on the main points you want the students to learn from the lecture. The questions can be fill-in-the-blank, multiple choice, or short answer. This quiz could be an exact duplicate of a quiz you used at the beginning of the lecture, a similar quiz, or a new quiz covering different issues (see the Quiz Time pauses, SP 10 and SP 1).
2. You can use a paper-and-pencil quiz, an audience response system quiz, or a quiz where students respond with a show of hands or by holding up color cards or letter cards.
3. Tell students that a nongraded quiz related to that day's topic will be given at the end of the lecture.
4. Provide opportunities for students to celebrate the gains they made in their responses to the quizzes from the beginning of class to the end of class.

5. It is often a good idea to add some questions that go beyond review of content such as, What do you value from this content? or How will you be more successful as a professional in your career as a result of learning this material?

Additional Suggestions

- Various forms of quizzing can be used for this opening pause. A team quiz in which students take the quiz in teams of two or three at the end of the lecture can be a good alternative to the individual quiz.
- Occasionally when you use a quiz for a closure activity, you may use a quiz as a starting pause as well (see the Quiz Time Start pauses SP 10 and SP 11).
- If you don't have a learning management system you are using in a face-to-face course, you might consider some options for quizzing, like Quia.com or Coursecanary.com. Of course, audience response systems allow immediate results. See Quiz Time Start—Audience Response System (SP 10).

Online Adaptation

The online course is well suited to use quizzes as ungraded activities to focus students at the beginning of learning, to refocus them midway through the module, or to wrap up the topic at the end. Learning management systems allow instructors to differentiate between quizzes that contribute to the grade and quizzes for formative assessment.

Key References and Resources

Angelo, T. A., & Cross, K. P. (1993). *Classroom assessment techniques: A handbook for college teachers* (2nd ed.). San Francisco, CA: Jossey-Bass.

Barkley, E. F., & Major, C. H. (2015). *Learning assessment techniques: A handbook for college faculty*. San Francisco, CA: Wiley.

Course canary. (2015). Retrieved from coursecanary.com

Hall, M. (2012, September 21). Teaching tips: Classroom assessment [Web log post]. Retrieved from ii.library.jhu.edu/tag/non-graded-assessment

Quia. (2017). Retrieved from www.quia.com

CLOSING PAUSE 49

ONE WORD AT THE DOOR

This is a good closure activity when there is limited end-of-class time. The instructor asks students to share one word or phrase they learned that day. This short closing pause allows teachers to build personal relationships, however brief, with students as well as to receive some quick feedback on what stands out in the students' mind.

Settings for Use

☑ Small classroom lecture
☑ Clinical or laboratory presentation
☑ One-on-one session
☑ Conference presentation/in-service education
☐ Keynote/large-group presentation
☐ Course/unit
☐ Online learning module

Characteristics

☑ Affirming/positive
☐ Physical/movement
☐ Activates prior knowledge/experience
☐ Focuses/refocuses
☐ Creates community
☐ Generates curiosity
☐ Metacognitive
☑ Reviews
☑ Celebrates
☐ Commits to action
☐ Provides a bookend

Procedure

1. At the end of the learning session, tell the students you will be standing at the door as they leave.
2. Ask students to tell you one word or concept learned from class as they leave.
3. Thank each student.
4. Although the feedback you receive may be fairly minimal, it can be helpful to see if the one most important objective you had for the session comes up the majority of time from the students as they pass by. If that objective does not come up frequently, this information can be helpful in planning the next learning session.

Additional Suggestions

- This activity works particularly well with a smaller class; obviously it could be difficult with a larger group. This activity can also work well with forms of learning other than the traditional class period, such as a laboratory session or a small-group orientation session. Saying individual good-byes is also a good way to build a positive classroom culture that contributes to enhanced learning environments.

- Some instructors like to provide a tangible thank-you to the students as they leave. A chocolate candy or other small item can accomplish a great deal toward maintaining that positive environment that enhances learning.
- Todd Finley (2015) suggests giving students cards to leave with the instructor that contain one of the following options:
  - Stop (I'm totally confused).
  - Go (I'm ready to move on).
  - Proceed with caution (I could use some clarification on . . .).

Key References and Resources

Angelo, T. A., & Cross, K. P. (1993). *Classroom assessment techniques: A handbook for college teachers* (2nd ed.). San Francisco, CA: Jossey-Bass.

Finley, T. (2015). *22 powerful closure activities*. Retrieved from www.edutopia.org/blog/22-powerful-closure-activities-todd-finley

CLOSING PAUSE 50

HOT POTATO

This popular child's game can be adapted to work well for any age group. You can use this closure pause following a single class session (as a review) or following a quarter's, semester's, or year's work (as a review for a comprehensive exam). In this activity students form a circle and toss an object (may be a potato, but a soft ball may be preferable) from student to student. The instructor gives the students a question to answer. It may be a concept question with a particular answer, or it may be a question with many right answers such as, What is one reason you are glad you were in class today? or How can the ideas in this course make you a more effective professional? The instructor plays music while the hot potato is tossed or handed from person to person, and when the music stops, whoever is holding the hot potato gives an answer to the question. When the music starts again, the object is again tossed from person to person until the music stops and another person answers the question. This activity is a highly successful way of motivating students to listen for important information during class and is also useful in reviewing for upcoming exams.

Settings for Use

- ☑ Small classroom lecture
- ☑ Clinical or laboratory presentation
- ☐ One-on-one session
- ☑ Conference presentation/in-service education
- ☐ Keynote/large-group presentation
- ☑ Course/unit
- ☐ Online learning module

Characteristics

- ☑ Affirming/positive
- ☑ Physical/movement
- ☐ Activates prior knowledge/experience
- ☑ Focuses/refocuses
- ☑ Creates community
- ☐ Generates curiosity
- ☐ Metacognitive
- ☐ Reviews
- ☐ Celebrates
- ☐ Commits to action
- ☐ Provides a bookend

Procedure

1. Come prepared with a soft ball (a hacky sack or small beach ball would work well) to toss around. You probably don't want a real potato, which might cause injuries if someone misses catching it.

2. Inform students at the beginning of class that an activity near the end of class will involve recall of information. This usually encourages students to pay extra attention during class.
3. Explain the activity to students. Tell them they are going to play a game of hot potato, and when the music stops, whoever is holding the potato will have the opportunity to respond to the question.
4. Provide the question you want students to be ready to answer and give them a little time to think about their answers.
5. Let them toss the ball or object around until the music stops or a buzzer goes off.
6. Let the individual holding the object respond to the question.
7. Continue in the time remaining.
8. Finish with applause for all the good answers.

Additional Suggestions

I have found it very effective to use a hot potato simulator. These pretend potatoes have a built-in timer, so after answering the question, the person holding it can turn the timer to zero and start passing the potato again. This is less complicated than using music that has to be turned on and off and is less arbitrary.

Key References and Resources

Bolen, J. (n.d.). *Hot potato: An ESL speaking game for kids*. Retrieved from eslspeaking.org/hot-potato-esl-speaking-game-for-kids

Lou, A. (n.d.). *ESL games in the classroom: Hot Potato*. Retrieved from www.mychiangmaievery thing.com/2014/07/esl-games-in-classroom-hot-potato.html

CLOSING PAUSE 51

THREE CLAPS

This short closure technique has the advantage of giving the instructor feedback on what the group has learned. It is an excellent alternative to the common way of closing a lecture by asking the audience for questions. Instead, the instructor prepares questions on content and attitude, resulting in a mix of questions that will ensure that students understand key concepts. The instructor also prepares questions that have no right response but elicit answers that fit a student's personal situation such as, What will your personal next step be after attending this lecture? When someone answers one of the instructor's questions, the instructor responds and then leads the class in clapping three times before proceeding to the next question.

Settings for Use

- ☑ Small classroom lecture
- ☑ Clinical or laboratory presentation
- ☐ One-on-one session
- ☑ Conference presentation/ in-service education
- ☐ Keynote/large-group presentation
- ☐ Course/unit
- ☐ Online learning module

Characteristics

- ☑ Affirming/positive
- ☐ Physical/movement
- ☐ Activates prior knowledge/ experience
- ☑ Focuses/refocuses
- ☑ Creates community
- ☐ Generates curiosity
- ☐ Metacognitive
- ☑ Reviews
- ☑ Celebrates
- ☐ Commits to action
- ☐ Provides a bookend

Procedure

1. Prepare a set of questions to use at the end of the learning session.
2. When you are ready, tell the class that you will let them know when they should clap their hands three times.
3. Ask each question one at a time and allow appropriate wait time (an ideal wait time is a minimum of two to five seconds) before calling on someone to answer.
4. Respond to the answer, perhaps with a clarifying comment, perhaps with an invitation for others in the group to add to the response. When you are satisfied with the responses, ask the group to join you in thanking the discussants by giving three claps.

5. Proceed with the second question and continue with the procedure.
6. You may wish to ask the entire group to applaud at the end, thanking everyone for their participation and their help in closing the learning session.

Additional Suggestions

I have sometimes used noisemaker props that can be purchased at online stores or party supply stores to add to the celebratory sense of appreciation and applause.

Key References and Resources

Rhode Island Novelty Hand Clappers. Available from http://www.rinovelty.com/ProductDetail/slhancl_3-hand-clapper--------------------2443

CLOSING PAUSE 52

ROUND CIRCLE

This pause is best used when learners are in small groups sitting at round tables. A sheet of paper containing a question is circulated around the table, and learners add their responses to the list. Small-group discussions are followed by a large-group discussion. Questions could include topical review questions or attitudinal questions. Examples of attitudinal questions are, What did you think was the most important idea from today's session? What do you most want to remember from the lecture today? What will you plan to do as a result of your being here today? Why are you glad you were here today? and How will today's class contribute to your professional success? A large-group discussion follows the small-group discussion.

Settings for Use

- ☑ Small classroom lecture
- ☑ Clinical or laboratory presentation
- ☐ One-on-one session
- ☐ Conference presentation/in-service education
- ☐ Keynote/large-group presentation
- ☐ Course/unit
- ☐ Online learning module

Characteristics

- ☐ Affirming/positive
- ☐ Physical/movement
- ☐ Activates prior knowledge/experience
- ☑ Focuses/refocuses
- ☑ Creates community
- ☐ Generates curiosity
- ☐ Metacognitive
- ☑ Reviews
- ☑ Celebrates
- ☐ Commits to action
- ☐ Provides a bookend

Procedure

1. Decide what question you would like the group to address at the end of the learning session. If you are using one question to circle the entire table, make it one that can be answered quickly. Don't forget to have a sponge activity for the rest of the group while they are waiting.
2. Prepare answer sheets, one for each learner, with the question at the top of the sheet. Make sure that the sheets are large enough for each of the respondents to write their response to the question as the sheets circle the table.
3. Instruct the learners to each write their response to the question and then pass it to the person on their right.

4. Allow the groups at their tables to talk together about their responses to the question.
5. Follow the small-group discussions with a large-group discussion before collecting the sheets.

Additional Suggestions

- A nice variation is to use a different question for each learner at the table.
- Another variation (this takes more time, so be careful about using it) is to start one sheet at each table with one question on it and have each learner at the table take turns answering the question, then pass the sheet around the circle a second time, allowing each person to read what the others have written and add additional comments. I rarely take this approach, as people can get bored waiting for their turn with the sheet. Be sure to have a sponge activity planned, so that individuals have something to occupy their time while waiting for their turn.
- This closing pause activity is similar to the Round Robin (MP 38).

Key References and Resources

Barkley, E. F., & Major, C. H. (2015). *Learning assessment techniques: A handbook for college faculty*. San Francisco, CA: Wiley.

Barkley, E. F., Major, C. H., & Cross, P. K. (2014). *Collaborative learning techniques: A handbook for college faculty*. San Francisco, CA: Jossey-Bass.

CLOSING PAUSE 53

ROTATING CIRCLES

This activity takes a little longer than many of the closing pauses, often as much as 10 to 12 minutes. First, each student develops a question about the content of the lesson. Second, the students form two circles, one inside the other, and pair up, answering each other's questions. When the signal is given, one of the circles rotates, and the process repeats itself. The activity allows students to interact with each other while reviewing content. Ideally, the instructor is able to wrap up with a large-group discussion before class concludes.

Settings for Use

- ☑ Small classroom lecture
- ☑ Clinical or laboratory presentation
- ☐ One-on-one session
- ☑ Conference presentation/in-service education
- ☐ Keynote/large-group presentation
- ☑ Course/unit
- ☐ Online learning module

Characteristics

- ☑ Affirming/positive
- ☑ Physical/movement
- ☐ Activates prior knowledge/experience
- ☐ Focuses/refocuses
- ☑ Creates community
- ☐ Generates curiosity
- ☐ Metacognitive
- ☑ Reviews
- ☑ Celebrates
- ☐ Commits to action
- ☑ Provides a bookend

Procedure

1. Explain the entire procedure thoroughly to the students before beginning the process.
2. Ask students to write one question about the class topic that has just concluded. Suggest that they try to write a question at a high level of the cognitive domain—not simply one requiring recall or basic understanding but moving into analysis, reasoning, or evaluation.
3. Assign each student number one or number two.
4. Place all the number one students in an outside circle and all the number twos in an inside circle so that each individual has a partner in the opposing circle.
5. Tell them that when you say "Go," they will have two minutes to ask each other their questions and try to answer each other's questions.

After the two minutes are up, the inside circle moves three people to the right and repeats the process.

6. When there are three minutes left in the class period, ask students to return to their seats and write what they learned about their question based on the answers they received from the other students.
7. During the final minute, ask the group to share their observations about the process.
8. Collect the questions and the student descriptions of what they learned.

Additional Suggestions

- This is an activity that works particularly well with a smaller class and a room with a large place for concentric circles. It doesn't lend itself to a large auditorium with fixed seating. The concept could be adapted to a fixed seating setting with a think-pair-share approach.
- Some instructors report using a few of the questions on their final exam.

CLOSING PAUSE 54

TIC-TAC-KNOW

This is an enjoyable pause that uses a commercial game called *Toss Across* (found in toy stores or online). The gameboard, based on tic-tac-toe, has nine rotating tiles. Each has an X on one side and an O on the other side, and tiles are flipped by tossing a beanbag. It provides a great review for students as well as good feedback on students' familiarity with the topics covered. The class is divided into two teams, an X and an O team. Each team takes turns tossing a beanbag at the game board. If a block is hit, that team gets an opportunity to answer a question. If the question is answered correctly, the team turns the hit block to either an X or an O. Once three Xs or Os in a row is achieved, that team is the winner.

Settings for Use

- ☑ Small classroom lecture
- ☑ Clinical or laboratory presentation
- ☐ One-on-one session
- ☐ Conference presentation/in-service education
- ☐ Keynote/large-group presentation
- ☐ Course/unit
- ☐ Online learning module

Characteristics

- ☐ Affirming/positive
- ☑ Physical/movement
- ☐ Activates prior knowledge/experience
- ☐ Focuses/refocuses
- ☐ Creates community
- ☐ Generates curiosity
- ☐ Metacognitive
- ☑ Reviews
- ☑ Celebrates
- ☐ Commits to action
- ☐ Provides a bookend

Procedure

1. Develop the questions you will use for this closing pause.
2. Place the nine-tiled game board where everyone can see it from the beginning of the class; this piques curiosity and tends to help students stay focused as they anticipate some sort of upcoming activity that will ask for their responses.
3. When you are ready for your closing pause, explain to the students how the game works and divide them into two teams.
4. Decide which team will be X, which will be O, and which gets to go first.
5. The first team will select one member to toss a beanbag at the game board. The objective is to hit one of the tiles. If the tile is hit, the

teacher asks the team a question. The group members can consult with each other before giving an answer.
6. If the answer is correct, the team gets to turn the tile to an X or an O.
7. The second team repeats the throw-question-turn sequence.
8. The game is over when three tiles in a row match or when the class exhausts all of the questions.
9. Allow the teams to congratulate themselves and the opposing team.
10. Give prizes, if desired. It is not necessary, as the fun of playing the game is reward enough.

Additional Suggestions

- You can modify the rules. For example, you can start by giving the team a question. If team members answer correctly, they get to throw the beanbag, but tiles aren't claimed by the team. Whatever happens with the throw stays that way. This can lead to a lot of fun when the X team answers correctly but ends up giving its tile to the opposite team because the throw resulted in an O, not an X. In this case Team X wouldn't get to change the tile but rather would end up with whatever the throw turned up.
- If you don't have access to the game, you can simply project a tic-tac-toe diagram on an overhead screen or draw one on a white board. When a team answers a question correctly, it chooses where to place the X or O.

Key References and Resources

Cardinal Toss Across Game. Available from www.amazon.com/Cardinal-Industries-6030002-Toss-Across/dp/B00CEZ1I46/ref=sr_1_1?ie=UTF8&qid=1486003526&sr=8-1&keywords=toss+across

CLOSING PAUSE 55

ROUND THE CIRCLE LEARNINGS

This can be an interesting small-group summary of what participants value from the session. It works best where classroom seating is flexible or where participants are already seated at tables in groups of not more than four or five. It combines renewing a sense of friendship and learning each other's names as well as giving each individual in the room an opportunity to answer one important question from the instructor about the learning session. Examples might be, What do you feel is the most important thing that you learned from this session today? or If you could only remember one thing from our class, what would it be? or What one thing will you review after you leave class today, so that you are sure you will not forget it? The members of the groups are instructed to go around their circles, give their names, and answer the question. After each person does this, they will then repeat how each person in their circle before them (by name) answered the question. For example, Person 3 will say, "My name is ______ and my answer to the question is ______. Before me, Carol answered the question like this ______, and Greg answered the question with this ________." The first person in each group who starts the activity obviously has the easiest challenge, having only to answer the question for themselves, whereas the last individual has the challenge of remembering each name and each lesson.

Settings for Use

- ☑ Small classroom lecture
- ☑ Clinical or laboratory presentation
- ☐ One-on-one session
- ☐ Conference presentation/in-service education
- ☐ Keynote/large-group presentation
- ☐ Course/unit
- ☐ Online learning module

Characteristics

- ☑ Affirming/positive
- ☐ Physical/movement
- ☐ Activates prior knowledge/experience
- ☐ Focuses/refocuses
- ☑ Creates community
- ☐ Generates curiosity
- ☐ Metacognitive
- ☐ Reviews
- ☐ Celebrates
- ☐ Commits to action
- ☐ Provides a bookend

Procedure

1. Decide ahead of time what your big question will be.
2. When it is time for your closure, tell the class to form small groups of three to five individuals and make a circle.
3. Sometimes it is interesting to determine for them who will be the person to start in each group (the person with the shortest or longest hair, the person with the brightest or dullest clothes, the person with the smallest or largest shoes, etc.).
4. Explain the process. They are to say something like, "Hi, my name is _______ and my answer to the question is ___________. The person before me was Sally and her answer was _______, and the person before her was James and his answer was ________."
5. They keep going until the last person around the circle has answered.
6. Finish up with applause from the groups for making it all the way around their circles.

Additional Suggestions

- Sometimes you can pull a surprise final round of this activity by asking the first person in the group, who had they easiest job because he or she had no one to remember, to see if he or she can go the full circle and review everyone's answers. If you do this, you will want to really celebrate those first people in each group.

Key References and Resources

Barkley, E. F., Major, C. H., & Cross, P. K. (2014). *Collaborative learning techniques: A handbook for college faculty*. San Francisco, CA: Jossey-Bass.

CLOSING PAUSE 56

SHUT THE BOX

This builds on the game with the same title[1], available for purchase from toy stores and online. To start the game, students are randomly selected to come to the front of the room and roll a pair of dice. They then select a question from the day's lecture from a box. After reading it aloud, they provide an answer. If the answer is correct, the students then can pull down tiles equaling the total number on the dice they rolled. The box is shut when all of the tiles are pulled down. Questions should reflect not only lecture content but also personal valuing; for example, What will you personally do with what you have learned today?

Settings for Use

- ☑ Small classroom lecture
- ☑ Clinical or laboratory presentation
- ☐ One-on-one session
- ☑ Conference presentation/in-service education
- ☐ Keynote/large-group presentation
- ☐ Course/unit
- ☑ Online learning module

Characteristics

- ☐ Affirming/positive
- ☑ Physical/movement
- ☐ Activates prior knowledge/experience
- ☐ Focuses/refocuses
- ☑ Creates community
- ☐ Generates curiosity
- ☐ Metacognitive
- ☑ Reviews
- ☑ Celebrates
- ☐ Commits to action
- ☐ Provides a bookend

Procedure

1. Purchase or make your own Shut the Box game.
2. Prepare four to eight questions covering the content of the learning session as well as questions dealing with application and personal use of the information.
3. Write the questions on small pieces of folded paper and place them in the box, along with the dice.
4. Save five to seven minutes at the end of the learning session for the closure activity.
5. Select a student through some form of random means.

6. The student will roll the die (or dice), according to the rules that accompany the game.
7. Students read aloud the question and provide an answer. If the group agrees with the answer, the student then pulls down the number tiles to equal the number rolled.
8. After all the number tiles are pulled down, the box is shut.

Additional Suggestions

- Instead of selecting individual students to come forward to roll the dice and answer the questions, divide the larger group into teams and allow them to select the person who will answer the question.
- Teams could also be allowed to add to or correct the answer provided by their selected team member.
- If you do not have a Shut the Box game, you can use any box with a lid. Simply place your questions in the box and have students come forward and answer the questions on the papers. When the last question is answered, the box is shut. In this case you would forego rolling the dice.
- Have one student at a time come roll the dice and read the question, but ask each student in the room to respond to the question on a card to be turned in. This will provide valuable feedback to the instructor on how all students are answering the questions.
- It may take playing the actual game to decide exactly how you want to deal with the game as a closure activity, keeping in mind the amount of time you wish to dedicate to it. You will want to determine how you respond to running out of questions before all tiles are dropped, rolling dice totals that do not work with the tiles remaining to be dropped, running out of time before all of the tiles are dropped, and so on. You can adjust the rules to fit your situation.

Online Adaptations

Instead of a physical box, create a box of questions in your online course. Use a quizzing function to allow them to respond to the questions, including those that go beyond reviewing content to application issues. When all the questions have been answered, the students "shut the box" on the module. You could also consider placing the students in a group chat room to discuss the questions. This would be especially powerful with the application questions.

Note

1. Shut the Box instructions are a copyright of Masters Traditional Games. Instructions and adaptations are used with permission.

Key References and Resources

Shut the box. (2017). Available from www.mastersofgames.com/rules/shut-box-rules.htm

CLOSING PAUSE 57

MUSICAL UNCHAIRS

In the well-known musical chairs game, music plays while participants walk in front of empty chairs with enough chairs for everyone except one. When the music stops, everyone sits. The participant who didn't find a chair is out. Another chair is removed, and the music continues until there is a winner. This version of musical chairs involves partners, and instead of sitting in chairs when the music stops, partners find each other. The last two people to find a partner when the music stops answer a pause question before sitting down and being declared out. The music continues until only one couple remains.

Settings for Use

- ☑ Small classroom lecture
- ☑ Clinical or laboratory presentation
- ☐ One-on-one session
- ☑ Conference presentation/ in-service education
- ☐ Keynote/large-group presentation
- ☐ Course/unit
- ☐ Online learning module

Characteristics

- ☑ Affirming/positive
- ☑ Physical/movement
- ☐ Activates prior knowledge/ experience
- ☐ Focuses/refocuses
- ☑ Creates community
- ☐ Generates curiosity
- ☑ Metacognitive
- ☑ Reviews
- ☑ Celebrates
- ☑ Commits to action
- ☐ Provides a bookend

Procedure

1. Tell the students what the question is that they should be prepared to answer. A good question might be, What is the most important thing you learned today? or What do you most want to remember from class today? or How will you be sure that you remember what you learned in class today?
2. Have everyone in the group find a partner. If you have an uneven number, create one group of three.
3. Have the students form two concentric circles, with their partner in the other circle.
4. When the music starts, one circle goes one way and the other circle goes the opposite way.

5. When the music stops, students must find their partner, grasp both of their partner's hands, and then both partners put their hands up in the air.
6. The last couple to put their hands in the air answers the pause question before they are declared out and sit down.
7. Play continues until the last couple standing answers the question and claims the prize.

Additional Suggestions

- If you have room and you have chairs, you could do this pause activity in the traditional way, using chairs, and having those left without a chair give their answer one at a time.
- If you find it difficult to play music, you could use any signaling device, such as a bell, a buzzer, a chime, or flipping a light switch. However, music is energizing and uplifting, which makes using music worthwhile.
- Because this pause uses physical activity, it lends itself well to a midpause and a closing pause.

CLOSING PAUSE 58

EXAM QUESTION CHALLENGE

With this activity, students select a concept from the lecture and develop a question about the concept. Students share questions and answers with a partner and then help revise each other's questions. Both students put their names and questions on a three-inch-by-five-inch card and turn them in. If a question is used in an upcoming exam or in some other way receives special merit, each student who wrote the question receives bonus points.

Settings for Use

- ☑ Small classroom lecture
- ☑ Clinical or laboratory presentation
- ☐ One-on-one session
- ☑ Conference presentation/ in-service education
- ☐ Keynote/large-group presentation
- ☑ Course/unit
- ☑ Online learning module

Characteristics

- ☑ Affirming/positive
- ☑ Physical/movement
- ☐ Activates prior knowledge/ experience
- ☐ Focuses/refocuses
- ☑ Creates community
- ☐ Generates curiosity
- ☐ Metacognitive
- ☑ Reviews
- ☑ Celebrates
- ☐ Commits to action
- ☐ Provides a bookend

Procedure

1. Allow adequate time (about 10 to 12 minutes minimum) at the end of class for this activity
2. Ask students to take a minute to look over the class objectives and their notes and decide on one topic they feel is important enough to write an exam question on.
3. Explain to the group that these questions are extremely important and will be evaluated, and a portion of the questions will merit bonus points.
4. Give them three-inch-by-five-inch cards to write their questions on.
5. Have them write one examination question—decide if you want a particular kind of question. Multiple-choice questions work particularly well for most courses with larger enrollments.

6. Ask students to stand. This is important. Then instruct them to move to another part of the room and pair up with someone that they do not sit near.
7. Have the students test each other with their questions. Give them a little time to grade each other's questions and suggest any improvements to their questions.
8. Write question author names on the back of the card and add the name of their partner.
9. Explain how bonus points will be awarded to the best questions. Usually instructors choose some of the questions to be added to the midterm or end of the course examination. Bonus points will be given to both students whose names appear on the card of the questions selected.
10. Now ask the students to raise their hands if they feel their partner wrote a question worthy of bonus points. Usually nearly all hands will go up.
11. Finally, ask them to drop their cards in a basket or box or hand them to you as they go back to their seats. Before they sit down, ask them to applaud their partners for their good questions and the assistance they received on their questions.

Additional Suggestions

- The instructor could tell the group that a certain percentage of the questions were good enough to appear on the final or midterm exam. Of course, the bonuses would still apply. Students might decide to organize themselves so that they all share their questions with each other to assist themselves in preparing for the exam.
- If you don't have exams coming up in the course, you can determine other ways to give bonus points. You can select the questions you feel are especially well done and post the names of the students who earned the extra credit. Alternatively, you could post the questions and allow the students to determine which of the questions merit bonus points. For example, I used this closure at the end of a five-hour workshop on pausing the lecture for good learning. It was nearly 10:00 p.m., and the students were pretty tired after an intense learning session and a long day. The 18 students in the class, mostly doctoral students who planned to teach or faculty members auditing the course, threw themselves wholeheartedly into the task of writing a good multiple-choice question on the topic of the evening. The competition aspect seemed to add a bit of excitement, and the room buzzed with energy as students shared

their cards with their partners and then sat down together to revise and improve each other's questions. I found that it was extremely important to do the following:

- Make sure that everyone stands up before being asked to find a partner; otherwise, they simply stay in their seats and turn to the person sitting next to them. I want them to have the benefit of a little extra oxygen, as well as the opportunity to get a fresh perspective they might not get if they choose a person with whom they are well acquainted (which is more likely if they are sitting next to that person, rather than across the room).
- Make sure that everyone knows that not only the person writing the question but also the partner who helps revise the question will be getting the bonus points. Then when you ask for a show of hands of who has a partner who has written an excellent question, all the hands will go up.
- Make sure to collect the cards before you allow participants to applaud. It is hard to clap hands when you have something in your hand.

Online Adaptation

This closure activity is excellent to wrap up an online module. The questions can all be posted, making an excellent review of the module. The questions could be placed into an ungraded quiz using the learning management system as an optional review of the material. Students could vote on the top five or so for the bonus points.

Key References and Resources

Barkley, E. F., & Major, C. H. (2015). *Learning assessment techniques: A handbook for college faculty*. San Francisco, CA: Wiley.

Barkley, E. F., Major, C. H., & Cross, P. K. (2014). *Collaborative learning techniques: A handbook for college faculty*. San Francisco, CA: Jossey-Bass.

A PENNY FOR YOUR THOUGHTS

In this simple adaptation of the minute paper, the instructor pauses at the end of the learning session and asks students to provide feedback on what they have learned. The phrase *a penny for your thoughts* is a colloquial way of saying "I am willing to give you something in return for sharing your thinking with me." Although a penny isn't much today, it is something. So you better be ready to give away your penny.

Settings for Use

☑ Small classroom lecture
☑ Clinical or laboratory presentation
☑ One-on-one session
☑ Conference presentation/in-service education
☑ Keynote/large-group presentation
☐ Course/unit
☐ Online learning module

Characteristics

☑ Affirming/positive
☐ Physical/movement
☐ Activates prior knowledge/experience
☐ Focuses/refocuses
☐ Creates community
☐ Generates curiosity
☐ Metacognitive
☑ Reviews
☑ Celebrates
☐ Commits to action
☑ Provides a bookend

Procedure

1. Go to the bank and purchase some brand new shiny pennies if possible.
2. Glue a penny on brightly colored cards on which you have printed "A Penny for Your Thoughts" as shown in Figure C.3.
3. Have a place for each person to write his or her name.
4. Hand out the cards at the end of your learning session.
5. Ask students to put their name on the card.
6. Tell them you will collect the cards, but you will return them.
7. Give them a few minutes to write down their thoughts about the lecture.
8. Collect the cards and look them over quickly before handing them back.

9. Write responses to their thoughts if you have time.
10. Return the cards, either before students leave or at the next session, if there is one.

Figure C.3. A penny for your thoughts sample card.

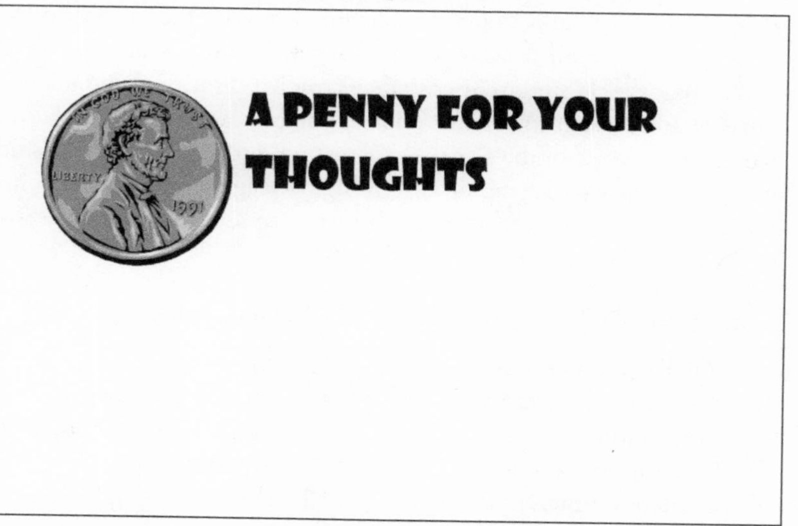

Additional Suggestions

- This works particularly well for a lay audience, whose members might be a bit overwhelmed if you asked them for a minute paper or anything else that sounds academic. This pause technique is not very threatening and gives individuals a chance to provide feedback while also taking home something that will remind them what they have learned.
- See the description of this activity in Chapter 5 (p. 63).

Key References and Resources

Angelo, T. A., & Cross, K. P. (1993). *Classroom assessment techniques: A handbook for college teachers* (2nd ed.). San Francisco, CA: Jossey-Bass.

CLOSING PAUSE 60

FIVE CONNECTIONS

This activity asks students to identify five ways the material presented in the lecture of the day (or the last few lectures) relates to contexts outside the classroom. After students studied Browning's monologues, Lang (2016a) asked them to list five popular songs in which the speaker does not represent the voice of the singer. A marketing instructor might ask students to identify product packaging or advertising. A religion or philosophy instructor might ask students to scan a news website for examples of a particular worldview or theosophy.

Settings for Use

- ☑ Small classroom lecture
- ☑ Clinical or laboratory presentation
- ☑ One-on-one session
- ☑ Conference presentation/in-service education
- ☐ Keynote/large-group presentation
- ☑ Course/unit
- ☑ Online learning module

Characteristics

- ☐ Affirming/positive
- ☐ Physical/movement
- ☑ Activates prior knowledge/experience
- ☑ Focuses/refocuses
- ☐ Creates community
- ☐ Generates curiosity
- ☐ Metacognitive
- ☑ Reviews
- ☑ Celebrates
- ☐ Commits to action
- ☐ Provides a bookend

Procedure

1. Plan about five minutes at the end of class for this pause.
2. Explain the connection you would like the students to make. It may be helpful to provide an example if the connection you are asking for is a bit difficult for them to conceptualize.
3. Explain how you would like students to list the connections, either on a piece of paper, an e-mail, text message, on a polling site such as Poll Everywhere or Kahoot!, on the course learning management system, or written on their class handout in a designated place at the end of the outline. Let the students know if they will be turning in their lists.
4. Explain that class will be over as soon as they have been able to think of five connections.
5. Discuss some of the students' responses before dismissing the class.

6. Be sure to allow students to leave on time by completing the discussion within the allotted time period. This may mean that not all students will finish their list of five when the discussion begins.

Additional Suggestions

- This closing pause can be adapted to many subjects and varying time periods. It could be longer or shorter than five minutes. The instructor may also ask for fewer than five connections, depending on the challenge of the task and the amount of time allotted.

Online Adaptation

This activity could be a closing pause assignment in the overall online module. Students would be given a place in the learning management system to submit their short document, sharing their connections.

Key References and Resources

Lang, J. M. (2016c). *Small teaching: Everyday lessons from the science of learning.* San Francisco, CA: Jossey-Bass.

CLOSING PAUSE 61

FOUR CORNERS WRAP-UP

This activity provides a review of a session concept or a response to a follow-up question by asking individuals in the class to look at four possible answers posted in the four corners of the room and to cluster themselves in the corner with the answer to the question that best represents their thinking. This pause aids in learning as the walking about the room increases blood flow and oxygenation to the brain, contributing to better learning; in addition, it allows for establishing community among the group as participants mingle with others in the room while selecting their answer to the question that has been posed.

Settings for Use

- ☑ Small classroom lecture
- ☑ Clinical or laboratory presentation
- ☐ One-on-one session
- ☑ Conference presentation/ in-service education
- ☐ Keynote/large-group presentation
- ☐ Course/unit
- ☐ Online learning module

Characteristics

- ☐ Affirming/positive
- ☑ Physical/movement
- ☐ Activates prior knowledge/ experience
- ☐ Focuses/refocuses
- ☑ Creates community
- ☐ Generates curiosity
- ☐ Metacognitive
- ☑ Reviews
- ☐ Celebrates
- ☐ Commits to action
- ☐ Provides a bookend

Procedure

1. Decide ahead of time what your question will be.
2. Post four possible answers in the four corners of the room.
3. Tell the group that you will post a question and that they will choose one of four answer options.
4. Instruct them to walk around the room to discover what has been posted in each corner.
5. Ask participants to stand in the corner that best represents their choice of the answer.
6. Give some time for the groups in each location to plan a short report about why they chose a particular answer; this can be especially

interesting if you have a range of choices, depending on where each group chooses to stand.

Additional Suggestions

- This closure activity can be particularly exciting if you create a case-based question with a selection of very plausible responses to the question. In a sense, you are receiving simultaneous responses to one specific question, giving yourself immediate, concrete feedback. Discussion can be extremely profitable if students feel that debate will be helpful in clarifying issues regarding the choice of a possible one best answer.
- If the instructor wants feedback on how the group is responding to the teaching methods, a question might simply ask for a response to a statement such as, I found class today to be . . .
    - o particularly stimulating.
    - o moderately interesting.
    - o somewhat interesting.
    - o not my favorite topic.

Key References and Resources

Barkley, E. F., & Major, C. H. (2015). *Learning assessment techniques: A handbook for college faculty*. San Francisco, CA: Wiley.

Halsey, V. (2011). *Brilliance by design: Creating learning experiences that connect, inspire, and engage*. San Fransisco, CA: Berrett-Koehler.

CLOSING PAUSE 62

TWO AND TWO CLOSURE

This pause is based on what Chuck Woolery used to tell his audience before he went on a commercial break on the 1980s television show *Love Connection*. He would tell the viewers, "We'll be back in two and two, so don't go away!" In this activity, the instructor stops class three to five minutes early and asks the students to take two minutes and two seconds for the following two questions: What was the most important thing you learned in class? and What will you do with this concept? Students can write their responses on a three-inch-by-five-inch card provided by the instructor or on a half sheet of paper, and turn them in.

The purpose is to give instructors a general idea of what the class thinks is important and how the participants plan to use what they have learned. The instructor can efficiently monitor how well the students are learning and what the students value. The feedback can also relay whether the students are learning big picture concepts or specific ideas or techniques. If instructors find that the students are learning something other than what was meant to be taught, they can decide whether any midcourse adjustments are warranted. The advantage of this technique for the student is that it ensures what is being learned is in line with what is being taught. If there are any discrepancies, then the instructor can make changes or corrections. This pause is simple, effective, and easy to use.

Settings for Use

- ☑ Small classroom lecture
- ☑ Clinical or laboratory presentation
- ☑ One-on-one session
- ☑ Conference presentation/in-service education
- ☑ Keynote/large-group presentation
- ☑ Course/unit
- ☑ Online learning module

Characteristics

- ☐ Affirming/positive
- ☐ Physical/movement
- ☐ Activates prior knowledge/experience
- ☐ Focuses/refocuses
- ☐ Creates community
- ☐ Generates curiosity
- ☐ Metacognitive
- ☑ Reviews
- ☑ Celebrates
- ☐ Commits to action
- ☐ Provides a bookend

Procedure

1. Plan about five minutes at the end of class and time at the beginning of the next class to discuss the results.
2. Give the two questions to the students.
3. Ask the students to take out a half sheet of paper.
4. Ask students not to put their name on their paper.
5. Explain the purpose of the exercise, then instruct students to answer the questions in the two- to five-minute window of time you give them. Provide examples of what kinds of answers you are looking for and when you plan to give them feedback.
6. Discuss the answers in small groups or in the larger class.
7. Collect the students' answers.

Additional Suggestions

- This pause can be carried into the beginning of the next class to review what was perceived to be important in the previous class. If several instructors share teaching for a class on different days, the papers can be very useful at the beginning of each new instructor's session, providing a bird's-eye view of what was learned in the previous session.
- This activity is especially helpful with lectures that cover a lot of different material.

Key References and Resources

Angelo, T. A., & Cross, K. P. (1993). *Classroom assessment techniques: A handbook for college teachers* (2nd ed.). San Francisco, CA: Jossey-Bass.

Kagan, S., & Kagan, M. (2009a). *Kagan cooperative learning.* San Clemente, CA: Author.

Riche, R. (2015). *3 2 1 performance feedback method.* Retrieved from www.linkedin.com/pulse/3-2-1-performance-feedback-method-richard-riche

CLOSING PAUSE 63

LECTURE WRAPPER

This closing pause is particularly valuable as a metacognitive experience, teaching students to think about how and what they are learning from the class session. Wrappers can be used after exams or homework assignments and can be an excellent short closing pause after a lecture as well. The wrapper requires just a few minutes to carry out but can have maximum impact. (This pause is described in Chapter 2, p. 29.)

Settings for Use

- ☑ Small classroom lecture
- ☑ Clinical or laboratory presentation
- ☐ One-on-one session
- ☐ Conference presentation/in-service education
- ☐ Keynote/large-group presentation
- ☐ Course/unit
- ☐ Online learning module

Characteristics

- ☑ Affirming/positive
- ☐ Physical/movement
- ☐ Activates prior knowledge/experience
- ☐ Focuses/refocuses
- ☑ Creates community
- ☐ Generates curiosity
- ☑ Metacognitive
- ☑ Reviews
- ☑ Celebrates
- ☐ Commits to action
- ☐ Provides a bookend

Procedure

1. Begin the class session by explaining active listening to the students. Tell them to take particularly careful notes during this lecture, looking for what they think are the key points, because they will have an opportunity to respond to an important question at the end. Sometimes it works to tell them they will have a quiz at the end of class. You can tell them it will be ungraded or just one question. Using the word *quiz* may increase tension, interest, or engagement. When tension is already high, avoid the word but use the ungraded or one-question aspect.
2. Give out three-inch-by-five-inch cards for the activity. Print the question on the card, project it on an overhead screen, or write it on the whiteboard.
3. Save a few minutes at the end for students to answer the following: What are the three most important ideas from today's class session?

4. Have students trade cards with a neighbor and compare their answers.
5. Discuss the process with the group. Did knowing ahead of time affect the way they engaged in the learning process? Would knowing the exact question ahead of time help them do a better job?
6. Collect the index cards.
7. Tell the students what the three major points were.
8. Allow time for some discussion. In particular, discuss any plans students can individually make to improve their ability to complete this activity.

Additional Suggestions

- It is often helpful to students to repeat this activity several times during a course.
- Generally, the instructor will provide less prompting as the activity is repeated. For example, the second and third time, the students might not be given a heads-up at the beginning of the class at all. This will teach them to begin planning for this kind of note-taking and to make self-monitoring a habit.
- Repeating the activity allows students to see if they are improving in their ability to pick up the instructor's main points.
- This is a particularly valuable activity when students take their own notes and are not given a handout that makes clear what the major points are, although it will work either way.
- When using this activity, encourage the students to disregard their notes.
- The questions can vary from asking for the three major points to asking for a number of related concepts, such as, What do you value most from the class session? or What concepts will be most helpful to you as you apply the lessons learned from today's session?

Key References and Resources

Glenn, D. (2009, May 1). Close the book. Recall. Write it down. *Chronicle of Higher Education, 55*(34), A1.

Karpicke, J. D., & Roediger, H. L. (2008). The critical importance of retrieval for learning. *Science, 319*, 966–968. doi:10.1126/science.1152408

Karpicke, J. D., & Blunt, J. R. (2011). Retrieval practice produces more learning than elaborative studying with concept mapping. *Science, 331*, 772–775. doi:10.1126/science.1199327

Retrieval practice. (2017). *Retrieve!* Retrieved from www.retrievalpractice.org

CLOSING PAUSE 64

QUAD FOLD CLOSURE

This closing pause provides a new way of looking back at the class session just finished. Students fold a piece of paper into four quadrants and answer questions, create a design, or ask a question in one of the four sections of the paper. These papers are then shared with a small group and finally turned in for the instructor for input and to be returned to the students.

Settings for Use

- ☑ Small classroom lecture
- ☑ Clinical or laboratory presentation
- ☑ One-on-one session
- ☑ Conference presentation/ in-service education
- ☐ Keynote/large-group presentation
- ☐ Course/unit
- ☐ Online learning module

Characteristics

- ☐ Affirming/positive
- ☐ Physical/movement
- ☐ Activates prior knowledge/ experience
- ☐ Focuses/refocuses
- ☑ Creates community
- ☐ Generates curiosity
- ☐ Metacognitive
- ☑ Reviews
- ☑ Celebrates
- ☐ Commits to action
- ☐ Provides a bookend

Procedure

1. Instruct learners to fold a piece of paper into four quadrants by folding it in half each way, thus creating four sections for writing.
2. Tell them they will have an opportunity to summarize the class session by answering four questions, one in each of the quadrants of the paper.
3. In the upper-left corner they describe what they learned.
4. In the upper-right corner students state why they think the learning was important.
5. In the bottom-left quadrant students can get creative and illustrate what they learned. For example, they may create a realistic diagram of a concept, a cartoon showing an important idea, or an abstract illustration of a portion of the day's content.
6. In the bottom-right quadrant students have an opportunity to ask questions or give indications of where they might follow up on what they learned in the class.

7. Large-group discussions allow students to share their summaries.
8. After completing this activity, students can turn in their papers to the instructor as they leave the class.
9. Figure C.4 is an example.

Figure C.4. Quad fold activity example.

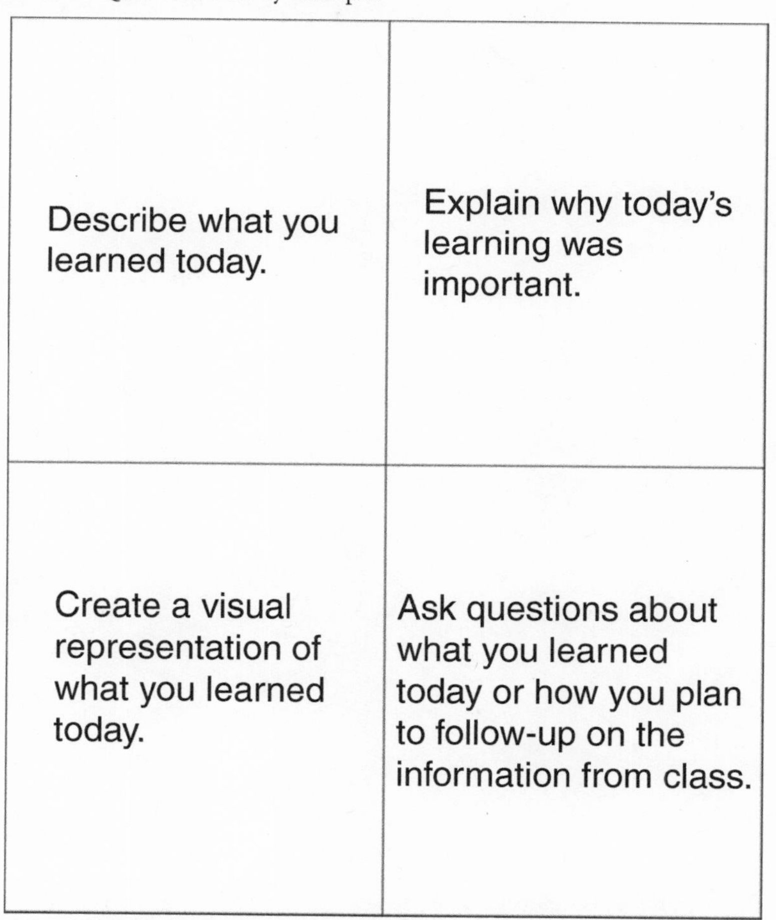

Note. Adapted from "What I Learned Today Quad-Fold Activity," 2017, literacyteacher.com/what-i-learned-today-quad-fold-activity. Copyright 2017 by LiteracyTeacher.com

Additional Suggestions

- Different questions from those in this description can be used.
- Students might be invited to find a partner to trade papers to see if they can answer their partner's questions and return the paper with the answers penciled in.

Key References and Resources

Barkley, E. F., & Major, C. H. (2015). *Learning assessment techniques: A handbook for college faculty*. San Francisco, CA: Wiley.

What I learned today quad-fold activity. (2017). Retrieved from literacyteacher.com/what-i-learned-today-quad-fold-activity

FIVE-STEP CLOSURE

This closing pause provides a new way of looking back at the class session. Students use nonverbal skills while exchanging ideas and obtaining information from each other. Students use a three-inch-by-five-inch card or a sticky note to answer a question about a class that is nearly over. They exchange cards with a series of other students, each viewing the other's card without saying anything. Finally they participate in a large-group discussion.

Settings for Use

- ☑ Small classroom lecture
- ☑ Clinical or laboratory presentation
- ☑ One-on-one session
- ☑ Conference presentation/in-service education
- ☐ Keynote/large-group presentation
- ☐ Course/unit
- ☐ Online learning module

Characteristics

- ☐ Affirming/positive
- ☑ Physical/movement
- ☐ Activates prior knowledge/experience
- ☐ Focuses/refocuses
- ☑ Creates community
- ☐ Generates curiosity
- ☑ Metacognitive
- ☑ Reviews
- ☑ Celebrates
- ☐ Commits to action
- ☐ Provides a bookend

Procedure

1. When the class is nearly over, tell the students they will have an opportunity to answer a question about the class and that they will be sharing their response with others in the class.
2. Give students a card or sticky note and give the question you want them to answer.
3. For this activity, it is best if the question can be answered with a few words. Examples of questions that might work well with this activity include the following:
   a. What is the most important concept we discussed in class today?
   b. What do you value most about our class discussion today?
   c. If you were going to explain what we learned in class today in one sentence to a child, what would you say?

   d. Describe what you learned in class today in an elevator talk. In other words, what could you share with someone in the time it would take to ride the elevator together?
   e. Indicate what you feel is the most valuable application of what we learned in class today.
   f. What helped you learn well in class today?
4. Give students the question to write their answer to on their card or sticky note sheet. Suggest they add a drawing or illustration to their answer.
5. Ask them to stand and take five steps in any direction.
6. Tell them to swap their cards with someone standing close by. They are not to say anything to each other, simply read what is written and smile at each other. Depending on the complexity of the question you have asked, this may take from 20 to 45 seconds.
7. Instruct students that when you say stop, they are to wait for further instructions.
8. Tell students to take five steps in any direction and then trade cards with another individual in the class, repeating the process.
9. Depending on the time remaining, you might have students repeat the sequence several times before returning to their seats.
10. Finish with a large-group discussion, asking students what they learned from viewing others' cards.
11. Collect the cards or sticky notes and post them where all the students can see them as they exit the class.

Additional Suggestions

- This activity could be changed to triads of students instead of dyads. In this case, students would share with two classmates before collecting their cards and continuing.
- Students could also form small groups and share their cards around their circle.

Key References and Resources

Coffman, S. (n.d.). *Door to door activity about dreams and goals.* Retrieved from www.greatexpectations.org/Websites/greatexpectations/images/pdf/practices/goalsetting/Door%20to%20Door%20activity.pdf

REFERENCES

Achor, S. (2011a). *The happiness advantage: Linking positive brains to performance* [Video file]. Retrieved from youtu.be/GXy__kBVq1M

Achor, S. (2011b). *The happiness advantage: The seven principles of positive psychology that fuel success and performance at work*. New York, NY: Random House.

Agarwal, P. K. (2017). *Retrieval practice*. Retrieved from www.retrievalpractice.org

Alber, R. (2011, May 24). *6 scaffolding strategies to use with your students*. Retrieved from www.edutopia.org/blog/scaffolding-lessons-six-strategies-rebecca-alber

Ambrose, S. A., Bridges, M. W., Di Pietro, M., Lovett, M. C., & Norman, M. K. (2010). *How learning works: Seven research-based principles for smart teaching*. San Francisco, CA: Jossey-Bass.

Angelo, T. A., & Cross, K. P. (1993). *Classroom assessment techniques: A handbook for college teachers* (2nd ed.). San Francisco, CA: Jossey-Bass.

Armstrong, E. (2016). *Program for educators in health professions*. Boston, MA: Harvard Macy Institute.

Armstrong, E., & Parsa-Parsi, R. (2005). How can physicians' learning styles drive educational planning? *Academic Medicine, 80*, 680–684.

Bain, K. (2004). *What the best college teachers do*. Cambridge, MA: Harvard University Press.

Barkley, E. F. (2010). *Student engagement techniques: A handbook for college faculty*. San Francisco, CA: Jossey-Bass.

Barkley, E. F., & Major, C. H. (2015). *Learning assessment techniques: A handbook for college faculty*. San Francisco, CA: Wiley.

Barkley, E. F., Major, C. H., & Cross, P. K. (2014). *Collaborative learning techniques: A handbook for college faculty*. San Francisco, CA: Jossey-Bass.

Bennett, B., & Rolheiser, C. (2001). *Beyond Monet: The artful science of instructional integration*. Toronto, Ontario, Canada: Bookstation.

Berns, G. S., McClure, S. M., Pagnoni, G., & Montague, P. R. (2001). Predictability modulates human brain response to reward. *Journal of Neuroscience, 21*, 2793–2798.

Bjork, R. A. (1994). Memory and metamemory considerations in the training of human beings. In J. Metcalfe & A. P. Shimamura (Eds.), *Metacognition: Knowing about knowing* (pp. 185–205). Cambridge, MA: MIT Press.

Bligh, D. A. (2000). *What's the use of lectures?* San Francisco: CA: Jossey-Bass.

Bloom, B. S. (Ed.). (1956). *Taxonomy of educational objectives; the classification of educational goals, by a committee of college and university examiners*. New York, NY: Longmans, Green.

Boffey, P. (June 14, 1962). The lecture system: Its value at Harvard. *The Harvard Crimson*. Retrieved from http://www.thecrimson.com/article/1962/6/14/the-lecture-system-its-value-at/

Bolen, J. (n.d.). *Hot potato: An ESL speaking game for kids*. Retrieved from eslspeaking .org/hot-potato-esl-speaking-game-for-kids

Bonwell, C. C., & Eison, J. A. (1991). *Active learning: Creating excitement in the classroom*. Retrieved from ERIC database. (ED336049)

Bowman, S. (2009). *Training from the back of the room*. San Diego, CA: Pfeiffer.

Bowman, S. (2011). *Using brain science to make training stick*. Glenbrook, NV: Bowperson.

Bozarth, J. (2011). *SURPRISE! Nuts and bolts*. Retrieved from www.learning solutionsmag.com/articles/622/nuts-and-bolts-surprise

Briggs, S. (2014). *20 simple assessment strategies you can use every day*. Retrieved from www.teachthought.com/pedagogy/assessment/20-simple-assessment-strategies-can-use-every-day/#

Broad, M. L., & Newstrom, J. W. (1992). *Transfer of training: Action-packed strategies to ensure high payoff from training investments*. Retrieved from ERIC database. (ED 366712)

Brookfield, S. D., & Preskill, S. (2005). *Discussion as a way of teaching: Tools and techniques for democratic classrooms* (2nd ed.). San Francisco, CA: Jossey-Bass.

Brown, P. C., Roediger, H. L., & McDaniel, M. A. (2014). *Make it stick: The science of successful learning*. Cambridge, MA: Belknap Press.

Burns, M. (2012). *Class tech tips*. Retrieved from classtechtips.com/2012/08/23/sticky-notes-for-a-tech-friendly-classroom

Cavanagh, S. R. (2016). *The spark of learning*. Morgantown: West Virginia University Press.

Chickering, A.W., & Gamson, Z.F. (eds). (1991). *Applying seven principles for good practice in undergraduate education*. San Francisco, CA: Jossey-Bass

Churchland, P. S., & Sejnowski, T. J. (1992). *The computational brain*. Cambridge, MA: MIT Press.

Clowes, G. (2017). *The essential 5: A starting point for Kagan Cooperative Learning*. Retrieved from www.kaganonline.com/free_articles/research_and_rationale/330/The-Essential-5-A-Starting-Point-for-Kagan-Cooperative-Learning

Coffman, S. (n.d.). *Door to door activity about dreams and goals*. Retrieved from www.greatexpectations.org/Websites/greatexpectations/images/pdf/practices/goalsetting/Door%20to%20Door%20activity.pdf

Common Cents. (1998). *Memory*. Retrieved from www.exploratorium.edu/exhibits/common_cents/index.html

ConcepTests. (2017). Retrieved from serc.carleton.edu/introgeo/interactive/conctest .html

Cooper, J. L., Robinson, P., & Ball, D. (Eds.). (2003). *Small group instruction in higher education: Lessons from the past, visions of the future*. Stillwater, OK: New Forums Press.

Course Canary. (2017). *Course Canary course design*. Retrieved from coursecanary.com

Cross, J. (2007). *Informal learning* (1st ed.). San Francisco, CA: Pfeiffer.

Cuseo, J. B. (2002). *Igniting student involvement, peer interaction, and teamwork: A taxonomy of specific cooperative learning structures and collaborative learning strategies*. Stillwater, OK: New Forums Press.

Davis, M., & Hult, R. E. (1997). Effects of writing summaries as a generative learning activity during note taking. *Teaching of Psychology, 24*, 47–50.

Deck, M. L. (1995). *Instant teaching tools for health care educators.* Maryland Heights, MO: Mosby.

Dennick, R., & Exley, K. (2004). *Small group teaching: Tutorials, seminars and beyond.* New York, NY: Routledge.

Dewey, J. (1910). *How we think.* USA: Heath & Co, Kindle Edition.

Dewey, J., & Dewey, E. (1915). *Schools of tomorrow.* Whitefish, MT: Kessinger Publishing.

Doyle, T. (2011). *Learner-centered teaching: Putting the research on learning into practice.* Sterling, VA: Stylus.

Dror, I. (2011). Brain friendly technology: What is it? And why do we need it?. In I. E. Dror (Ed.), *Technology enhanced learning and cognition* (Vol. 27, pp. 1–7). Philadelphia, PA: John Benjamins.

Dunn, J. (2012, August 10). *The 100 best video sites for educators.* Retrieved from www.edudemic.com/best-video-sites-for-teachers

Eagan, M. K., Stolzenberg, E. B., Berdan Lozano, J., Aragon, M. C., Suchard, M. R., & Hurtado, S. (2014). *Undergraduate teaching faculty: The 2013–2014 HERI Faculty Survey*. Los Angeles, CA: Higher Education Research Institute, UCLA.

Effective classroom practices. (2017). Retrieved from www.brown.edu/about/administration/sheridan-center/teaching-learning/effective-classroom-practices/entrance-exit-tickets/accessed2/1/17

Egawa, K. (2004). *Sharing from graffiti boards: Learning assessment.* Retrieved from www.readwritethink.org/files/resources/lesson_images/lesson305/graffiti-sharing.pdf

Eggleston, T. J., & Smith, G. E. (2002). Parting ways: Ending your course. *APS Observer, 15*(3), 15–16.

Entry ticket. (n.d.). Retrieved from www.theteachertoolkit.com/index.php/tool/entry-ticket/accessed2/1/17

Exit tickets: Checking for understanding. (2015). Retrieved from www.edutopia.org/practice/exit-tickets-checking-understanding

Feinberg, J. (2014). Wordle. Retrieved from www.wordle.net

Fenker, D., & Schütze, H. (2008, December 17). Learning by surprise. *Scientific American.* Retrieved from www.scientificamerican.com/article/learning-by-surprise

Finkel, D. L. (2000). *Teaching with your mouth shut.* Portsmouth, NH: Boynton/Cook.

Finley, T. (2015). *22 powerful closure activities.* Retrieved from www.edutopia.org/blog/22-powerful-closure-activities-todd-finley

Fletcher, J., Najarro, A., & Yelland, H. (2015). *Fostering habits of mind in today's students.* Sterling, VA: Stylus.

Flisti. (n.d.). Retrieved from flisti.com

Floyd, T. (2014, October 5). *Untitled presentation*. Presented at San Diego, CA

Follett, K. (1989). *Pillars of the earth*. New York City, NY: William Morrow.

Four square feedback. (n.d.). Retrieved from wvde.state.wv.us/abe/file-cabinet/Core_Sessions/Four_Square_Feedback.doc

Garside, C. (1996). Look who's talking: A comparison of lecture and group discussion teaching strategies in developing critical thinking skills. *Communication Education, 45*, 212–227. doi:10.1080/03634529609379050

Glenn, D. (2009, May 1). Close the book. Recall. Write it down. *Chronicle of Higher Education, 55*, A1.

Gruber, M. J., Gelman, B. D., & Ranganath, C. (2014). States of curiosity modulate hippocampus-dependent learning via the dopaminergic circuit. *Neuron, 84*, 486–496.

Grundy, L. (2015). *9 high-yield instructional strategies by Robert J. Marzano*. Retrieved from www.3plearning.com/9-high-yield-strategies-robert-j-marzano

Hake, R. R. (1998). Interactive-engagement versus traditional methods: A six-thousand-student survey of mechanics test data for introductory physics courses. *American Journal of Physics, 66*, 64–74.

Hall, M. (2012, September 21). Teaching tips: Classroom assessment [Web log post]. Retrieved from ii.library.jhu.edu/tag/non-graded-assessment

Halsey, V. (2011). *Brilliance by design: Creating learning experiences that connect, inspire, and engage*. San Francisco, CA: Berrett-Koehler.

Harrington, C. (2014, December 9). The power of pausing [Web log post]. Retrieved from blog.cengage.com/power-pausing

Harrington, C., & Zakrajsek, T. *Dynamic lecturing: Research-based strategies to enhance lecture effectiveness*. Sterling, VA: Stylus Publishing.

Hartley, J., & Davies, I. K. (1978). Note taking: A critical review. *Programmed learning and educational technology, 15*(3), 207–224.

Hassard, J., & Dias, M. (2009). *The art of teaching science* (2nd ed.). New York, NY: Routledge.

Heath, C., & Heath, D. (2007). *Made to stick: Why some ideas survive and others die*. New York, NY: Random House.

Honeycutt, B. (2016). *FLIP the first 5 minutes of class: 50 focusing activities to engage your students*. Retrieved from barbihoneycutt.com/store/home/12-50-proven-activities-ebook.html

Howard, B. (2017). *Cooperative learning structures improve performance and attitudes of high school journalism students*. Retrieved from www.kaganonline.com/free_articles/research_and_rationale/312/Cooperative-Learning-Structures-Improve-Performance-and-Attitudes-of-High-School-Journalism-Students

Howard, P. (1994). *Owner's manual for the brain*. Austin, TX: Leorinian Press.

Hunter, M. (1994). *The Madeline Hunter model of mastery learning*. Retrieved from https://www.scribd.com/document/296042948/Dr-Madeline-Hunter-Article1

Inside/outside circles. (n.d.). Retrieved from www.theteachertoolkit.com/index.php/tool/inside-outside-circles

Inside/outside circles. (2006). Retrieved from carla.umn.edu/articulation/polia/pdf_files/insideoutsidecircles.pdf

Jensen, E. P. (2005). *Teaching with the brain in mind* (2nd ed.). Alexandria, VA: American Society for Curriculum and Development.

Jensen, E. P. (2008). *Brain-based learning: The new paradigm of teaching* (2nd ed.). Thousand Oaks, CA: Corwin Press.

Johnson, B. (2012). Tools for teaching: The amazing sticky note. Retrieved from www.edutopia.org/blog/sticky-note-teaching-tool-ben-johnson

Johnson, D. W., Johnson, R. T., & Smith, K. A. (1998). *Active learning: Cooperation in the college classroom*. Retrived from ERIC database. (ED449714)

Johnston, S., & Cooper, J. (1997). Quick-thinks: The interactive lecture. *Cooperative Learning and College Teaching, 8*(1). Retrieved from https://tomprof.stanford.edu/posting/818

Kagan. [Kaganvideo]. (2014, June 12). *What is Kagan?* [Video file]. Retrieved from youtu.be/D-yzgJtgVrg

Kagan, S. (1992) *Cooperative learning.* (2nd ed.): San Juan Capistrano, CA: Resources for Teachers.

Kagan, S., & Kagan, M. (2009a). *Kagan cooperative learning*. San Clemente, CA: Author.

Kagan, S., & Kagan, M. (2009b). Round robin. *Kagan cooperative learning.* San Clemente, CA: Author.

Kagan, S., Kagan, M., & Kagan, L. (2015). *59 Kagan structures: Proven engagement structures*. San Clemente: CA: Author.

Kahoot! (n.d.). Retrieved from getkahoot.com

Kaplan, J. (2014, September 17). *Round robin*. Retrieved from www.betterevaluation.org/en/evaluation-options/roundrobin

Karpicke, J. D. (2012). Retrieval-based learning: Active retrieval promotes meaningful learning. *Current Directions in Psychological Science, 21*, 157–163.

Karpicke, J. D., & Blunt, J. R. (2011). Retrieval practice produces more learning than elaborative studying with concept mapping. *Science, 331*, 772–775. doi:10.1126/science.1199327

Karpicke, J. D., & Roediger, H. L. (2008). The critical importance of retrieval for learning. *Science, 319*, 966–968. doi:10.1126/science.1152408

Kimball, S. M., & Milanowski, A. (2009). Examining teacher evaluation validity and leadership decision making within a standards-based evaluation system. *Educational Administration Quarterly, 45*(1), 34–70.

King, A. (1993). From sage on the stage to guide on the side. *College Teaching, 41*(1), 30–35. doi:10.1080/87567555.1993.9926781

Kolb, D. A. (2014). *Experiential learning: Experience as the source of learning and development*. Upper Saddle River, NJ: Pearson Education.

Kornikau, R., & McElroy, F. (1975). *Communication for the safety professional.* Chicago, IL: National Safety Council.

Kroski, E. (September 11, 2014). *Polling the classroom: 4 free polling tools to keep students engaged.* Retrieved from http://ellyssakroski.com/polling-the-classroom-4-free-polling-tools-to-keep-students-engaged/

K-W-L chart. Retrieved from www.readwritethink.org/classroom-resources/printouts/chart-a-30226.html

Lang, J. M. (2016a, January 11). Small changes in teaching: The first 5 minutes of class, advice. *Chronicle of Higher Education*. Retrieved from www.chronicle.com/article/Small-Changes-in-Teaching-The/234869

Lang, J. M. (2016b, March 7). Small changes in teaching: The last 5 minutes of class, advice. *Chronicle of Higher Education*. Retrieved from www.chronicle.com/article/Small-Changes-in-Teaching-The/235583

Lang, J. M. (2016c). *Small teaching: Everyday lessons from the science of learning* (1st ed.). San Francisco, CA: Jossey-Bass.

Lee, G. [Lee RebelTech]. (2013, October 31). Kagan structure: Stand up, hand up, pair up [Video file]. Retrieved from www.youtube.com/watch?v=7rCTJoTSTJc

Lou, A. (n.d.). *ESL games in the classroom: Hot potato*. Retrieved from www.mychiangmaieverything.com/2014/07/esl-games-in-classroom-hot-potato.html

Lovett, M. (January 29, 2008). *Teaching metacognition*. Presentation to the Educause Learning Initiative Annual Meeting. Retrieved from https://serc.carleton.edu/NAGTWorkshops/metacognition/teaching_metacognition.html

Lucero, R. (2017). *Closure activities: Making that last impression*. Retrieved from tilt.colostate.edu/teachingResources/tips/tip.cfm?tipid=148

Lutsky, N. (2010). Teaching psychology's endings: The simple gifts of a reflective close. In D. S. Dunn, B. B. Beins, M. A. McCarthy, & G. W. Hill IV (Eds.), *Best practices for teaching beginnings and endings in the psychology major: Research, cases, and recommendations* (pp. 331–349). New York, NY: Oxford University Press.

Lyman, F. (1987). Think-pair-share: An expanding teaching technique. *Maa-Cie Cooperative News, 1*(1), 1–2.

Lynette, R. (2012). *Quiz, quiz, trade*. Retrieved from minds-in-bloom.com/quiz-quiz-trade

Major, C. H., Harris, M. S., & Zakrajsek, T. (2016). *Teaching for learning: 101 intentionally designed educational activities to put students on the path to success.* New York, NY: Routledge.

Marken, R. (2008). *Silences*. Ottawa, Ontario, Canada: Council of 3M National Teaching Fellows of the Society of Teaching and Learning in Higher Education.

Marzano, R. J. (2012). Art and science of teaching: The many uses of exit slips. *Educational Leadership: Students Who Challenge Us, 70*(2), 80–81.

Matthews, G. (n.d.). *Study focuses on strategies for achieving goals, resolutions.* Retrieved from www.dominican.edu/dominicannews/study-highlights-strategies-for-achieving-goals

Mazur, E. & Hilborn, R.C. (1997). Peer instruction: A user's manual. *Physics Today, 50*, 68.

McConnell, D., Steer, D., Borowski, W., Dick, J., Foos, A., Knott, J., . . . Horn, S. V. (2004). ConcepTest: Waves. Retrieved from https://serc.carleton.edu/download/images/857/Waves.jpg

McCullough, D. (2017, April 17). Interview by C. Rose. *The American Spirit, CBS This Morning* [Television broadcast]. New York, NY: Columbia Broadcasting System.

McIntyre, G. (2013, January 25). *Rally coach* [Video file]. Retrieved from youtu.be/mNvAHN_x1hY

McIntyre, G. (2013, February 4). *Stand up, hand up, pair up* [Video file]. Retrieved from www.youtube.com/watch?v=NoUxq_clsEA

McKeachie, W. J. (1994). *Teaching tips: Strategies, research, and theory for college & university teachers* (9th ed.). Lexington, MA: D. C. Heath.

McKeachie, W. J., & Svinicki, M. (2013). *McKeachie's teaching tips* (14th ed.). Independence, KY: Cengage.

Medina, J. (2011). *Brain rules: 12 principles for surviving and thriving at work, home and school.* Seattle, WA: Pear Press.

Mednick, S. C., Nakayama, K., Cantero, J. L., Atienza, M., Levin, A. A., Pathak, N., & Stickgold, R. (2002). The restorative effect of naps on perceptual deterioration. *Nat Neurosci, 5*, 677–681.

Mehta, N. (n.d.). *The flight instructor.* Retrieved from www.clevelandclinic.org/cclcm/edu/flight/instructor1.htm

Meier, D. (2000). *The accelerated learning handbook: A creative guide to designing and delivering faster, more effective training programs.* New York City, NY: McGraw-Hill.

Merrill, M. D. (1991). Constructivism and instructional design. *Educational technology, 31*(5), 45–53.

MicroPoll. (2017). Retrieved from www.micropoll.com

Miller, S. (2017). *50 ways to use Twitter in the classroom.* Retrieved from www.teachhub.com/50-ways-use-twitter-classroom

Millis, B. J. (2010). *Cooperative learning in higher education: Across the disciplines, across the academy.* Sterling, VA: Stylus.

Millis, B. J., & Cottell, P. G. (1998). *Cooperative learning for higher education faculty.* Phoenix, AZ: Oryx Press.

National Education Association. (2017). *K-W-L (know, want to know, learned).* Retrieved from www.nea.org/tools/k-w-l-know-want-to-know-learned.html

Nelson, C. E. (2010). Want brighter, harder working students? Change pedagogies! Some examples, mainly from biology. In B. J. Millis (Ed.), *Cooperative learning in higher education: Across the disciplines, across the academy.* Sterling, VA: Stylus.

Neuman, S. B. (2001). The role of knowledge in early literacy. *Reading Research Quarterly, 36*, 468–475.

Nilsen, C., Odahlen, B., Geller, L., Hintz, K., & Borden-King, L. (2011, February). *Fifty ways to teach your students.* Paper presented at the the 30th Annual Conference on the First Year Experience, Minot, ND. Retrieved from www.minotstateu.edu/cetl/_documents/50WaystoTeachYourStudents.pdf

Nilson, L. (2013). *Creating self-regulated learners: Strategies to strengthen self-awareness and learning skills.* Sterling, VA: Stylus.

Ogle, D. M. (1986). KWL: A teaching model that develops active reading of expository text. *Reading Teacher, 39*, 564–570.

Pastötter, B., & Bäuml, K.-H. T. (2014). Retrieval practice enhances new learning: The forward effect of testing. *Frontiers in Psychology, 5*, 1–5. doi:10.3389/fpsyg.2014.00286

Penner, J. G. (1984). *Why many college teachers cannot lecture: How to avoid communication breakdown in the classroom.* Retrived from ERIC database. (ED261638)

Pescosolido, B. (1999). *The social worlds of higher education: Handbook for teaching in a new century* (Vol. 2). Thousand Oaks, CA: Pine Forge Press.

Pike, B., Pike, R. W., & Busse, C. (1995). *101 games for trainers: A collection of the best activities from Creative Training Techniques Newsletter.* Amherst, MA: Human Resource Development.

Pike, R. W. (2003). *Creative training techniques handbook: Tips, tactics, and how-to's for delivering effective training* (3rd ed.). Amherst, MA: Human Resource Development Press.

Poll everywhere. (2007). Retrieved from www.polleverywhere.com

Polldaddy. (n.d.). Retrieved from polldaddy.com

Prochaska, J. O., & DiClemente, C. C. (1984). *The transtheoretical approach: Crossing traditional boundaries of therapy.* Homewood, IL: Dow Jones-Irwin.

Puzzle games daily. (n.d.). Retrieved from free.puzzlegamesdaily.com/index.jhtml?partner=^BK8^xdm002&k_clickid=_kenshoo_clickid_&gclid=CK-N78rWxNECFd6IswodJwgGbA

Quia. (n.d.). Retrieved from www.quia.com

Quiz. (n.d.). Retrieved from www.quiz.com/en

Qzzr. (n.d.). Retrieved from www.qzzr.com

Retrieval practice. (2017). *Retrieve!* Retrieved from www.retrievalpractice.org

Riche, R. (2015). *3 2 1 performance feedback method.* Retrieved from www.linkedin.com/pulse/3-2-1-performance-feedback-method-richard-riche

Rock, D. (2008). SCARF: A brain-based model for collaborating with and influencing others. *NeuroLeadership Journal, 1*(1), 44–52.

Rossi, E. L., & Nimmons, D. (1991). *The 20-minute break: Using the new science of ultradian rhythms.* Los Angeles CA: Tarcher.

Ruhl, K. L., Hughes, C. A., & Schloss, P. J. (1987). Using the pause procedure to enhance lecture recall. *Teacher Education and Special Education, 10*(1), 14–18. doi:10.1177/088840648701000103

Russell, I. J., Hendricson, W. D., & Herbert, R. J. (1984). Effects of lecture information density on medical student achievement. *Journal of Medical Education, 59*, 881–889.

Shut the box. (2017). Retrieved from www.mastersofgames.com/rules/shut-box-rules.htm

Silberman, M. L. (1996). *Active learning: 101 strategies to teach any subject.* Boston: Allyn and Bacon. Retrieved from ERIC database (ED424243).

Simons, D., & Chabris, C. (2010). Selective attention test [Video file]. Retrieved from youtu.be/vJG698U2Mvo

Sipe, A. (n.d.). *Lesson closure with examples or 40 ways to leave a lesson.* Retrieved from www.stma.k12.mn.us/documents/DW/Q_Comp/40_ways_to_leave_a_lesson.pdf

Solem, M. S. (2016). Displaying knowledge through interrogatives in student-initiated sequences. *Classroom Discourse, 7*(1), 18–35.

Sousa, D. A. (2006). *How the brain learns*. Thousand Oaks, CA: Corwin Press.

Starting Point. (2017). *Think-pair-share*. Retrieved from serc.carleton.edu/introgeo/interactive/tpshare.html

Stewart, R. (2015, March 13). Using exit tickets as an assessment tool [Web log post]. Retrieved from www.scholastic.com/teachers/blog-posts/rhonda-stewart/using-exit-tickets-assessment-tool

Straker, D. (2008). *Surprise and learning*. Retrieved from changingminds.org/explanations/learning/surprise_learning.htm

Stuart, J., & Rutherford, R. (1978). Medical student concentration during lectures. *The Lancet, 312*, 514–516.

Sztabnik, B. (2015). The 8 minutes that matter most. Retrieved from www.edutopia.org/blog/8-minutes-that-matter-most-brian-sztabnik

Thelin, J. R. (2011). *A history of American higher education* (2nd ed.). Baltimore, MD: John Hopkins University Press.

3-2-1. (n.d.). Retrieved from www.theteachertoolkit.com/index.php/tool/3-2-1

3-2-1. (2016). Retrieved from www.facinghistory.org/resource-library/teaching-strategies/3-2-1

Ting-A-Kee, M. (n.d.). WIIFM: What's in it for me [Web log post]. Retrieved from rationalizedthoughts.blogspot.com/2007/07/wiifm-whats-in-it-for-me.html

Tomm, T. T. (1999). *Forensic science starters*. Retrieved from http://sciencespot.net/Pages/classforscistarters.html

Udvari-Solner, A., & Kluth, P. (2007). *Joyful learning: Active and collaborative learning in inclusive classrooms*. Thousand Oaks, CA: Corwin Press.

University of Nebraska–Lincoln Office of Graduate Studies. (2017). *Quick tips for teaching*. Retrieved from www.unl.edu/gradstudies/current/teaching/tips

Wakeford, L. (2017). Sample exit tickets. Retrieved from www.brown.edu/about/administration/sheridan-center/teaching-learning/effective-classroom-practices/entrance-exit-tickets/sample

Ward, T. (2017). *On course workshop: Six ways to use quick writes to promote learning forum*. Retrieved from oncourseworkshop.com/life-long-learning/six-ways-use-quick-writes-promote-learning

Weaver, R. L. P., II. (2008, November 25). *Speech speed vs. thought speed: Managing effectiveness* [Video file]. Retrieved from youtu.be/uGY0oV5MlF0

Weimer, M. (2012, November 19). Deep learning vs. surface learning: Getting students to understand the difference. *Faculty Focus*. Retrieved from www.facultyfocus.com/articles/teaching-professor-blog/deep-learning-vs-surface-learning-getting-students-to-understand-the-difference

Weimer, M. (2012). The ideal Professor vs. the typical professor. *Faculty Focus*. Retrieved from https://www.facultyfocus.com/articles/teaching-professor-blog/the-ideal-professor-vs- the-typical-professor/

Westervelt, E. (2016). *A Nobel laureate's education plea: Revolutionize teaching*. Retrieved from www.npr.org/sections/ed/2016/04/14/465729968/a-nobel-laureates-education-plea-revolutionize-teaching

What I learned today quad-fold activity. (2017). Retrieved from literacyteacher.com/what-i-learned-today-quad-fold-activity

Wieman, C. E. (2014). Large-scale comparison of science teaching methods sends clear message. *Proceedings of the National Academy of Sciences of the United States of America, 111*, 8319–8320. doi:10.1073/pnas.1407304111

Wiggins, G. P., & McTighe, J. (2005). *Understanding by design.* Retrieved from www.christina.k12.de.us/literacylinks/elemresources/comprehension/techniques.pdf

Wilson, K., & Korn, J. H. (2007). Attention during lectures: Beyond ten minutes. *Teaching of Psychology, 34*, 85–89. doi:10.1080/00986280701291291

Wolfe, P. (2001). *Brain matters.* Alexandria, VA: Association for Supervision and Curriculum Development.

WordSearch.com. (n.d.). Retrieved from thewordsearch.com/cat/good-to-know

Workshop.on.ca. (2006). *Graffiti.* Retrieved from www.eworkshop.on.ca/edu/pdf/Mod36_coop_graffiti.pdf

Worthen, M. (2015, October 17). Lecture me. Really. *New York Times.* Retrieved from www.nytimes.com/2015/10/18/opinion/sunday/lecture-me-really.html?_r=0

Yee, K. (n.d.). Interactive Techniques. Retrieved from http://www.usf.edu/atle/documents/handout-interactive-techniques.pdf

YouTube. (2017). Retrieved from www.youtube.com

Yuhas, D. (2014, October 2). Curiosity prepares the brain for better learning. *Scientific American.* Retrieved from www.scientificamerican.com/article/curiosity-prepares-the-brain-for-better-learning/#

ABOUT THE AUTHOR

Gail Taylor Rice is a professor in the School of Allied Health Professions at Loma Linda University, where she also directs faculty development. She has held professorial positions at three universities in seven schools and has graduate degrees in nursing, public health education, educational psychology, and higher education administration and leadership. She serves on several editorial boards for professional journals and boards for professional societies. Rice has taught for the Harvard Macy Institute Program for Education in the Health Professions since 2010 and presents regularly for the annual University of Southern California's Keck School of Medicine's Innovations in Medical Education conference. She presents workshops, seminars, and courses for organizations and campuses worldwide and has published books and articles for peer-reviewed journals on various topics relating to creative, effective teaching in higher education and health professions education.

INDEX

This book is for anyone seeking ways to get students to better learn the content of their course, take more responsibility for their work, become more self-regulated as learners, work harder and smarter during class time, and engage positively with course material. As a teaching method, flipped learning becomes demonstrably more powerful when adopted across departments. It is an idea that offers the promise of transforming teaching in higher education.

Stylus

22883 Quicksilver Drive
Sterling, VA 20166-2102

Also available from Stylus

Dynamic Lecturing
Research-Based Strategies to Enhance Lecture Effectiveness
Christine Harrington and Todd Zakrajsek

Foreword by José Antonio Bowen

Series Preface by Todd Zakrajsek

"Finally, a book that lifts lecturing out of the land of ill-repute and positions it squarely in the midst of active learning strategies. Harrington and Zakrajsek present a plethora of simple strategies, based on numerous research studies, that will actively engage students in learning. This is a must-read for faculty who want to use lecturing as a tool to improve students' critical thinking and problem solving skills." —***Saundra McGuire****, Director Emerita, Center for Academic Success, Louisiana State University*

Is the lecture an outmoded teaching method that inhibits active learning or is it a potentially powerful tool that is an essential part of every teacher's repertoire?

This book presents up-to-date research on the different types of lecture, on what constitutes effective lecturing, and on the impact of lecturing when done appropriately and well. It fills the void in professional development resources on how to lecture, validating the practice when it's aligned with the educational mission of creating engaged learning environments.

FLIPPED **LEARNING**

A Guide for Higher Education Faculty

ROBERT TALBERT
Foreword by JON BERGMANN

Flipped Learning
A Guide for Higher Education Faculty
Robert Talbert

Foreword by Jon Bergmann

"Think you know what flipped learning is? Think again. I had to. It's not about technology, recording your lectures, or physical classrooms. This is why you have to read Robert Talbert's *Flipped Learning*. It's the definitive book on the pedagogy, with a new and refreshing perspective. Talbert relates flipped learning to theories of motivation, cognitive load, and self-regulated learning and gives step-by-step directions for flipping your course, along with plenty of examples, answers to typical questions, and variations for hybrid and online courses." *—Linda B. Nilson, Director Emeritus, Office of Teaching Effectiveness and Innovation, Clemson University*

(Continued on preceding page)